401(k)s & IRAs

401(k)s & IRAs

by Ted Benna
with Brenda Newmann

A Wiley Brand

401(k)s & IRAs For Dummies®

Published by:

John Wiley & Sons, Inc.
111 River Street
Hoboken, NJ 07030-5774
www.wiley.com

For general information on our other products and services, please contact our Customer Care Department within the U.S. at 877-762-2974, outside the U.S. at 317-572-3993, or fax 317-572-4002. For technical support, please visit https://hub.wiley.com/community/support/dummies.

Wiley publishes in a variety of print and electronic formats and by print-on-demand. Some material included with standard print versions of this book may not be included in e-books or in print-on-demand. If this book refers to media such as a CD or DVD that is not included in the version you purchased, you may download this material at http://booksupport.wiley.com. For more information about Wiley products, visit www.wiley.com.

Library of Congress Control Number: 2021946256

ISBN 978-1-119-81724-6 (pbk); ISBN 978-1-119-8725-3 (ebk); ISBN 978-1-119-81726-0 (ebk)

SKY10034606_052722

Contents at a Glance

Table of Contents

Introduction

Bumper stickers I'd love to see: "I'd Rather Be Managing My 401(k)" and "Honk if you love your IRA." Made you snicker? I agree. Most of us have better things to do with our time than planning for retirement. You probably *wouldn't* rather be managing your retirement accounts — you'd rather take in a movie, watch a ball game, or pursue your favorite hobby. But it's hard to enjoy yourself if you're plagued by a nagging worry that you could end up destitute in retirement. Spending some time thinking about and planning for your retirement can pay you big dividends down the road.

The concept of retirement has changed dramatically over the last decade or so. Social Security seems less than secure, and it was never meant to cover all your retirement needs, anyway. Most people can't count on receiving a traditional fixed pension from their employer. The burden of retirement planning falls squarely on your shoulders at a time when you're living longer and need more money to finance retirement.

I have good news for you. Although you *do* have to take responsibility for your own retirement saving, you *don't* have to let retirement planning take over your life. Investing a bit of time now in ways I explain in this book should enable you to eventually sit back and relax.

There are lots of places where you can find basic information about all the different types of 401(k) and IRA plans, but finding insight into which one may be best for your business is challenging. I include that in this book. I also include ways I have found to utilize these plans to provide benefits comparable to a 401(k) without all the fees and complications of a 401(k).

About This Book

Don't let the title fool you. *401(k)s and IRAs For Dummies* is a useful book that explains the basic rules — and even some obscure ones about various retirement account options. I include information that's completely up to date, including new rules that went into effect in 2020 with the enactment of the Secure Act, which adds some benefits to 401(k) plan participants. The CARES act was passed in 2020 in response to the COVID-19 crisis.

This book explains essential 401(k) and IRA rules in easy-to-understand language so that you can manage your retirement accounts in a way that leaves you better off in the long run.

This book also explains how to manage risk in your investments and minimize the chances of big losses.

I give examples to show why you should start saving for retirement as soon as you can, because the longer your money stays in your 401(k) and IRA, the bigger your potential nest egg. In fact, if you take only one message away from this book, I hope that it's "Save as much as you can as early as you can, and invest it sensibly."

I explain basic principles of long-term investing to help you decide which investment options are right for you. I also give you guidelines to figure out how much you need to save for retirement, and then, after you retire, how to manage withdrawals from your accounts so that your money can last. These are important concepts for 401(k) and IRA investors, but they're equally important for everyone else.

WARNING

I have to say this loud and clear: Nothing in this book should be taken as tax advice or investment advice for your specific situation. Everyone is unique, and all I can do is explain some of the more important rules and give you guidance to help you make your own decisions.

Also, because the rules are so complicated, I explain the general rules but leave some of the more technical exceptions to your own expert advisors. I know that most people want someone to tell them exactly what to do, but our lawyers won't let me do that. You need to consult an investment advisor or tax advisor for advice on your specific situation. But rest assured, reading this book will help you understand the advice that you receive and may save you money by enabling you to have fewer and shorter meetings with your advisors!

I explain things in a way that's easy to understand; I go into as much detail as necessary for a basic understanding, but no more, and I refer you to additional resources. And heck, I created the first 401(k) plan. How much more authoritative can you get?

To make the content more accessible, it's divided into six parts:

>> Part 1, "The ABCs of 401(k)s and IRAs"

>> Part 2, "401(k) Basics"

>> Part 3, "Here Come the IRAs"

>> Part 4, "Saving and Investing"

>> Part 5, "Money In, Money Out"

>> Part 6, "Helping Small Employers"

>> Part 7, "The Part of Tens"

I think the titles are pretty self-explanatory, but if you're wondering what a Part contains, check out the Part Page at the beginning of that Part for a quick glimpse of the contents.

Foolish Assumptions

This book is for readers who are either thinking about participating in a 401(k), IRA, or other retirement plan, or who already are participating in a retirement plan but have doubts about what they're doing. I assume that you have an idea that it's important to save for retirement, but you're not sure whether you're doing it right or how to get started.

You may also be self-employed or a small business owner looking for options for your own retirement plan and to start a plan for your employees.

I try to make things as simple as possible, but I can't avoid throwing in some math. I assume that you understand some basic economic principles, such as inflation and earning a return on an investment.

For more information about the general investing concepts I cover, I recommend the latest editions of *Investing For Dummies* and *Mutual Funds For Dummies*, both by Eric Tyson (Wiley Publishing, Inc.), as well as other resources listed throughout the book.

Icons Used in This Book

Throughout this book, you'll find helpful icons that highlight particularly useful information. Here's a quick rundown on what they all mean.

TIP

Pay attention to this because it may save you time, money, or aggravation.

REMEMBER

Importantissimo. Commit this information to memory.

WARNING

Ignoring this information may result in painful financial consequences.

TECHNICAL STUFF

You don't have to know this detailed information, but it wouldn't hurt. Skip it if you're in a hurry or not interested. (There aren't many of these.)

Beyond the Book

In addition to the abundance of information and guidance related to retirement plans in this book, you get access to even more help and information online at Dummies.com. Check out this book's online Cheat Sheet for fun and helpful additional information. Just go to www.dummies.com and search for "401(k)s & IRAs For Dummies Cheat Sheet."

Where to Go from Here

The beauty of *401(k)s & IRAs For Dummies* is that I've organized it so that you can start reading anywhere without risking total confusion. Here are a few suggested starting points, depending on why you picked up the book.

>> If you're completely new to the subject, start at the top with Chapter 1 to get an overview of retirement saving and plans.

>> If you're changing jobs and want to know what to do with the money in your employer's 401(k) plan, head to Chapter 7.

>> If you need to take money out of your 401(k) for an emergency, to put a down payment on a home, or to pay for college expenses, you can find information to help in Chapter 14.

>> If you're just starting to realize the need and benefits of saving for retirement, go to Chapter 11.

>> If you need knowledge about investments and investing, Chapters 13 and 14 are the place to go.

>> If you're entirely happy with your retirement fund and the investments in it, give a copy of this book to someone who isn't!

Something else you'll find in this book that you probably won't find elsewhere is the section on retirement plans from an employer's point of view, with tips for small-business owners on choosing a plan. This isn't easy because there are so many options.

1

The ABCs of 401(k)s and IRAs

Explore the reasons for tax-advantaged retirement plans and compare and contrast the two basic types — 401(k)s and IRAs.

See how and how much you can benefit from tax considerations when you invest in your future through an IRA or 401(k).

Continue planning for the future by naming beneficiaries to your retirement plans and figuring out how best to pass along your money to benefit both you and them.

Chapter **1**

Explaining IRAs and 401(k)s

M y primary goal is to help people concerned about having enough money to successfully retire. Even young people, for whom retirement would normally be low on the priority list, have jumped on the retirement savings bandwagon. They're the smart ones, because in some respects, *how long* you save is more important than *how much* you save.

Looking forward to not having to work is a worthy goal, but remember the paychecks cease when you stop working. Having enough income to sustain yourself during the next 20 to 30 years isn't easy. Your plans may be disrupted before you reach your planned retirement age. The current COVID-19 pandemic is an example.

Exploring the Basics of Retirement Savings Plans

A retirement plan lets you put some of your income away now to use later, presumably when you're retired and not earning a paycheck. This process may not appeal to everyone; human nature being what it is, many people would rather spend their money now and worry about later when later comes. That's why the federal government approved tax breaks to enjoy now — or in April, anyway. Uncle Sam knows that your individual savings are going to be an essential part of your retirement and wants to give you an incentive to participate.

Currently, you have several options for saving for your retirement:

» Joining a 401(k) plan, which is an employer-sponsored plan that takes an amount you determine out of your paycheck or automatically enrolls you to contribute and deposits your contributions into your 401(k) account

» Starting an IRA, an individual retirement account, on your own and determining your contribution amount and schedule on your own

» Joining an IRA-based employer-sponsored retirement plan that takes an amount you determine out of your paycheck and deposits your contributions into an IRA

» Your employer automatically contributes a percentage of your pay to a retirement plan

» If you're a solo entrepreneur, setting up a 401(k) or IRA-based plan that may include either employee contributions, employer contributions, or both

I guess you can open a savings account and put money into that, or stick money under your mattress, but neither of these methods will beat 30 to 40 years of inflation, and the mattress method is open to many hazards — fire, flood, boll weevils, and so on. You also won't get any tax breaks (unless you're hiding money that hasn't been taxed, in which case you'll probably have legal problems to worry about).

The next sections explain both 401(k) and IRA plans.

Getting down to 401(k) basics

When you sign up for a 401(k) plan, you agree to let your employer deposit some of your paycheck into the plan as a *pre-tax* contribution or as a Roth after-tax contribution or a combination of the two. You put money into your 401(k) plan through a *payroll deduction*.

Your employer is also permitted to sign you up without your approval, but you have the right to override the percentage you're automatically enrolled to contribute, including totally opting out. Your employer is required to give you advance notice before automatically enrolling you.

The beauty of a 401(k) is that it makes saving easy and automatic, and you probably won't even miss the money you put into your retirement account.

I cover the four types of 401(k)s in this book:

>> A regular 401(k) is sponsored by your employer. Your 401(k) is funded by contributions deducted from your paycheck and deposited into your account. Check out the chapters in Part 2 for information about regular 401(k)s.

>> Several types of 401(k) serve the self-employed and other small business owners. I go into detail about the following plans in Chapter 19:

- Safe harbor 401(k)
- Solo 401(k)
- Qualified automatic contribution arrangement (QACA) 401(k)

Your employer may set up its own 401(k) or adopt one using a pooled plan provider (PPP) to set up a pooled employer plan (PEP) or become part of a multiple-employer plan (MEP). I cover the different rules for these plans in Chapter 19.

REMEMBER

Your employer may throw in some extra money known as a matching contribution. You don't pay federal income tax on any 401(k) money until you withdraw it.

401(k) plans are like snowflakes — each one is unique. If you're looking for a standard 401(k) plan, be aware that there's no such animal. Each company creates its own plan, and some are better than others. Part 2 goes into detail about all the aspects of 401(k)s.

Federal laws govern many aspects of 401(k) plans, but employers are allowed to be more restrictive with their plan rules. For example, the contributions your employer allows may be less than what Uncle Sam permits.

TECHNICAL STUFF

The 401(k) gets its memorable name from the section of Internal Revenue Code (IRC) that governs it. Section 401 of the IRC applies to pension, profit sharing, and stock bonus plans.

A 401(k) plan must satisfy the IRC in both form and operation to be a qualified plan. The rules and regulations governing these plans are massive and complex. Fortunately, your employer deals with making sure the plan you're offered meets IRC standards. You just have to worry about upholding your end of the arrangement, which this book helps you do.

To meet IRC standards, an employer must adopt a lengthy plan document (150 to 175 pages) and have it approved by the Internal Revenue Service (IRS). The document specifies

>> Who's eligible to join the plan

>> When they're eligible

>> How much eligible employees may contribute

>> The type and amount of any employer contributions

>> When the employer contribution belongs to the participant

Each plan's operation must satisfy all the applicable rules and regulations. This includes legislative requirements enacted by Congress and regulations issued by the governmental agencies that have jurisdiction, which include the Treasury Department, the Department of Labor (DoL), and the Securities and Exchange Commission (SEC). The IRS and DoL conduct audits to determine whether an employer is in full compliance.

Introducing IRAs

An IRA, or *individual retirement account*, is a tax-advantaged way to save for retirement. This is how the government helps workers save for retirement whenever their employers don't offer a retirement plan.

This book includes information about all the different types of IRAs:

>> Traditional IRA

>> Roth IRA

>> Spousal IRA

>> Rollover/Conduit IRA

>> Inherited IRA

Head to Part 3 for details about all these IRAs.

The eligibility rules for a pre-tax traditional IRA depend on whether you or your spouse are covered by an employer-sponsored retirement plan. Otherwise, anyone with earned income can open a traditional IRA. (I cover tax issues and tax terms in Chapter 2.)

With a traditional IRA, you can make contributions on your own anytime up to the date you file your tax return and claim a deduction for your contributions. You don't get a tax deduction when you contribute to a Roth IRA.

Both a traditional IRA and Roth IRA are invested at a financial institution you select. Your money grows without being taxed with both types of IRA. All withdrawals from a traditional IRA are taxable, and a 10 percent penalty tax is imposed if you withdraw the money prior to age 59½ for any reason other than those that exclude you from the penalty tax. Withdrawals from a Roth IRA aren't taxable if you follow the rules.

A LITTLE RETIREMENT HISTORY

Did you know that IRAs were permitted long before 401(k)s? What you know as a traditional pre-tax IRA was included in the Employee Retirement Income Security Act (ERISA) passed by Congress on September 2, 1974. That IRAs were included in ERISA is especially surprising because ERISA's primary purpose was to strengthen the defined-benefit pension system.

Originally, you could own an IRA only if you weren't covered by an employer-sponsored retirement plan. If you were covered by an employer-sponsored plan, no matter how many or how few benefits the plan provided, you were not eligible to contribute to an IRA.

For example, you can lose all the benefits you earned under an employer-provided pension plan if you left before completing 20 years of service. Or you may have been a participant in an employer-funded profit-sharing plan by an employer that did not make any contributions to the plan or perhaps only small contributions. The 1981 Economic Recovery Tax Act removed the inequity of such situations resulting in the expansion of IRAs to most individuals who have earned income including those covered by employer-sponsored plans.

The Taxpayer Relief Act of 1997 added an additional option — Roth after-tax IRAs. Another step was to expand the Roth option by adding it to 401(k)s during 2006, giving 401(k) participants the option of making pre-tax contributions, Roth after-tax contributions, or some of each.

The traditional IRA and Roth IRA have income thresholds that make higher income earners ineligible to contribute. Participants in 401(k)s are eligible to make Roth contributions regardless of how high their incomes are.

You may be surprised to hear that your author, known as the father of 401(k), thinks there are better alternatives to a 401(k) for solo entrepreneurs, small family businesses, and many other small employers. These IRA–based plans include the following:

>> Payroll-deduction IRA

>> SEP IRA

>> SIMPLE IRA

Chapter 18 includes detailed information about these plans, including why they may be better than a 401(k).

Comparing and Contrasting IRAs and 401(k)s

IRAs and 401(k)s are both retirement savings plans, but after that the resemblance gets dim. Both plans offer

>> Pre-tax contribution options

>> A Savers Tax credit for employees who contribute subject to income limits (Chapter 2 lists the credits and restrictions.)

>> The ability to grow your money tax-free until you withdraw it

Contrasts between 401(k)s and IRAs are numerous and include the following:

>> An IRA generally offers more investment choices than a 401(k). Depending on how much choice you like to have, this can be good or bad.

Your employer picks the investments offered in a 401(k), so your options with a 401(k) are limited unless your plan includes a brokerage option compared with the range of investment vehicles you can find for an individual IRA. A 401(k) is thus a disadvantage if you prefer total investment flexibility. On the positive side, your employer is supposed to select investments that are in the sole best interest of participants. Some employers strive to do this, but many don't. (Many employers have in fact been sued for failing to do so.)

>> If you have money in a 401(k) plan, you can be forced to withdraw the money when you reach the plan's normal retirement age, usually 65, unless you're still working for that employer. With a traditional IRA, you're required to start

taking minimum distributions only after you turn 72. A Roth IRA never requires you to take withdrawals (unless you inherited it).

>> Money held in a 401(k) may be more secure from your creditors than money in an IRA. IRA protection depends on state law, while 401(k)s are protected by federal law.

>> 401(k) and employer-sponsored IRA plans may include an employer contribution. Whatever amount your employer contributes is a bonus you don't get with a personal IRA.

Federal laws govern many aspects of 401(k) plans, but employers are allowed to be more restrictive with their plan rules. For example, the contributions your employer allows may be less than what Uncle Sam permits.

STARTING THE FIRST 401(K) PLAN

Paragraph (k) was added to Section 401 via the Tax Revenue Act of 1978. It was only a page and a half long, and it certainly was not expected to be a big deal. It was added by Congress to resolve a battle between Congress and the Treasury over cash-deferred profit-sharing plans. The effective date of this new IRC paragraph was January 1, 1980. This date passed without a rush of employers implementing these plans. I was redesigning the retirement program of a Philadelphia area bank during the fall of 1980. I was drawn to this section of the code as I was considering what the bank was trying to accomplish. It was during this process that I came up with the idea of using this section of the IRC to form a new type of employee retirement savings plan. One with an employer matching contribution and employee pre-tax contributions. Section 401(k) did not include a provision for either type of contribution, but it also did not prohibit them.

The bank's attorney did not want them to be the pioneers adopting the first 401(k) savings plan. I was part of The Johnson Companies at the time. We implemented the first 401(k) savings plan for our employees effective January 1, 1981, a year after Section 401(k)'s effective date.

This started the launch of employee pre-tax 401(k) plans. Millions of workers have already retired and are enjoying their 401(k) benefits, and millions of active workers are contributing to their plans; however, more than half the private workforce works for employers that do not offer a 401(k) or any other retirement plan.

Accentuating the Positive

Saving for your own retirement may seem like an unnecessary irritation, but it's very rewarding when you reach the age when you need it. Facing retirement with your only income coming from Social Security is a sure way to tarnish the gold of your golden years.

If you're fortunate enough to work for an employer who matches a portion of your contribution to your 401(k), you have even more reasons to be a very happy saver.

Saving up

From what people have told me over the years, the biggest benefit of participating in a 401(k) plan is that it turns spenders into savers. Most people want to save for the future, but having money left at the end of the month is tough. Saving becomes your priority with a 401(k). You decide how much of your gross pay to put into the plan and live your daily life on what's left.

These days, it's easier than ever to transfer a certain amount every week, month, or paycheck to a retirement account, especially if you're able to participate in a 401(k). Chapters 11 and 12 have pointers for finding ways to save.

TIP

You may face a strong temptation to invade your emergency savings when the first significant emergency hits or you see something you really want to buy. Pulling money from a savings account is easy, but getting money out of a 401(k) isn't easy at all. So, if you want long-term savings immune from impulse buys, go with a 401(k).

If you're one of the lucky ones, you're eligible to contribute to both a 401(k) and an IRA. You are probably also eligible to make Roth contributions either inside or outside the 401(k).

Getting employer contributions

Being able to contribute to a plan that has employer contributions is a big benefit of a 401(k) and employer-based IRA plans. For example, if your employer contributes $0.25 for each $1.00 you contribute limited to the first 6 percent of pay that you contribute, you should strive to contribute 6 percent of your pay, so you get the full employer contribution. Of course, if your employer contributes $1 for each $1 you contribute to the 401(k), that's the best-case scenario regardless of other factors.

TIP

Payroll deduction is magical, so take advantage of putting money into a 401(k), a payroll deduction IRA, or a SIMPLE IRA if you have the opportunity. A payroll deduction IRA may include employer matching contributions to encourage employees to contribute. A SIMPLE IRA must include employer contributions. A personal IRA isn't an effective alternative unless you're highly disciplined about managing your money.

IN THIS CHAPTER

» **Understanding why you get tax breaks**

» **Getting a handle on tax terms**

» **Taking credit when you can**

» **Scoping Social Security issues**

» **Paying taxes before and after you retire**

» **Being prepared for changes in the tax code**

Chapter 2

Taxing Issues

I t's up to you — no one else — to plan for a successful retirement. Government policy makers want you to have the resources to retire successfully so that you don't become a burden to society. With that goal, the government gives you and your employer tax incentives to encourage you to save and your employer to offer retirement plans to make saving easy.

This chapter talks about the whys and hows of taxes as they relate to retirement accounts.

Realizing the Reasons for Tax Breaks

I hope it's not news to you that Social Security was never intended to provide an adequate level of retirement income. The additional amount you need to retire comfortably must come from other sources. Lawmakers encourage setting aside money for retirement by providing tax breaks and incentives.

What the government gains

Society is stronger if older people are financially secure. Having sufficient resources to provide for themselves eliminates the need for federal and state governments to sustain senior citizens via Medicaid, food stamps, subsidized housing, and other programs.

If people are forced to continue working into their seventies and eighties, that makes it more difficult for teenagers and other younger workers to find employment because both groups are likely to compete for jobs in the service and retail industries.

Having money to spend beyond the bare necessities — going out to eat, buying a new car (even if it's just new to you), taking vacations, and engaging in other leisure activities — boosts the economy, which in turn provides employment to other workers.

Retirement saving is good for seniors and good for the country.

What you gain

By participating in a retirement saving plan, you do yourself several favors:

>> You put away money so that you can enjoy your retirement without financial worries.

>> If you can contribute pre-tax wages, you put off paying taxes until you spend the money. You may even work for an employer that adds money to your account. I talk about 401(k) plans in Part 2.

>> You can deduct qualified traditional IRA contributions when you file your taxes.

Saving so that you have money to live on in your later years is its own reward. Being able to kick back and enjoy the fruits of many years of labor is part of why you work in the first place.

Benefiting from tax advantages while you save is the icing on the retirement cake. The next sections touch on these.

Benefiting from an employer-sponsored plan

Some folks can take advantage of employer-sponsored retirement benefit plans. Most public employers still offer traditional pension plans that provide a stream of monthly lifetime pension income.

If you're self-employed, you can start your own retirement plan — the chapters in Part 5 offer information on small business plans.

You can put 25 percent or more of your earned income into an IRA-based retirement plan. If set up properly, you can save federal and state income tax, local wage tax, as well as Social Security tax. The combined tax savings if your marginal federal income tax rate is 22 percent will be 40 to 50 percent of the amount you save. A $10,000 contribution can produce $4,000 to $5,000 of tax savings.

TIP

You're one of the fortunate ones if you're covered by an employer-funded non-401(k) plan, also known as a *pension*. There are two types of employer-funded pension plans:

>> **Traditional defined benefit plan:** This type of plan pays a lifetime monthly income after retirement. The plan isn't very valuable unless you spend a lot of years working for the same employer. The value of the benefits you earn are low during your twenties and early thirties. The value of the benefit you earn during your twenties is usually less than $1,000 per year if you earn $50,000 annually. The value increases the longer you stay and the closer you get to retirement.

>> **Cash balance plan:** In this type of plan, the employer contributes a specific percentage of pay for younger employees — typically 3 percent, so $1,500 per year if you earn $50,000 annually. You may have to stay with the employer for three years to get this benefit.

Deducting IRA contributions

If you work for an employer that doesn't offer any plan, you're probably eligible to contribute to an IRA. You can contribute $6,000 annually if you are under age 50 plus an additional $1,000 if you are age 50 and over. You can deduct the amount you contribute on your Form 1040 when you file your tax return. These are the 2021 limits.

WARNING

You may not be eligible to contribute to a traditional IRA if your spouse is covered by an employer-based retirement plan. See "Paying attention if your spouse has a plan" later in the chapter.

Talking Tax Terms

Being an effective and efficient manager of your own money means being familiar with taxes and tax terms. The next sections explain common tax terms it pays to be familiar with, particularly when dealing with an IRA.

Earning your income

Earned income includes the amount you receive from working for someone. Wages, commissions, tips, bonuses, and taxable fringe benefits all count as earned income, as does income from running a business or a farm.

Earned income may also include untaxed military pay, taxed alimony, and disability benefits. Untaxed alimony, child support, Social Security benefits, unemployment, and wages earned by penal institutional inmates are excluded. Your contributions to an IRA can't exceed your earned income except for contributions to a spousal IRA that come from the employed spouse's earned income.

Combining your income

Your *combined income* is what determines how much of your Social Security benefit is taxable.

Your combined income is the total of

» Your adjusted gross income

» Your nontaxable interest

» Half your Social Security benefits

Adjusting your income with AGI

Whether it rings an immediate bell or not, you're familiar with figuring your *adjusted gross income* (AGI) at tax time. The IRA defines AGI as "gross income minus adjustments to income." Your AGI is equal to or less than the total amount of income you had for the tax year depending on the adjustments you're allowed. Income sources that contribute to your AGI include

» Wages on a W-2 or 1099 form

» Self-employed income on a Schedule C

» Interest and dividends

» Alimony from an ex-spouse (for agreements prior to 2019)

» Capital gains

» Rental income

» Retirement distributions

» Other earnings subject to income tax

By the time you get to the bottom of the first page of your tax form, you have figured your AGI.

You have many opportunities to take tax deductions on your tax return. Some deductions reduce your income to determine your AGI; these are referred to as *adjustments to income*. Some current permitted adjustments to your AGI include educator expenses, student loan interest, and IRA contributions. But be aware that tax laws change every year.

Your *modified adjusted gross income*, or MAGI, is your AGI plus specific add backs of untaxed income. For example, you aren't taxed on foreign investment income, but your MAGI includes that income.

In a nutshell, your AGI reflects your income; your MAGI is a more complete picture of your financial resources. It's confusing and one of the many reasons I don't prepare my own tax return.

Figuring your marginal tax rate

The United States has a graduated tax structure rather than one flat rate in which all taxable income is subject to the same rate. Your income is subject to different tax rates. Your tax rate increases as your taxable income increases.

The more your taxable income, the higher your taxes. You pay a lower rate on the bottom tier of your earnings and pay increasing rates on higher amounts. Table 2-1 shows tax tiers for 2021.

So, if you're single and have $75,000 of taxable income, you pay 10 percent on $9,950, 12 percent on $9,951 to $40,525, and 22 percent on $40,526 to $75,000. So, 22 percent is your *marginal tax rate* — the rate you pay on the top portion of your income.

TABLE 2-1

2021 Tax Tiers by Income

Single with Income Up To	Married Filing Jointly with Income Up To	Tax Rate
$9,950	$19,900	10%
$40,525	81,050	12%
$86,375	172,750	22%
$164,925	$329,850	24%
$209,425	$418,850	32%
$523,600	$628,300	35%
over $523,600	over $628,300	37%

Source: Internal Revenue Service

Getting Credit for Contributions

You get an immediate tax break when you make pre-tax contributions to a 401(k) because your taxable pay is reduced by the amount you contribute. You actually authorize your employer to reduce your pay when you join a 401(k). The taxes withheld are reduced; therefore, the reduction in your take home pay is less than the amount you decide to contribute. You don't get this advantage with Roth contributions to your 401(k) because they're post-tax contributions.

Deducting IRA contributions

You get a tax reduction when you contribute to a traditional IRA and you file a tax return: Your taxable income is reduced by the amount you contributed. You may also get an additional tax benefit via a tax credit from the government.

If you're covered by a retirement plan at work, use the information in Table 2-2 to see whether your modified AGI affects the amount of your deduction. These are the 2021 limits.

The amount you can contribute to a Roth IRA is limited by your MAGI as shown in Table 2-3.

If you file separately and did not live with your spouse at any time during the year, your IRA deduction is determined under the "Single" filing status.

TABLE 2-2

2021 IRA Deduction Limits

Your Filing Status	Your Modified AGI	Your Deduction
Single or **head of household**	$66,000 or less	Up to your contribution limit
	More than $66,000 but less than $76,000	Partial deduction
	$76,000 or more	No deduction
Married filing jointly or **qualifying widow(er)**	$105,000 or less	Up to your contribution limit
	More than $105,000 but less than $125,000	Partial deduction
	$125,000 or more	No deduction

Source: Internal Revenue Service

TABLE 2-3

Roth IRA Deduction Limits

Filing status	2020 MAGI	2021 MAGI	Contribution
Single or **head of household**	<$124,000	<$125,000	Full contribution
	>$124,000 and <$139,000	>$125,000 and <$140,000	Partial contribution
	>$139,000	>$140,000	No contribution
Married filing jointly or **qualified widow(er)**	<$196,000	<$198,000	Full contribution
	>$196,000 and <$206,000	>$198,000 to <$208,000	Partial contribution
	>$206,000	>$208,000	No contribution
Married filing separately	<$10,000	<$10,000	Partial contribution
	>$10,000	>$10,000	No contribution

Source: Internal Revenue Service

Paying attention if your spouse has a plan

The amount of your contributions to an IRA that you can deduct on your tax form may be limited if you or your spouse are covered by a retirement plan.

IRS standards for determining whether you or your spouse are covered by your employer's retirement plan include the following:

>> Your employer has a recognized contribution plan, including a 401(k) plan, profit sharing, stock bonus, or money purchase pension plan. A *money purchase pension plan* is one that an employer contributes to for the employee's benefit. The employee is barred from contributing but may be able to choose what the funds are invested in.

A *defined benefit plan,* which is, oddly enough, a pension plan with defined benefits, that you're eligible to participate in within the tax year counts.

>> Contributions or forfeitures (a fancy way of saying losses or withdrawals) were registered in your plan during the calendar year or plan year. The contributions may be to a SEP or SIMPLE IRA plan — I talk about those plans in Chapter 20.

TIP

One way to tell whether you're covered in an employer-sponsored retirement plan is to check your W-2. If Box 13, the retirement plan box, is checked, you're covered.

Table 2-4 shows how big a deduction you can take if you or your spouse has an employer-based plan. This table applies even if you or your spouse decides not to contribute to the plan that is available at work.

TABLE 2-4   ## Deduction Limits if Spouse Has an Employer-Sponsored Plan

Filing Status	2020 MAGI	2021 MAGI	Deduction
Single or **head of household**	<$65,000	<$66,000	Full deduction
	>$65,000 and <$75,000	>$66,000 and <$76,000	Partial deduction
	>$75,000	>$76,000	No deduction
Married filing jointly or **qualified widow(er)**	<$104,000	<$105,000	Full deduction
	>$104,000 and <$124,000	>$105,000 and <$125,000	Partial deduction
	>$124,000	>$125,000	No deduction
Married filing separately	<$10,000	<$ 10,000	Partial deduction
	>$10,000	>$10,000	No deduction

Source: Internal Revenue Service

Earning extra credit according to income

Congress approved an extra tax break to encourage low- and moderate-income earners to contribute to retirement accounts. This tax credit, called the Saver's Tax Credit, is available to those who contribute to a 401(k), a traditional IRA, and/or a Roth IRA.

The saver's credit is available if you meet all three conditions:

>> You're 18 or older.

>> You're not a full-time student.

>> You're not claimed as a dependent on someone else's return.

You were a student if, during any part of five months of the tax year, you

>> Were enrolled as a full-time student at a school.

>> Took a full-time, on-farm training course given by a school or a state, county, or local government agency.

REMEMBER

A school includes technical, trade, and mechanical schools. It doesn't include on-the-job training courses, correspondence schools, or schools offering courses only through the internet.

The amount of the credit is 50 percent, 20 percent, or 10 percent of your contributions up to $2,000 — $4,000 if you're married filing jointly. Eligibility and the amount of the credit is tied to your adjusted gross income. You can't claim the credit if you make more than $33,000 or $66,000 if you're married and file jointly. Table 2-5 shows the credit amount in 2021.

TABLE 2-5 **2021 Saver's Tax Credit Rates**

Married Filing Jointly	Head of Household	Other Filers	Credit Rate
Up to $39,500	Up to $29,625	Up to $19,750	50%
$39,501–$42,000	$29,626–$32,250	$19,751–$21,500	20%
$42,001–$66,000	$32,251–$49,500	$21,501–$33,000	10%
More than $66,000	More than $49,500	More than $33,000	0%

Source: Internal Revenue Service

The actual calculation of the tax credit has a few more rules that apply, and the amount of your tax credit may be further reduced by any plan withdrawals you (or your spouse) may receive (or have received in the past two years).

TECHNICAL STUFF

You must complete and file Form 8880 to get the credit. Request a copy from your employer or get one from www.irs.gov.

Taxing Income at Retirement

The amount of your taxable income at retirement is an important factor because if you're like most retirees, you have much less taxable income when you don't get a paycheck any longer. Social Security benefits are a large portion of most retirees' income, and they will be for you, too, unless you have substantial assets or significant taxable income from other sources when you retire.

Fun fact: Social Security benefits weren't taxable until 1984. Today, however, you can pay tax on up to 85 percent of your Social Security benefit — even though you pay federal income taxes on the amount you contribute to Social Security during all the years you work.

This comment used to get people attending my speaking engagements turning their heads, so let me explain: Both your federal income tax and Social Security taxes are computed as part of your gross income. This means you pay federal income tax on your Social Security taxes when you are working and paying them in. You also may have to pay taxes on 85 percent of your Social Security benefits after you retire.

Table 2-6 shows the portion of your Social Security benefit taxable in 2021.

TABLE 2-6   **Tax Rates on Social Security Benefits in 2021**

Filing Status	0% for Income	50% for Income	85% for Income
Single	Under $25,000	$25,000 to $34,000	Over $34,000
Married Filing Jointly	Under $32,000	$32,000 to $44,000	Over $44,000

Source: Internal Revenue Service

Taxes on your Social Security benefits come into play only if your combined income exceeds $25,000 for a single person and $34,000 for marrieds. If you're a single taxpayer whose combined income exceeds $34,000 for 2021, 85 percent of your Social Security benefit is taxable. The 85 percent threshold for joint returns is $44,000.

Middle-income workers are the ones who need tax help the most: Lower-income earners receive a much larger percentage of their wages from Social Security, and top earners in large, publicly owned companies receive their big payoffs through employer-funded non-qualified retirement benefits and stock option plans.

An employee currently making $30,000 who retires at the normal Social Security retirement age will receive 45 percent to 50 percent of this amount in Social Security income. Financial pros say you need 70 percent of your pre-tax income as retirement income. So, this retiree needs only 20 percent to 25 percent of non-Social Security income to accomplish this — roughly $225,000 to $250,000 in retirement savings. This is equal to 7.5 to 8.3 times the worker's $30,000 pre-retirement income.

An employee in the same situation with a $100,000 salary will receive 25 to 30 percent of this amount in Social Security income. This is a much smaller percentage of pay than the $30,000 wage earner even though both employees were paying 7.65 percent of their incomes in FICA tax prior to retirement (assuming they both work for an employer that also pays 7.65 percent). Making matters worse, a self-employed individual earning $100,000 must pay 15.3 percent in FICA taxes.

The $100,000 wage earner has been paying 3.3 times as much in FICA taxes but will receive only 1.7 times as much in benefits. This wage earner also will need sufficient assets to replace 40 to 45 percent of pre-retirement income to hit the 70 percent threshold. That will take $1,000,000 to $1,125,000 of assets — 10 to 11 times the worker's pre-retirement income.

A self-employed person earning $100,000 will pay $15,300 in FICA taxes, or 6.7 times as much as the as an employee earning $30,000. Despite paying many times more in FICA taxes, the self-employed person receives only 1.7 times as much in Social Security benefits. This is one of the reasons why I am so passionate about helping solo entrepreneurs and small family businesses set up a plan that will give them the biggest tax break — because they deserve it. Oh, and by the way, up to 85 percent of your Social Security benefits may be taxable for self-employed and other workers.

TECHNICAL STUFF

Tax-qualified retirement plans have maximum benefit limits. Non-qualified plans have no maximum benefit limits, so the only restriction on how much benefit top cats can get is determined by the company's board of directors.

Some more information about Social Security inequity:

>> **Paying taxes twice:** Have you ever considered the fact that you're taxed twice by the federal government on the Social Security taxes you pay? Everyone I tell this to gives me a strange look, but I'm only talking the truth.

Your Social Security tax is determined using your gross income. So is your federal income tax; so your annual income is used to determine both taxes.

>> **Paying to be self-employed:** The self-employed are required to pay 15.3 percent in FICA (Federal Insurance Contribution Act) taxes. A 22 percent federal income tax rate, plus a 2 percent state income tax, a 1 percent local wage tax, plus the 15.3% FICA tax results in a combined 40.3 percent rate.

Income and tax levels before and after retirement are fairly stark.

For example, assume you retired at the end of 2020 having earned $75,000 during 2020. Your Social Security benefit for 2021 should be approximately $25,000 if you qualify for full benefits. You need a $1,000,000 retirement nest egg to generate $40,000 per year of additional retirement income assuming a typical recommended 4 percent withdrawal rate (4 percent of $1,000,000). So, you start out 2021 with $10,000 less income than you had in 2020 but only the $40,000 withdrawn from your retirement account may be taxable.

REMEMBER

All things considered, it's improbable that tax rates will increase to a point where your tax rate on a substantially lower amount of taxable income will be higher than your current rate. This is why the highly promoted Roth tax advantage is a myth: Most retirees are in a lower tax bracket when they retire than when they were working.

REMEMBER

You still have tax deductions after you retire, which can reduce your AGI significantly since you don't have salary income. The standard deduction for a single taxpayer is $12,000.

Table 2-7 shows how 2020 and 2021 compare tax-wise for a single person who retired at the end of 2020.

TABLE 2-7   **Comparing Taxable Income after Retirement**

2020 Taxable Income		2021 Taxable Income	
Salary	$75,000	IRA withdrawal	$40,000
IRA deduction	+ $7,000	85% of Social Security	+ $21,250
Standard deduction	− $12,400	Standard deduction	− $12,550
Taxable income	= $55,600	Taxable income	= $48,700

Source: Internal Revenue Service

The amount of your taxable income is likely to be much less after you retire unless you have a larger retirement nest egg than $1,000,000 or significant taxable income from other sources.

Staying Alert to Changes in Tax Law

I remember well during the early days of the Roth IRA how retirement savers were encouraged by most financial pros to pay tax now rather than after they retire because Roth IRAs provided a big tax advantage. How well did this advice work out? Well, you win with the Roth option only if taxes are higher when you take out your money than when you put it in.

Table 2-8 shows the tax rates applicable to single and marrieds filing jointly during 1998 (the year after Roth IRAs became effective) and 2021.

TABLE 2-8   **Comparison of 1998 and 2021 Tax Rates**

Income 1998 Single	Income 1998 Married Filing Jointly	Tax Rate	Income 2021 Single	Income 2021 Married Filing Jointly	Tax Rate
Up to $25,349	Up to $42,349	15%	Up to $9,950	Up to $19,900	10%
$25,350 to $61,399	$42,350 to $102,299	28%	$9,951 to $40,525	$19,901 to $81,050	12%
$61,400 to $128,099	$102,300 to $155,949	31%	$40,526 to $86,375	$81,051 to $172,750	22%
$128,100 to $278,449	$155,950 to $278,449	36%	$86,376 to $164,925	$172,751 to $329,850	24%
Over $278,449	Over $278,449	39.6%	$164,926 to $209,425	$329,851 to $418,850	32%
			$209,426 to $523,600	$418,851 to $628,300	35%
			Over $523,600	Over $628,300	37%

Source: Internal Revenue Service

A single tax filer in 1998 would have been taxed at a 28 percent rate on taxable income above $25,350. The 2021 rate for taxable income above this level is 12 percent. The tax rate was 28 percent for a married couple filing jointly during 1998 on taxable income above $42,350 compared to 12 percent during 2021. So, it definitely did not benefit you to invest in a Roth IRA in 1998 and take money out in 2021. Check out Chapter 10 for more on Roth IRAs.

REMEMBER

There's no guarantee that retirement tax exemptions will be available in their current form in the future. Tax laws change all the time.

POLITICS AND TAX HISTORY

You may shake your head as I get into the different types of 401(k)s and IRAs wondering how saving for retirement got to be so complex and confusing. Well, the programs, rules, and regulations have evolved over many decades in patchwork fashion. The 16th Amendment passed on July 2, 1909, established Congress's right to impose a federal income tax. This is considered the predecessor of the current U.S. tax code. There were nearly 10,000 code sections in 2020. Who knows how many more we will get in 2021 and beyond.

The expansion of the traditional IRA to include employees covered by employer-sponsored retirement plans occurred during the Reagan administration. President Reagan was in favor of increasing savings and capital formation. Congressman Jack Kemp spearheaded that effort. I had the opportunity to meet with Congressman Kemp to discuss this issue. I warned him that 401(k) would cost $4 to $5 billion per year in lost tax revenue within a couple of years. (It was projected to cost a few million when it was enacted.) I also told him IRAs did not need to be expanded because 401(k) was going to result in a lot more savings than expanded IRAs. My input was ignored resulting in IRA expansion being enacted.

Then came the mid-1980s tax reform effort. The conflict between what is good policy and politics is why we get bad tax legislation. The intent of President Reagan's tax reform act was to do a massive overhaul of the tax code. The initial version would have eliminated 401(k) even though it was successfully creating a lot of new savings and capital formation. This was proposed as a back-door way to increase tax revenue. It took a massive lobbying effort from 401(k) participants to prevent this from happening; however, the maximum employee contribution limit was reduced from $30,000 to $7,500 per year.

President Donald Trump also suggested that perhaps 401(k) pre-tax contributions should be eliminated during the early stage of his tax change legislation. The reaction was sufficiently negative to stop that effort.

The Biden administration will be forced to deal with ways to increase tax revenues eventually. It remains to be seen what alterations to the current system will be proposed.

Chapter **3**

Naming Beneficiaries and Planning for the Future

I want to say right up front that passing along money in your retirement account is complex stuff. I only cover the basics here. Please keep in mind that I'm not the one who created the rules; I'm just the one telling you about them.

Get a qualified tax advisor who has experience dealing with these issues to help you. I recommend either an accountant or tax attorney. A fee-for-service financial planner is another option. I don't recommend a financial advisor who receives compensation from your investments because their opinions can be influenced by the compensation they receive. They also aren't likely to be knowledgeable enough to provide the help you need.

Deciding Who Gets Your Savings When You're Gone

When you establish an IRA or join a 401(k), one of the first actions you take is to name beneficiaries to your account. You have to be a little more specific than "my spouse" or "the cousin we call Junior." Be prepared to provide some details about the people you want to leave your assets to, including

>> Name

>> Address

>> Social Security number

You may be asked to say how your beneficiaries are related to you, whether that's by blood ties or just friends.

If you want to name a charity as your beneficiary, you need the name, employer identification number, relationship (charity), and address. You also need your spouse's properly signed consent if the charity is a primary beneficiary.

KEEP YOUR HEIRS AWARE

I was reminded as I was writing this chapter how important it is to keep heirs informed about financial matters. I have given free financial help to a few widows over the years and have often been told how difficult getting financial stuff together was because their spouses had handled all the finances and never discussed any of the details with them.

This personal reminder led me to provide a detailed written update for my heirs. I included a summary of assets, where they are located, and what to do after I am gone. This summary is included in the envelope that contains my will. I also told my heirs where they can find my will.

My will, like yours, governs who gets my assets that aren't controlled by specific beneficiary designations. My IRA and life insurance have named beneficiaries I designated. Any other assets are distributed to the heirs named in my will. The instruction letter to my heirs doesn't have any impact on who gets what, but it lets my heirs know what assets there are — bank, brokerage, and IRA accounts — and how to access them.

TIP

Naming beneficiaries and keeping them updated assures the benefits will go to those you want to get them. Most 401(k) plans have default beneficiary provisions that apply if none of your named beneficiaries is still living, so your money may go to someone you never intended to have it. Your spouse is the first default beneficiary because this is what the law requires.

IRAs don't have default beneficiary provisions; therefore, these assets become part of your estate subject to probate if you don't have a living beneficiary. The benefit recipient will be decided by the court — not you.

Detailing the Distribution

Probate is the legal process of administering an estate. Probate doesn't apply to assets such as 401(k) and IRA accounts and life insurance when you have one or more living beneficiaries properly filed with the organization responsible for paying out these funds:

>> For a 401(k), the employer or the service provider designated by them

>> For an IRA, the financial organization that holds the IRA account

>> For an insurance policy, the insurance company that issued the policy

Distributions from a 401(k) are made by the financial organization that holds the money. The employer is responsible for notifying the beneficiaries when death occurs; however, the beneficiary will probably have to start the process by informing the employer when the death involves a former employee.

Your employer has an interest in helping a deceased 401(k) participant's beneficiaries get the money out of the plan, but there is a limit to how much effort the employer will put into tracking down a beneficiary. An employer will be aware of the death of an active employee but isn't likely to know that a former employee who left the company many years ago and left money sitting in the 401(k) has died. This becomes an even greater problem when businesses are sold, restructured, or otherwise transform because your ties back to the business become much weaker.

The administrative process for other assets is determined by whether you have a will. If you do, probate involves proving that your will is legally valid. After that, the executor you named in your will is responsible for executing your instructions and paying applicable taxes.

WARNING

Passing without a will leaves your entire estate in the hands of a judge for assets that don't have a living named beneficiary.

You may also pass assets to a trust when you die rather than directly to individual beneficiaries. A trust is a good idea if you're leaving money to minor children. You name the trustee who is responsible for managing the assets in the trust. The trustee can be a bank that offers trust services or an individual. The trust you establish also details how the assets may be used and when, if ever, they will be distributed to the beneficiary. Income earned on the trust assets is usually distributed each year to the beneficiary. The trustee can also be given discretion to distribute amounts from the principal to the beneficiary as needed.

The financial organization that holds an IRA won't know when an account holder dies unless it is informed of this fact.

TIP

Include information about your 401(k) and/or IRA accounts with your will and other end-of-life documents and make sure your heirs know where to find them when the time comes.

Talking Timing and Taxes

The Secure Act passed on December 20, 2019, changed the rules for inherited retirement accounts passed on during or after 2020. Now 401(k) and traditional IRA accounts must be fully distributed within ten years after the account holder's death. That means the recipient of your 401(k) and/or your IRA account must withdraw the entire amount within ten years after your death unless one of the exceptions applies. How much and when to withdraw money during that period is up to the beneficiary: They can take everything out at once or withdraw funds throughout the ten years.

REMEMBER

As with all government regulations, there are some exceptions to this ten-year rule: They include a surviving spouse, disabled person, chronically ill person, a child who hasn't reached the age of majority, and a person not more than ten years younger than you. A surviving spouse may be able to leave the money in the 401(k) and take lifetime distributions.

Your 401(k) plan doesn't have to give your beneficiaries the option to keep the money in the 401(k). It may require them to take a lump sum distribution, which is fully taxable as ordinary income in the year distributed except for your Roth contributions and the investment gains on them.

WARNING

The tax liability is a significant issue for a beneficiary who has a high level of taxable income. A beneficiary who already has significant income may be pushed into a higher tax bracket as a result of an IRA distribution.

Your beneficiaries may transfer the taxable portion into an inherited traditional or Roth IRA. With a traditional IRA, the beneficiary avoids paying tax until they take distributions from the inherited IRA. The same rules apply as for any other traditional IRA. For example, in most circumstances, a 10 percent penalty tax applies if money is withdrawn by someone who is younger than 59½. The Roth contributions and investment gains can be transferred into an inherited Roth IRA and continue benefiting from tax-sheltered investment growth.

Any Roth contributions to a 401(k) and investment gains on those contributions shouldn't be transferred into an IRA because no taxes are owed.

REMEMBER

Converting the taxable portion of the distribution into a Roth IRA means paying taxes during the year of the conversion. The taxable portion includes your pre-tax contributions, employer contributions, and investment gains on these contributions. The beneficiary may use part of the distribution to pay the applicable taxes, which results in less money going into the inherited Roth IRA. The beneficiary can use other sources to pay the taxes and can then transfer the entire taxable distribution into the inherited Roth IRA.

The beneficiary receiving the 401(k) distribution then names beneficiaries for either type of inherited IRA.

REMEMBER

Distribution options within a 401(k) are possible only if the plan permits them. For example, the plan may require a mandatory lump-sum distribution to the beneficiaries. I advise my 401(k) clients to permit only lump-sum distributions because participants and beneficiaries have similar options via an IRA rollover as they do if the money is left in the 401(k). They are able to defer having to pay taxes by rolling the money into an inherited IRA.

Passing along Company Stock

The applicable laws are complex when it comes to employer stock held in your 401(k) account. The value of the stock when you received it in your 401(k), the *cost basis*, is taxable to you as additional income during the year the stock is distributed. The plan's administrator is required to provide the value of the stock when it was contributed. Your beneficiaries can get a huge tax break if you retain the stock and have it pass to your beneficiaries.

Imagine you have a retirement account with $100,000 of employer stock and the cost base is $40,000. You have to pay income tax on the $40,000 cost base if you roll over the stock into a brokerage account instead of an IRA. This way you avoid paying income tax on the $60,000 increase in value that has occurred over the years. You can avoid paying any tax on the gains until shares of the stock are sold. When you sell any shares of the stock, the gains will be taxed at the capital gains tax rate rather than at your income tax rate. This gives you a tax break as long as capital gains tax rates are less than income tax rates. You lose this advantage if you transfer the stock into an IRA.

You can sell portions or all of the stock anytime you want after the transfer into the brokerage account. Say you sell $10,000 worth of the stock shortly after the stock is transferred into the brokerage account when the total value of the stock is still $100,000. This means you will be selling 10 percent of the shares. The cost base for those shares is $4,000 (10 percent of $40,000). You won't owe any tax on this portion because you already paid tax when the stock was transferred into the brokerage account. The increase in value taxable as a capital gain is $6,000 (10 percent of the increase in value). You have to pay capital gains tax on the $6,000 gain.

The risk of having a large amount invested in only one stock during your retirement years needs to be considered before you decide to go this route. You can sell all or some of the stock after you retire at any time to reduce this risk. You can, for example, pay tax on the $40,000 value, transfer all shares into a brokerage account, and decide to sell 5 percent or some other percent each year. Normally you must hold stock for one year to have the gain taxed as a capital gain. The one-year requirement doesn't apply in this instance.

Passing as much of the stock as possible to your heirs provides them an additional major tax advantage. Your beneficiaries get the stock at a stepped-up value for tax purposes. Using the $100,000 example, they don't have to pay any tax on the $60,000 increase in value of the stock. They also don't have to pay any tax on any additional increase in value during the time the shares were transferred out of your 401(k) account into your brokerage account.

They pay capital gains tax only on any increase in value of the shares after they receive them and only when they sell the shares. If the stock is worth $200,000 when you die and if your heirs promptly sell the shares at the same value, they don't have to pay any tax. That means no taxes are ever paid on the $160,000 increase in value of the stock that occurred after the shares were contributed into your 401(k) account.

WARNING

Reducing your investment risk can backfire on your heirs. Say you transfer company shares into an IRA and then sell the shares to reduce your investment risk by investing the money in a diversified portfolio. The entire value of your portfolio is taxable to your beneficiaries as additional income at their personal tax rates. The amount of tax they must pay can be substantial, particularly if they have lots of earned income. You reduced your investment risk by selling the stock and investing in other things, but your beneficiaries must pay a lot of taxes.

The situation is different if you need to convert your entire 401(k) account into a stream of income that will last the rest of your life. Selling all or a large portion of the stock so you can properly diversify your investments may be the best decision.

Starting the Roth Clock

A Roth IRA offers estate-planning opportunities because the entire account can be retained until death without any required minimum distributions. The account can grow without any tax on the investment gains during the account holder's enter lifetime. If your contributions to a 401(k) plan are made to a Roth account, the required minimum distribution rules still apply, and you will be required to withdraw part of your account each year.

TIP

The five-year Roth IRA requirement is a great reason to establish a Roth IRA soon if you have significant 401(k) and/or IRA accumulations. A Roth IRA must be in existence for at least five years before you can avoid paying taxes on the investment gains you withdraw. Even if you put just $1,000 into it, you start the five-year clock ticking, which will make your beneficiaries thankful.

Having living beneficiaries for your 401(k) and IRA at the time of your death enables these funds to go to these individuals promptly after your death. Otherwise, these funds have to go through probate, which will delay the transfer and result in unnecessary fees.

Qualifying Your Charitable Giving

Another estate-planning issue worth considering if you're approaching retirement or have already retired and successfully accumulated a lot more in a tax-deferred 401(k) or a traditional IRA than you need for your retirement is a qualified charitable distribution, or QCD.

Giving a good QCD

Essentially, making a QCD means transferring money from an IRA directly to a qualified charity — in IRA terms, a *qualified charitable entity,* or QCE. You can search to see whether an organization is recognized as a suitable donation recipient at apps.irs.gov/app/eos/. After you identify the charity you want to donate to, get in touch with them to find out how to make a direct-transfer QCD.

You can't make a QCD from funds held in a 401(k) account. The 401(k) account holder must transfer funds from the 401(k) account into a traditional IRA or make the QCD from other funds held in a traditional IRA.

Donor-advised funds, including other supporting charitable entities and private foundations, don't qualify for QCDs. A *donor-advised fund* is a charitable investment account for the sole purpose of supporting charitable organizations. Major financial organizations like Vanguard and Fidelity operate donor-advised funds. The money or other assets transferred into these funds are invested for tax-free growth, and you may recommend grants to virtually any IRS-qualified public charity. However, the fund makes the donation, not you, and you can't mark your contribution as a QCD.

Linking RMDs and QCDs (and minding your Ps and Qs)

Qualified charitable distributions (QCDs) are tied to required minimum distributions (RMDs). The RMD is, as the name implies, a distribution you must take each year from an employer-sponsored retirement plan, traditional IRA, SEP, or SIMPLE IRA starting when you turn 72. If you own 5 percent or more of the company holding the retirement plan, you must start taking the minimum amount when you turn 70½. If you're an actively employed individual and don't own 5 percent or more of the business, the age 72 requirement doesn't apply to you.

REMEMBER

The amount you give to a charity must not exceed your RMD unless you're in the age 59½ to age 72 gap period.

The Secure Act increased the age at which you must start taking RMDs from 70½ to age 72. However, age 70½ was retained as the minimum age at which a QCD is permissible. That means a traditional IRA account holder who is over age 70½ can make a QCD without taking any other distribution.

You can make up to $100,000 per year of QCDs to one or more QCEs. Between ages 70½ and 72, the QCD will not be taxable if it is made directly to the QCEs. After age

72, the amount of QCDs may not exceed the RMD for that year. For example, if your RMD for 2022 is $15,000, this is the maximum permissible QCD for that year.

Roth IRAs are exempt from RMDs except when inherited by a non-spouse of the account holder.

A QCD may be counted toward your RMD, but there is a "gotcha" to avoid. The applicable RMD for the year must be satisfied first. So, make the QCD first before you withdraw other funds.

Assume you want to make a $10,000 QCD during 2022 and your RMD for 2022 is $20,000. You also want the QCD to count toward your RMD. To do that, you must first have $10,000 transferred to the applicable eligible charitable entities. You may then withdraw the additional $10,000 needed to satisfy the RMD any time during 2022. Doing it in this manner lets you satisfy the RMD rules and pay tax on only the $10,000 paid to you.

The situation gets much dicier when a husband and wife are both required to take RMDs from retirement accounts they each have. There isn't any tax penalty if you withdraw more than the RMD in any year, but there is a 50 percent tax penalty for not withdrawing enough.

Giving tax free

Funds leaving an IRA for a qualified charity aren't taxable because the distribution isn't income. This results in a lower adjusted gross income than a regular withdrawal from your IRA that is then given to charities.

For example, assume you give $5,000 annually to QCEs. Taking funds from your IRA to do this will increase your adjusted gross income by $5,000 because an itemized deduction doesn't reduce adjusted gross income. The QDC benefit is also in addition to the standard deduction, which is $12,550 for a single taxpayer and $25,100 for a married couple filing jointly. Many individuals no longer receive a tax break for charitable donations because they take the standard deduction rather than itemizing deductions. Using a QCD is a way to get a tax break for your charitable giving.

Using QCDs to make charitable contributions may also result in having to include a smaller portion of your Social Security benefits as taxable income. The rules applicable to tax on your Social Security benefits are covered in Chapter 12. Your adjusted gross income is the first item included in determining how much, if any, of your Social Security benefits will be taxable.

QCDs aren't limited to just those who have more retirement account assets than they know they'll need. They can be beneficial to anyone who supports charitable organizations.

Being a Beneficiary

If you're a beneficiary of someone else's retirement plan, you have to do a little bit of work and maybe some contemplation about how to handle your windfall.

Before you get access to the funds, you most likely have to fill out a form that asks for some or all of the following information:

>> The name of the *decedent* (the person who died and left you the account)

>> The decedent's Social Security number

>> The decedent's account number

>> Your name and contact information

>> Your Social Security number and date of birth

>> The account number the funds are going into

Keep this information handy; you'll need most of it when you open your beneficiary IRA.

REMEMBER

Opening an inherited IRA means you need to name your own beneficiaries. See the "Deciding Who Gets Your Savings When You're Gone" section earlier in this chapter for the information you need for that form.

Deciding — or being told — what to do with the money

A surviving spouse has the option of retaining an existing IRA and designating it as their own or rolling the money into their own IRA. All IRA rules apply when a spouse transfers an IRA that is inherited into their own current IRA or a new IRA. This includes the early withdrawal tax penalty prior to age 59½ unless the withdrawal is for one of the permitted exceptions. A surviving spouse can also roll over into their own 401(k) account if the plan permits. All rules applicable to 401(k) apply following the transfer, including required minimum distributions.

Non-spousal beneficiaries must open a separate inherited IRA because a rollover into an existing IRA is considered a taxable distribution.

All other beneficiaries must take full distribution of the IRA benefits they inherit within ten years. The actual deadline is December 31 following the tenth anniversary of the deceased's death. For example, the deadline is December 31, 2031, if the deceased died on February 3, 2021. Any amount may be withdrawn at any time during the ten-year period. Leaving the entire amount invested to grow tax-free until being withdrawn is another option. The entire amount can be withdrawn in a lump sum just prior to the deadline. All amounts withdrawn will be taxable, so that plays a part in deciding how and when to take withdrawals.

REMEMBER

Mingling inherited 401(k) or IRA accounts with another IRA isn't permitted.

The 10 percent early distribution penalty doesn't apply for a lump-sum payment if the beneficiary is a surviving spouse, minor child, disabled person, or chronically ill individual no more than ten years younger than the deceased.

TIP

If you're the beneficiary of a Roth IRA, you can leave the balance to grow tax free for the entire ten-year period before you're required to withdraw the money. You can also withdraw any amount during this ten-year period as desired. If the Roth IRA was at least five years old when you inherit it, withdrawals during this ten-year period aren't taxable.

Saying no to the money

A beneficiary may *disclaim*, or refuse, all or part of an inherited IRA. Generally, if you reject an IRA inheritance you do it because

>> You know the other beneficiaries have greater financial needs.

>> You're already in a high tax bracket and accepting the money would push you into an even higher rate.

If you disclaim an IRA, you pay no taxes on the money because it was never really yours.

Stretching an inherited IRA

Any beneficiary other than a minor child may elect to take life expectancy distributions from an inherited IRA. If you choose this option, you receive regular benefit distributions, usually monthly or quarterly, in a fixed amount. You can understand why this distribution plan is sometimes called a stretch IRA.

The minimum amount to be withdrawn is determined by using a life expectance mortality table. Most major financial institutions that hold IRA accounts can determine the proper amount. Using an accountant who is familiar with these requirements is another possibility. This is not a good DIY project due to the big tax penalty if the withdrawals are too small.

2

401(k) Basics

Realize that contributing to a 401(k) brings various benefits from tax credits to tax deferrals, and maybe contributions from your company.

Discover all you need to know about joining a 401(k) — how, when, whether you can, or whether you're automatically in.

Look into the fees you pay related to your 401(k) and hope your employer is smart enough to pay administrative costs for you.

Explore options for your 401(k) when you leave your job. Decide whether to take your money to a new plan, keep it where it is, or convert it to an IRA.

Chapter **4**

Checking the Benefits of a 401(k)

In the 40-plus years 401(k) plans have been available, millions of Americans have used them to save for retirement. Because Social Security alone won't provide adequate retirement income and fewer companies offer a traditional pension plan, 401(k)s have become an essential part of the average worker's retirement plans.

Even young people, for whom retirement is normally low on the priority list, have jumped on the retirement savings bandwagon. They're the smart ones, because in some respects, how long you save is more important than how much you save.

The 2008 market crash caused 401(k) plans to come under fire because owners saw large drops in their accounts. Some blamed the 401(k) itself, but that's like blaming the messenger who brings you bad news. Those who didn't panic and kept making their usual 401(k) contributions have done well. If you take the time to understand and follow basic investing principles (which I talk about in Chapters 13 and 14), your 401(k) can grow into a nest egg that can help you retire comfortably.

REMEMBER

The beauty of a 401(k) is that it makes saving easy and automatic, and you probably won't even miss the money you save.

How much your 401(k) will be worth when you retire depends on a number of factors, such as how much you contribute, what investments you choose, what return you get on those investments, whether your employer makes a contribution, and whether you withdraw money early.

Realizing What a 401(k) Does for You

A 401(k) plan lets you put some of your income away now to use later, presumably when you're retired and not earning a paycheck. This procedure may not appeal to everyone; human nature being what it is, many people would rather spend their money now and worry about later when later comes. That's why the federal government approved tax breaks for 401(k) participants to enjoy now. Uncle Sam knows that your individual savings are going to be an essential part of your retirement, and he wants to give you an incentive to save.

When you sign up for a 401(k) plan, you agree to let your employer deposit some of the money you earn into the plan as a pre-tax contribution, Roth after-tax contribution, or a combination of the two, instead of paying it to you. (You always pay tax on contributions before they go into a Roth account; see Chapter 9 for more on Roths.) Your employer may even throw some money, known as a *matching contribution*, into your 401(k). You don't pay federal income tax on any of this money except the Roth contribution until you withdraw it. (I talk about matching contributions in the upcoming "Gets you matching funds from your employer" section.)

WARNING

Of course, there's a catch. Some 401(k) plans don't allow you to withdraw money while you're still working. Even if your plan does allow withdrawals, if you're under 59½ years old, those withdrawals can be difficult and costly. I talk about taking out money before you retire in Chapter 16.

The next sections cover the benefits of what a 401(k) does for you.

Lowers how much tax you pay

A 401(k) lets you pay less income tax in two ways:

REMEMBER

>> **Lower taxable income:** You don't have to pay federal income tax on the money you contribute with pre-tax contributions to your 401(k) plan until you withdraw it from the plan.

If you're making contributions to a Roth 401(k), you must pay tax now on the amount you put into the plan. (See Chapter 9 for details about Roth retirement accounts.)

>> **Tax deferral:** You don't pay tax on your 401(k) investment earnings each year. You pay tax on your pre-tax contributions, any employer contributions, and your investment gains on these contributions only when you make withdrawals.

The investment gains on your Roth contributions are never taxed if you follow the rules.

The government provides these big tax breaks in an attempt to avoid having a country full of senior citizens who can't make ends meet. (Nice to know the government's looking out for seniors, huh?)

Lower taxable income

The money you contribute to a 401(k) except for Roth contributions reduces your *gross income* or *taxable income* — and lowers your pay before tax and some other deductions. When you have lower taxable income, you pay less of the following income or wage taxes:

>> **Federal taxes:** These taxes increase as your taxable income increases — for 2021, the marginal rate for most workers is either 12 or 22 percent, and the top tax rate is 37 percent. (Chapter 2 has more information about retirement-related tax issues.)

>> **State taxes:** Many states impose their own income or wage taxes, ranging from less than 1 percent to as much as 13.3 percent in 2021, depending on the state.

>> **Local/municipal government taxes:** Many local and municipal governments also have income or wage taxes. The top city wage tax rates are almost 4 percent.

In every state except Pennsylvania, you aren't required to pay state income tax on your 401(k) contributions if you opt for pre-tax contributions. Your contributions are also exempt from most local wage taxes. Check with your local tax authorities if you're not sure what the rules are.

TECHNICAL STUFF

Taxes that you can't avoid paying because everybody has to pay them on gross income (including 401(k) contributions) are Social Security/Medicare (FICA) and unemployment (FUTA) taxes. The only way to avoid these taxes is if you're a sole proprietor and set up a plan funded with employer contributions rather than employee salary-reduction contributions.

Check the following hypothetical to see how you save money when you contribute some of your pay pre-tax to a 401(k). Consider the following hypothetical example:

>> Your gross pay is $3,000 each pay period.

>> You're in the 22 percent federal tax bracket.

>> Your state income tax is 2 percent, your local income tax is 1 percent, and your FICA taxes are 7.65 percent.

FICA tax is 7.65 percent up to $142,800 for 2021 — split 6.2 percent for Social Security and 1.45 percent for Medicare. All income above $142,800 is subject to the 1.45 percent Medicare tax for 2021. There's a cap on the maximum amount of your income subject to Social Security tax but no cap on the amount subject to Medicare tax.

>> You don't live in Pennsylvania, so contributions you make to a 401(k) plan are exempt from federal, state, and local tax.

You have the option to contribute to a retirement plan. Table 4-1 shows the difference to your bottom line when you choose to participate. The right side shows what happens when you hypothetically make a 6 percent, or $180, per paycheck pre-tax contribution to a 401(k) plan. Your FICA/FUTA taxes remain the same, but other taxes are lower because they're based on a lower income (your gross income minus your retirement contribution). Here's how it breaks down:

TABLE 4-1   **Take-Home Pay without and with 401(k) Contributions**

	Without 401(k) Contributions	With 401(k) Contribution
Gross pay	$3,000	$3,000
Retirement contribution	$0	$180
Federal income tax withheld	$350	$310
State income tax withheld	$60	$56
Local wage tax withheld	$30	$28
FICA taxes withheld	$230	$230
Take-home pay	$2,330	$2,196

You invested $180 for your retirement, but your take-home pay is reduced by only $134. For the time being, you're up $46 that would otherwise have gone to the government. You don't have to pay these taxes until you withdraw your money from the plan. As a general rule in this tax bracket, if you contribute $1, your take-home pay is reduced by only about 75 cents.

Another way of looking at it: Without a 401(k) plan, taxes eat away the money you can save.

Say you want to put 10 percent of your earnings into retirement savings. You earn $75,000 per year, so you want to set aside $7,500 for your retirement fund. Your total tax rate is 32.65 percent — 22 percent federal income tax plus 7.65 percent

FICA plus 2 percent state income tax plus 1 percent local wage taxes — so it takes almost 16 percent of your gross income, or $11,136, to have 10 percent left to invest for retirement.

You have to earn $11,136 in order to have $7,500 left after paying taxes — bummer. The following table lays out this scenario:

Pre-tax earnings required	$11,136
Federal income tax	– $2,450
State/local wage tax	– $334
FICA taxes	– $852
Amount left to save	$7,500

Now assume that your employer offers a 401(k) plan, and you can save the $7,500 pre-tax in your 401(k) account. In this case, the only tax you have to pay at the time you make the contribution is FICA. As a result, you need to earn only $8,121 in order to be able to contribute $7,500 to the 401(k) plan — $7,500 plus the 7.65 percent FICA tax, which is $621. Check out the difference:

Pre-tax earnings required	$8,121
Federal income tax	$0
State/local wage tax	$0
FICA taxes	– $621
Amount left to save	$7,500

Without a 401(k) plan, it takes you $11,136 in pre-tax income to save $7,500 after taxes. When you can save pre-tax money in your 401(k), it takes only $8,121 to save the same $7,500. In other words, with a 401(k), it costs less of your current earnings to save the same amount. Pretty good deal, don't you think?

Even better, you can also avoid the $621 FICA taxes if you are self-employed and set up an employer-funded plan. That means you only need $7,500 to invest $7,500 into a retirement account.

TIP

Some plans allow you to make *after-tax* contributions that aren't Roth contributions. You don't get the initial tax break of lower taxable income, but you do benefit from deferring taxes on your investment earnings. The earnings are taxable when they are withdrawn with this type of after-tax contribution.

Tax deferral

In addition to the income tax savings on your contributions, you also save when it comes to paying tax on your investment earnings.

The gains in your 401(k) aren't taxed annually, as they would be in a regular bank savings account, a personal mutual fund account, or a *brokerage account* (which you may use to buy and sell stocks and other investments). With a 401(k), you defer paying taxes on your investment earnings until you withdraw the money.

Figure 4-1 shows how tax-deferred compounding lets your money grow faster than it would in a taxable account. It compares the results of investing $7,500 at a 9 percent return in a tax-deferred account with investing $5,050 in a taxable account ($5,050 = $7,500 less income tax) at a 9 percent return.

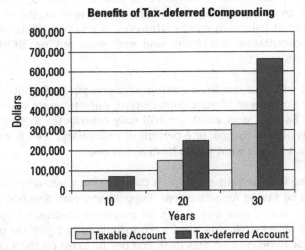

Benefits of Tax-deferred Compounding

FIGURE 4-1:
Positive impact of tax-deferred compounding.

Gets you matching funds from your employer

Whoever said there's no such thing as a free lunch didn't know about *employer matching contributions* — money that your employer contributes to your 401(k) if you contribute to the plan. (Not all employers make this type of contribution, but many do.)

The most common formula is for the employer to put in 50 cents for every dollar you contribute up to 6 percent of your salary. Employers may make higher (dollar-for-dollar, for example) or lower (25 cents on the dollar, for example) matching contributions and may match higher or lower percentages of salary. There's no set rule, and some employers are more generous than others. But after an employer sets the formula for the matching contribution, it must meet the commitment until it amends the *plan document* unless the document permits the employer to make variable employer matching contributions. (The plan document is the official document detailing the plan's rules.)

So, if your employer puts in 50 cents for every dollar you put in up to 6 percent of your salary, the most your employer will contribute is half of 6 percent, or 3 percent of your salary. You get this full 3 percent only if you contribute 6 percent or more of your salary.

For a concrete example, say you earn $50,000 a year. Six percent of your salary is $3,000. For every dollar you contribute to your 401(k) plan up to $3,000, your employer will contribute 50 cents. So, if you contribute $3,000, your employer contributes an additional $1,500, and you end up with $4,500 after only contributing $3,000 of your own money. However, if you contribute only $1,000, your employer contributes just $500, and you miss out on $1,000 in employer contributions.

How much will your employer contribute if you put in $4,000? If you answered $2,000, or 50 percent of your contribution, unfortunately you're wrong. If you contribute $4,000, your employer still only contributes $1,500 if the matching funds apply only to $3,000, or 6 percent of your salary. (Yes, it was a bit of a trick question, but I don't want you to be disappointed.)

You can also include your employer's contribution when determining how much you should be saving for retirement. Suppose you earn $50,000 and want to put aside 10 percent in your 401(k). If your employer contributes up to 3 percent of your salary as a match, you need to contribute only 7 percent of your salary to achieve your 10 percent savings goal. You pay no taxes on the 3 percent employer contribution until you withdraw it from the 401(k), so the math works out as follows:

Your contribution of 7 percent:	$3,500
Employer 3 percent matching contribution:	± $1,500
Total contribution:	= $5,000

TIP

An employer matching contribution gives you an incentive to save, and it can give your savings a powerful boost. It makes sense for you to contribute at least the full amount that your employer will match.

You typically have to work for your employer for a certain period of time before you can leave the company without losing your employer's contributions. I talk about that in the upcoming "Vesting: When Your Employer's Contribution Is Yours to Keep" section later in this chapter.

REMEMBER

The employer matching contribution can be the single most important feature of your 401(k) plan. The more you get from your employer, the less you have to save out of your own paycheck to achieve an adequate level of retirement income. In fact, if your employer offers a matching contribution, make sure that you contribute enough to your plan to get it all. If you don't, this money will be lost to you. Keep in mind that it's easier to contribute the amount needed to get the full employer matching contribution if you utilize pre-tax rather than Roth contributions.

Note: Some employers make what's called a *variable* or *discretionary matching contribution* — a hybrid of profit-sharing and matching contributions. You have to contribute to your 401(k) to get it, as with an ordinary matching contribution, but the amount of the contribution varies at the discretion of your company. For example, the amount of your matching contribution may depend on the success of your company from one year to the next.

Makes room for a little something extra: Employer non-matching contribution

Some employers contribute to their employees' 401(k) accounts (or to another plan) whether the employee contributes or not in what's called a *non-matching contribution*. For example, your employer may deposit a profit-sharing contribution into the 401(k) on your behalf, either alone or in addition to a matching contribution. In a good year, for example, your employer may contribute 5 percent of each eligible employee's pay as a profit-sharing contribution, plus a 25 percent of 401k deferral or 50 percent of 401k deferral matching contribution. You get the 5 percent no matter what, but you only get the additional matching contribution if you put some of your salary into the plan. In a bad year, the company may only make the matching contribution and forgo the profit-sharing contribution, or it may even forgo both contributions!

A company may also make *a non-matching employer contribution* that's not based on its financial results. The employer may contribute a specific percentage of your pay each year — typically between 3 and 5 percent — regardless of whether the company does well. A non-matching employer contribution is frequently used when a company has discontinued a defined-benefit pension plan in favor of a defined-contribution arrangement including a cash-balance plan.

Automatic contributions may also be made in what's called a *Safe Harbor 401(k)* or a *Qualified Automatic Contributions Arrangement* (QACA). These are two types of 401(k) plans that don't have to pass certain federal nondiscrimination tests that are part of the law governing 401(k)s. Details about all types of 401(k) plans are included in Part 5.

Allows you to save without tears

A big benefit of signing up for your 401(k) plan is that you don't have to think about the fact that you're saving. "Out of sight, out of mind" is what happens to most people — they don't even miss the money, because it's taken out of their paycheck before they have a chance to spend it.

REMEMBER

This semi-forced savings is one of the most valuable benefits of 401(k) plans. The payroll deduction has the power to convert spenders into savers. Most people are unable to save over a long period of time if they have to physically write the check or make the deposit each pay period. Saving becomes the last, not the first, priority. Many participants have said that the 401(k) has helped them save thousands of dollars that they otherwise would have spent carelessly.

It's a good idea to increase your 401(k) contributions if you get a raise or a bonus. In fact, do it right away so that you don't get used to spending the extra money.

Vesting: When Your Employer's Contribution Is Yours to Keep

When your employer puts money into your 401(k) plan, that money doesn't necessarily belong to you right away. Most companies require that you stay employed with them for a certain amount of time before the contributions *vest*, or are yours to keep if you leave your job. They use this requirement to encourage you to stay on the job.

The employer contributions are generally deposited in the account right away, earning a return on your behalf even before they vest. If you leave your job before the employer contributions vest, you forfeit those contributions plus any earnings on them.

REMEMBER

The contributions you make from your salary are always yours to keep, and you can take them with you when you leave. Vesting applies only to contributions made by your employer.

Your employer can't make you wait forever to vest. There are maximum lengths of time for matching and non-matching contributions. What are they? Keep reading to find out.

Vesting of employer contributions

Employer contributions, whether matching or non-matching, must generally become yours to keep in one of the following two ways:

>> All at once on a specified date within three years

>> Gradually over six years

The first method is known as *cliff vesting*. With this method, you go from 0 to 100 percent vested after three years of service, at the most (the period can be shorter). The second is called *graded vesting*, or *graduated vesting*. With this method, you must go from 0 to 100 percent vested by increases of 20 percent over a period of six years at the most.

Table 4-2 shows a comparison of the two vesting schedules, looking at the maximum number of years of service that an employer can generally require.

An employer may choose a faster vesting schedule (and may even choose to have your matching contributions 100 percent vested at all times).

TABLE 4-2

Longest Allowed 401(k) Matching Contribution Vesting Schedules

Years of Service	Cliff	Graduated
Less than 2	0%	0%
2 but less than 3	0%	20%
3 but less than 4	100%	40%
4 but less than 5	100%	60%
5 but less than 6	100%	80%
6 or more	100%	100%

Making exceptions (You knew this was coming, right?)

A few other situations may cause immediate vesting of matching and non-matching employer contributions no matter how many years you have worked at the company. These situations are as follows:

>> If your employer terminates your 401(k) plan

>> If you reach normal retirement age (an age defined by the plan, but usually age 65)

>> If you die before you leave the company

>> If you become disabled, as defined in the plan

>> If you're among a substantial portion (such as more than 20 percent) of plan participants who are laid off due to the closing of a plant or division, or are otherwise part of a large layoff

>> If your employer needs to make contributions to pass one of the nondiscrimination tests for a regular 401(k)

TECHNICAL STUFF

Employer contributions to a Safe Harbor 401(k) must be fully vested at all times. Employer contributions to a QACA 401(k) must be fully vested after two years.

To find out which rules apply to you, check your summary plan description.

Letting the Pros Work for You

Have you ever wished that you could hire a professional money manager to handle your investments? A 401(k) lets you take a step in that direction by offering *mutual funds.*

Mutual funds are investments that let you pool your money with the money of hundreds or thousands of other investors. An investment expert called the *fund manager* decides how to invest all this money, trying to get the best return on your investment based on the fund's *investment objective.* Because the fund manager invests your money along with the money contributed by other investors in the fund, they have more money to invest and can spread it around to different companies or sectors of the economy. This *diversification* helps reduce the amount of risk that you take with your investments. (I talk more about selecting investments, including mutual funds, in Chapter 13.)

What does this mean for you? If you choose your fund carefully, you benefit from a professional money manager who's seeking the best return for the fund's investors, based on the fund's investment objectives.

In most cases, your employer is responsible for choosing the mutual funds (and any other investments) offered by your 401(k) plan. More than 8,000 mutual funds are registered in the United States. If your employer does a good job of narrowing the offering down to a handful, it can save you a lot of time.

BUYING MORE WHEN PRICES ARE LOW

When you invest a specified amount at regular intervals, as you do with automatic 401(k) contributions from your paycheck, you're using an investment strategy called *dollar cost averaging.* (You didn't know you were that smart, did you?) This investment strategy may lower the average price that you pay for your investments. How? Because you're spending the same amount each time you invest, you end up buying more shares of your investments when prices are low and fewer shares when prices are high. By averaging high and low prices, you reduce the risk that you will buy more shares when prices are high.

Of course, if stock prices only go up for the entire time you invest, this strategy won't work. But if you contribute to a 401(k) over a long period of time, there will likely be periods when prices go down. It's important to keep contributing when the value of your investments drop because additional shares purchased when prices are lower help your account grow when prices rebound.

Rather than rely on choices made by their employer, however, some investors prefer to choose their own investments, such as individual stocks, mutual funds, or other investments that aren't included in their plans. Some 401(k) plans offer a *brokerage window* that allows you to choose your own investments. But you generally pay an extra fee if you use this feature. Chapter 13 has more details on brokerage windows.

You have the sole responsibility as an IRA investor for deciding where to invest your IRA contributions.

Protecting Your Money

Investing money always involves some risks, but money in a 401(k) plan is protected in some ways that money in an ordinary savings account, brokerage account, or IRA isn't. The next sections explain the safeguards.

Meeting minimum standards

A federal law called ERISA, the Employee Retirement Income Security Act, governs 401(k) plans. Passed in 1974, ERISA sets minimum standards for retirement plans offered by private-sector companies. Some nonprofits also follow ERISA rules, but local, state, and federal government retirement plans, as well as church plans, don't have to.

ERISA requirements include

>> Providing information to you about plan features on a regular basis, including a *summary plan description* outlining the plan's main rules, when you enroll in the plan and periodically thereafter.

>> Defining how long you may be required to work before being able to sign up for the plan or before employer contributions to the plan are yours to keep if you leave your job.

>> Detailing requirements for the *plan fiduciary,* essentially including anyone at your company or the plan provider who has control over the investment choices in the plan. (A fiduciary who breaks the rules may be sued by participants.)

REMEMBER

This last point, *fiduciary responsibility*, is important to understand. Essentially, it means that anyone who has a decision-making role in your 401(k) plan's investments is legally bound to make those decisions in the best interests of the plan participants (you and your co-workers), and not in the best interest of the company, the plan provider, or the fiduciary's cousin Joe. For example, the committee in charge of choosing a 401(k) provider shouldn't choose Bank XYZ just because the company president's cousin runs the bank.

But this doesn't necessarily mean that you can sue your employer if your 401(k) doesn't do well. (Keep in mind that lawsuits are often costly and won't endear you to your employer.) If you lose most of your money because you make bad investment decisions or the stock market takes a nosedive, but your employer has followed ERISA rules, your employer isn't liable. Your employer may gain limited protection through something called *404(c)*. Without going into too much detail, Section 404(c) of ERISA requires your employer to provide you with specific information about your plan, including information about the investment options, and allows you to make changes in your investments frequently enough to respond to ups and downs in the market. In return, you assume liability for your investment results.

Avoiding losses in bankruptcy

Many people wonder whether their 401(k) money is at risk if their employer goes out of business. The answer is usually no, with a few caveats:

>> If the money is in investments that are tied to your employer, such as company stock, and the employer goes bankrupt, you may lose your money. (This is a compelling argument for you to limit the amount of your 401(k) that you invest in a single stock.)

>> In the case of fraud or wrongdoing by your employer or the trustee of the 401(k) account, your money may be at risk. (The trustee would be personally liable to return your money, but that's no help if they have disappeared.)

These situations are rare; what's more, your employer is required to buy a type of insurance — a *fidelity bond* — when it sets up the plan that may enable you to recoup at least some of your money in the event of dishonesty. (Fidelity bonds generally cover 10 percent of the amount in the entire plan, or $500,000, whichever amount is smaller.)

>> Part of your money may be lost if your employer goes out of business or declares bankruptcy before depositing your contributions into the trust fund that receives the 401(k) money that is deducted from your paycheck.

REMEMBER

Federal law says that if you declare personal bankruptcy, your creditors generally can't touch your 401(k). They may be able to get at your other savings, but your 401(k) should be protected. Exceptions include if you owe money to the IRS or if a court has ordered you to give the money to your ex-spouse as part of a divorce settlement. In both of those cases, your 401(k) money is vulnerable.

Watching Out for Potential Pitfalls

The tax advantages you get with a 401(k) have a flip side: rules. Rules about when you can take your money out, whether you have to pay a penalty, and even what you can invest in. All of these are out of your control after you decide to contribute to a 401(k) plan. The following sections tell you what pitfalls to watch out for.

Earning more may mean contributing less

If you earn enough to qualify as a highly compensated employee, your contributions to your 401(k) plan may be limited to only a few percent of your salary. Many 401(k) plans are required to pass *nondiscrimination tests* each year to make sure that highly paid employees as a group aren't contributing a lot more to the plan than their lower-paid colleagues. In requiring these tests, Congress is looking out for the little guy and gal. Chapter 12 explains how these tests work and who qualifies as "highly compensated."

Being at the mercy of your plan

A well-administered, well-chosen, flexible 401(k) plan can be a wonderful benefit. A poorly administered plan with bad investment choices and little flexibility can be a nightmare. I've heard stories of companies that don't invest employee contributions on time or that take money from the plan; companies that don't let employees contribute the maximum permitted; and companies where employees pay useless fees for a plan because the managers who set it up were incompetent, uninformed, or even criminals.

In most cases, the tax benefit of a 401(k) is a good enough reason to take advantage of the plan offered by your employer. However, if the investments offered by the plan are truly bad, the fees charged are exorbitant, or the administration of the plan is questionable, you may be better off investing your retirement money elsewhere until you have a better 401(k).

Chapter **5**

Signing Up for a 401(k)

occasionally hear from people who are self-employed or whose employers don't offer a retirement plan who want to know how they can open a 401(k) account. Unfortunately, it's not that simple. Unlike an IRA that you can open on your own, a 401(k) is only available through your employer.

Most companies aren't currently required to offer 401(k) plans (or any retirement plan, for that matter), but a growing number of states are requiring employers to do so. The fact that your employer offers a 401(k) doesn't mean that you're automatically eligible to contribute, though. Before joining your employer's 401(k) plan, you must fulfill your employer's eligibility requirements.

The information in this chapter can help you understand the paperwork you need to fill out when you sign up for your 401(k) plan. It also explains how much you're allowed to contribute, whether you're just signing up or whether you've been participating for years.

Exploring Your Eligibility

Your employer isn't required to let all employees join the 401(k) plan immediately. What's more, certain groups of employees can be excluded altogether. When interviewing for a job, be sure to ask what the rules are for the company's 401(k) plan.

As a new hire, you may be able to participate immediately, you may have to wait up to a year before you're eligible to join the plan — but no longer than 18 months — or you may never be eligible to participate in the plan.

For example, an employer can exclude employees who are younger than age 21 and those who haven't completed a year of service. Plus, the company may not offer a 401(k) plan to employees in every division of the company.

Sometimes you play a waiting game

Some companies require you to work there for a year before you can join the 401(k). Just be aware that different definitions of "year" are possible. For example, a year can mean

» Twelve months of continuous employment regardless of the number of hours worked.

» At least 1,000 hours of work during the course of 12 months of employment.

This hours-of-service method for determining a year of service is pretty simple: The employer sets the number of hours worked before you can join the company's 401(k) plan. That number is 1,000. So, you need to work 1,000 hours during your first 12 months of employment to be eligible to join a 401(k).

If you don't work 1,000 hours during your first 12 months, you can become eligible if you work at least 1,000 hours during a subsequent 12-month period.

Most employers shift the 12-month period to a calendar year because this is an easier way to track hours worked. You need credit for a year of service to be able to join the 401(k).

If you're a full-time employee, you work 1,000 hours in 25 40-hour weeks. So, if you work just 20 hours a week, you get to 1,000 work hours in 50 weeks, which is within a 52-week year (just in case you weren't paying attention).

The Secure Act passed in 2020 also requires employers to permit long-term, part-time employees to participate in 401(k) plans. These employees must work at least 500 hours in three consecutive years and be 21 or older to be eligible. Ask the human resources department for more information.

If you have to work 1,000 hours in one year to become eligible for the plan, you don't need to work 1,000 hours in subsequent years to remain in the plan. However, the number of hours you work in subsequent years may affect your eligibility to receive employer contributions. It may also affect how soon those contributions *vest*, or become your property. (See Chapter 4 for more on matching contributions and vesting.)

Sometimes you can't join at all

Employers are allowed to exclude certain employees from participating in the 401(k) plan. These employees include

» **Union employees covered by a collective bargaining agreement:** Federal law prohibits employers from offering any retirement or other benefit plan to union members that hasn't been agreed on through collective bargaining. This includes 401(k) plans — even those funded entirely by employee contributions. Labor laws require union employees who want a 401(k) to include it in their contract demands.

Union managers often prefer traditional defined-benefit pension plans, which guarantee benefits at retirement. This is the main reason that 401(k) coverage is lower among union employees. It's also why 401(k) plans for union employees typically don't include an employer matching contribution — the employer is already contributing to the defined-benefit plan.

» **Nonresident aliens:** Employers are allowed to exclude employees who live outside the United States and aren't U.S. citizens from participating in the plan. However, employees who are residents of the United States (including green card holders) but are not U.S. citizens can't be excluded simply because they're not U.S. citizens.

» **Leased employees:** *Leased employees* are people who work for a company temporarily, often placed through an agency.

» **Specific categories of employees:** Under certain circumstances, an employer may exclude a specific category of employee, such as hourly workers or the employees of a specific business unit, from participating in the 401(k) plan. Generally, an employer can legally exclude a group if it makes up less than 30 percent of all employees.

For example, your plan may permit only salaried workers to participate, and exclude hourly wage earners, if the hourly workers account for only 10 percent of the staff. However, even if the 30 percent test isn't satisfied, a variety of other exceptions may apply. Determining the categories of employees that may be excluded can be very complicated.

Finally, you may be excluded if you're under 21. The exclusion has to apply to all employees under 21, though; an employer can't permit some to participate and not others.

Sometimes you're automatically in

Many 401(k) plans use what's called *automatic enrollment.* Eligible employees are automatically signed up for the plan unless they refuse in writing. A percentage of salary is deferred into the plan for automatically enrolled employees and often is deposited in the most conservative investment option. The percentage is usually set between 3 and 6 percent by the employer and doesn't usually go above 10 percent. Employers must follow the applicable automatic enrollment rules to receive a special tax credit available. (Head to Chapter 18 for more on employer tax credits.)

You can change your contribution percentage at any time including opting out of the plan.

The Department of Labor has designated certain funds to be Qualified Default Investments for retirement accounts. Included as a prudent investment option are Target Date Funds (TDFs) that automatically invest and rebalance for the target year — you invest in one that matches the year you turn 65. A TDF is a balanced fund with a mix of stock and bond funds.

Your 401(k) plan may also permit your employer to automatically increase your contribution percentage each year. If so, you're permitted to override such increases by providing a written request.

If your plan has automatic enrollment, make the effort to come up with an investment plan to diversify your money among different investments. (A TDF is diversified from the get-go, so you don't need to seek diversity if you're enrolled in a TDF.) Also, consider contributing more than the amount your employer automatically deducts, which is likely to be too small to build up a sufficient nest egg.

Making Your Entry Date

Your employer is in control of when you can actually join the 401(k) plan once you become eligible. Your employer sets what are known as *entry dates,* the dates you can sign on to the 401(k). Entry dates are chosen for administrative reasons.

The maximum you have to wait is 18 months, but within that limit, your employer decides how many entry dates to offer and when they occur. For example, you may have two opportunities per year, January 1 and July 1; one each quarter on January 1, April 1, July 1, and October 1; or one each pay period.

Newly eligible employees are often invited to attend a meeting to explain various plan details and investment options. Limiting the number of such meetings can be a factor for limiting the number of entry dates.

Smart employers commonly permit new employees to join a 401(k) plan immediately. Excluding new hires from participating for 12 to 18 months may discourage prospective employees from accepting a new job, especially ones who have been contributing to a 401(k) at their previous employer.

You can join the plan on any entry date after you become eligible, and I advise you to start contributing to the plan as soon as you can. If you don't do that for some reason, you can enter the plan on any entry date that occurs after first becoming eligible.

Deciding How to Invest Your Money

After you decide how much to invest, you need to decide where to invest your money. Your enrollment papers typically include something called an *investment election form* (see Figure 5-1), which lists the investment options offered by your 401(k) plan. You need to specify the percentage of your contribution you want in the options you choose.

The percentages on your investment election form must add up to 100 percent.

If you're not sure right away what to invest in, don't use that as an excuse to put off signing up for the plan. At a minimum, find out if your plan offers a money market fund. A money market fund generally earns some interest and is the least likely to lose value, so it's a good short-term investment. Keep in mind that money market funds don't have as good a potential for long-term growth as stocks or bonds. Until you decide on a plan for investing your money, you can have your contributions deposited into a money market option. (You can read more about how to select investments in Chapter 13.)

If you want to change your investments, you can probably do so at any time by accessing your account online. Check to see whether this is how your plan operates.

WAGE DEFERRAL AGREEMENT
SAMPLE COMPANY 2 401K PLAN

Section 1: PARTICIPANT INFORMATION

Last Name	First Name	MI	Social Security Number

Address - Number and Street   City   State   Zip

Date of Birth: _____/_____/_____   Date of Hire: _____/_____/_____

Current Marital Status: ☐ Single ☐ Married

( )_____   ( )_____
Work Phone   Home Phone

Section 2: PARTICIPANT ELECTIONS

The Election is effective for the first pay period beginning on or after _____/_____/_____.

You may elect to make three types of contributions under the Plan: (i) pre-tax regular 401(k) contributions, (ii) after-tax Roth contributions, and (iii) traditional after-tax contributions:

☐ **Regular 401(k) contributions.** You are hereby authorized to reduce my regular wages by ____% or $_____ each pay period for contribution on a pre-tax basis to the Sample company 2 401k Plan.

☐ **Roth contributions.** You are hereby authorized to deduct ____% or $_____ each pay period from my regular wages for the purpose of making a Roth Contribution on an after tax basis to the Sample company 2 401k Plan.

PLEASE NOTE: The combined amount entered for regular 401(k) contributions and Roth contributions may not be more than one hundred percent (100%) of your compensation. The IRS maximum for pre-tax regular 401(k) contributions and after-tax Roth contributions in 2021 is $19,500. However, if you are age 50 or over, you may defer an additional amount up to $6,500 in Catch-up Contributions.

☐ **Traditional After Tax contributions.** You are hereby authorized to deduct ____% or $_____ each pay period from my regular wages for contribution on an after tax basis to the Sample company 2 401k Plan.

PLEASE NOTE: The amount entered may not be more than seventy-five percent (75%) of your compensation. The total combined Elective Deferrals and Traditional After Tax amounts may not exceed seventy-five percent (75%) of your compensation.

Section 3: STATEMENTS OF UNDERSTANDING

Please read and check off all boxes below:

☐ I have completed, understood, and agree to the terms in the Agreement and have read the Summary Plan Description in full.

☐ I understand that I may elect to start, increase or reduce my elections effective as of the dates established pursuant to Plan Administrator procedures. However, I may revoke my election at any time by so advising the Plan Administrator and may start, increase or reduce my election during the 30 day period following receipt of the Safe Harbor Notice. If I revoke my election, I may resume contributions only as of the dates specified above.

☐ I understand that I must give the Plan Administrator sufficient time to process any change or revocation of an election. I understand that this Wage Deferral Agreement will be processed in a timely manner, typically within a 15 day period.

☐ I understand that the election indicated on this agreement will continue into succeeding Plan Years unless I revoke or change the election in accordance with the rules listed above and in the Summary Plan Description.

☐ I understand that this agreement supersedes and nullifies any prior wage deferral agreements under this Plan.

Dated:_____   Signature:_____

I do not wish to have deferrals withheld from my wages and contributed to the Plan at this time.
Date:_____   Signature:_____

FIGURE 5-1:
Sample 401(k) investment election form.

IN THIS CHAPTER

» **Digging into the fees**

» **Paying plan advisors**

» **Finding information**

» **Seeking changes to your plan**

Chapter **6**

Paying Attention to Administrative Issues

4 01(k) plans involve a lot of number crunching and record keeping. Someone has to keep track of how much money is in each person's account and where the money is invested. Someone also has to produce your monthly, quarterly, or annual account statement. The plan needs to carry out federally required testing and reporting. These administrative functions need to be paid for, and guess who pays for them? You're right, for most plans, you do.

Your employer has the option of paying all non-investment fees or having you pay them. You don't usually pay them directly; instead, you pay them indirectly as charges to your account. In most instances you won't see these charges because they're buried by reducing your investment return, or they are deducted from participant accounts and appear on their account statements.

Figuring on the Fees

A 401(k) plan provides a service to you, and as with most services, it's not free. You're charged various fees and expenses for the administration of the plan, your account, and your investments inside the account. These charges aren't unusual, but you want to assess whether you're paying a reasonable amount.

Most employers hire an outside firm to handle administrative functions. In many cases, the *service provider* (the financial company that offers your plan's investments) also handles the recordkeeping and some other administrative services. But your employer may also hire separate companies — one to provide the investments and another to handle the administration of the plan.

Smaller plans typically have a financial organization that receives all contributions, invests them, provides the recordkeeping, and pays plan benefits. The employer may hire a third-party administrator to perform the other administrative functions. An investment advisor may help your employer build the investment menu and help you pick your investments.

WARNING

For years financial writers have asked me to explain how fees work. One I remember was determined to peel off the layers. I wished him good luck. When he called me back a few months later, he was very frustrated that he hadn't succeeded.

Chapters 18 and 19, which cover plans from an employer's perspective, have a lot of information about fees because the employer is responsible for knowing what they are. The major issue is whether the employer pays any of the fees or whether the participants pay them all. When the employer pays all fees except the true investment management fees, it makes things pretty simple because the employer is billed for all the non-investment fees. Otherwise, who pays what and how is very fuzzy.

Finding the fees

You may not realize that you're paying administrative fees. The expense may be clearly shown on your statement, or it may be hidden and simply reduce your investment return. For example, if the investment and administrative fees for your plan total 1 percent of plan assets annually, your investment return is reduced by 1 percent.

Figuring out exactly what your fees are can be harder than it sounds. You don't get a bill that lists exactly how much you're paying in fees — participants don't see the bill. Nor will you necessarily see an entry on your 401(k) statement that reports all fees deducted. Instead, you have to do some detective work to find out what you're paying.

A participant with a $100,000 account balance will pay $1,500 if the plan has total fees equal to 1.5 percent of total plan assets. A participant with a $5,000 account balance will pay only $75. Participants don't get any tax break for fees paid from their accounts. Employers get to deduct these fees and have Uncle Sam share some of the cost. Better yet, employers may get tax credits to help them start and maintain a retirement plan. See Part 5 for more from the employer's perspective.

TECHNICAL STUFF

Most 401(k) fees are expressed in *basis points*. One hundred basis points equals 1 percent. How much is 150 basis points? If you said 1.5 percent, you're right. Fifty basis points equals 0.5 percent.

Understanding the fees

It's worth the effort to discover what administrative costs you pay for your plan. In most cases, fees are deducted from your investment return — the money being earned by your investments. The higher the fees, the more they reduce your eventual balance.

401(k) fees can be tricky to understand because of the way plans are put together. A large number of people provide services to 401(k) plans including attorneys, accountants, record keepers, financial advisors, mutual fund companies, insurance companies, and more. Generally, you have a fixed administrative cost and variable costs associated with individual investment choices. Many plans are administered by financial companies that combine some or all of these fees and charge all participants' accounts the same percentage fee. (In this case, the higher your account balance, the higher the dollar amount you pay.)

For example: Say you and your spouse each contribute $5,000 a year to 401(k) plans from age 30 to age 65. You both earn an average 8 percent return on your investment (before fees). Your spouse's plan charges 1 percent in fees annually. Your plan charges 2 percent. Do you think this 1 percentage point will make a big difference in the end value of your accounts? You bet it will. Your spouse will have $641,000. Assuming everything else is equal, you'll have $521,000 — $120,000 less! Higher fees don't mean you will be getting better investments.

TECHNICAL STUFF

If you keep up on financial news, be aware that the investment return you receive for a fund held in your 401(k) account won't match the return you see reported in financial publications. For example, if you invest in a mutual fund that has a 0.5% investment management fee on your own outside the plan, the 0.5 percent is the only fee you pay. But if your 401(k) plan fees are 2 percent of plan assets due to the additional services that are required, you lose out on 1.5 percent of investment earnings. Your investment return net of expenses would be 1.5 percent higher if you purchased the fund outside the 401(k) plan.

Mutual funds can have multiple share classes — sometimes more than ten — each with a different expense ratio. As a result, you can't know what investment fee you're paying unless you know the share class. This difference in share classes makes it difficult to check your fund's performance because the returns shown in newspapers and elsewhere are class specific.

There are 14 different share classes according to Morningstar. The net investment return is different for each share class making it much more difficult to compare funds. Each one may have a different fee structure. Morningstar provides an array of investment research and investment management services.

The common types of services subject to fees include the following:

>> **Record-keeping and other administrative functions:** The plan pays people to keep track of each participant's account and the investments held in the account. Other administrative tasks include the following:

- Doing compliance testing

- Processing investment changes requested by participants

- Providing summary annual reports to participants and completing and filing Form 5500 — an annual return that must be filed for the plan

- Performing the independent audit that is required for plans with more than 100 participants

- Making plan document amendments and restatements as requested by the employer or as required by the IRS

>> **Financial advising:** This is done by an advisor, a person who helps your employer pick and oversee the plans investment menu.

>> **Investment management:** The mutual funds where your contributions are invested charge fees.

>> **Benefit transactions:** You may have to pay a fee to receive a benefit distribution such as a hardship withdrawal or a plan loan.

>> **Education and advice:** Yes, the fees paid to have someone educate you about the plan can be charged to the plan. The plan also pays to provide support to participants online, via phone, and/or in person.

Paying the fees

The biggest issue with paying fees is who pays — you or your employer. Fees are easy to determine when the employer pays all the non-investment fees because the employer is billed directly. No mystery in this case. If your employer pays, you can invest directly in the mutual funds and any other investments with the same fees you'd pay if you invested in an IRA.

When participants pay all the fees, it's very difficult to sort out how much the various parties are paid. The charged fees are split up among the record keeper, the financial advisor, and the third-party administrator.

The financial advisor is retained by the employer to get the best deal; however, there is a direct conflict of interest when the investment advisor is paid a percentage of the plan assets. This often results in the advisor selecting mutual funds with higher expense ratios that may also include an additional wrap fee because the higher the fees, the more the investment advisor is paid. (See the later section "Unwrapping wrap fees" for more about wrap fees.)

When you participate in a 401(k) plan, you should receive a fee disclosure notice that can help you determine the fees paid by you and your account.

REMEMBER

There's no "right" amount of fees to pay — although, if you're paying more than 1 percent of your account balance, you're probably paying too much. As with just about everything in investing, you have trade-offs to consider; if your plan charges relatively high fees but provides many useful services, you may be satisfied.

Total fees for plans with more than $100 million of plan assets can be as low as 0.15 percent. More than 0.5 percent is probably too high. Total fees paid by the participants for plans in the $10-to-$100 million range should generally range between 0.5 and 1.0 percent.

Fees are usually higher for plans with less than $10 million in assets. An alternative that should be considered by such employers is for the employer to pay the non-investment fees because those with the largest account balances are paying most of the fees from their tax-deferred accounts.

REMEMBER

Annual administrative fees in the $1,000 to $2,000 range aren't unusual for a plan with only ten participants. The average would be $200 per participant if there are ten participants, making the total administrative fees $2,000, but this doesn't mean that each participant pays $200 if the fees are paid from plan assets.

Typically, participants with higher balances pay more of the administrative fees. A participant with a $100,000 account balance may pay $1,500, while a participant with a $5,000 account balance pays only $75. The participant with the $100,000 account balance is helping subsidize the administrative costs for other participants.

Annual administration fees aren't investment-related expenses that vary by account size; they're expenses that are generally equal for all participants regardless of account size. Each participant will likely be charged a percentage of their account. For example, say your plan has 100 participants. The total administrative fee is $10,000 (100 × $100 each). If all participant accounts added together are worth $5 million, with some people having $200,000 in their accounts and others having $10,000, the plan fee is 0.2 percent of each person's account. (The $10,000 administrative fee is 0.2 percent of $5 million.) The people with a $200,000 balance pay $400, while the people with $10,000 balances pay $20.

So, participants with larger account balances subsidize the fees of those with smaller account balances. This amazes me because those with the larger account balances are usually the business decision makers. Paying these fees from their plan accounts substantially reduces what they will accumulate in their accounts. The employer can pay this fee and receive a tax deduction for doing so. The participant with the $200,000 account balance is paying $400 from his tax-sheltered account and gets no tax break for doing so.

If you think that your plan fees are too high, you don't necessarily have to abandon your 401(k), especially if your alternative is not saving for retirement at all. At least contribute enough to get the employer matching contribution, and explore other ways to save for retirement, such as an IRA. (Part 3 has more information about IRAs.)

Paying extra for extra services

If your plan offers special services, such as loans or hardship withdrawals, you'll probably have to pay a fee when you take advantage of them. For example, you may be charged one fee when you take out the loan and a separate annual fee for each year that it takes you to repay it. You may even have to pay a fee for the privilege of taking your money out of the plan when you change jobs or retire. These fees are commonly in the $50 to $100 range.

You usually have to pay these fees yourself because you trigger the transactions.

Checking on small business challenges

A small business has options for offering owners and employees retirement plans, just like the big companies; however, small businesses have additional compliance issues to consider. The most significant are the "top heavy" rules that apply to plans where key employees own more than 60 percent of total plan assets. See Chapter 18 for more details about these constraints.

As a small business owner, you have a range of 401(k) types and employer-sponsored IRA plans to investigate to determine which best suits your company's needs — or in the case of a 401(k), your employees' needs. Chapters 18 and 19 go into these choices in detail.

LEAVING NO-FEE FANTASYLAND

Some representatives of financial organizations tell employees who have 401(k) plans that they don't pay any fees. If someone tells you this, don't believe them. No organization that runs a 401(k) plan does so for free. The question is *how* participants pay the fee — not whether they pay one. You don't actually write a check to pay a fee, but the reduction in your investment return is a powerful form of payment.

When the stock market was strong throughout the 1990s, participants were indifferent to fees. It was hard to get worked up about an extra 0.5 percent in fees when net investment returns were 15 percent or higher. In a down market, that half a percentage point looks a lot more important, which is why things began to change after the 2008 market crash. Many employers have been sued by their participants due to excess fees, poorly performing funds, and other reasons. As a result, fees have been declining but they are still extremely high among some smaller employers. Not long ago, I helped a small employer whose participants were paying 2.75 percent per year restructure their plan to reduce the participant fees to 0.15 percent and to save the employer $1,500 per year in fixed fees and to eliminate other fees.

Small employers can provide a plan with costs as low as or even lower than those offered by the largest employers. The way to do this with a 401(k) is for the employer to pay all the non-investment fees. Chapter 19 covers how to do this in detail. Surprisingly, it is easy for a small employer to set up an IRA-based plan with fees that are lower than those paid by the largest employers — ones with billions of dollars of 401(k) plan assets — because these plans don't have any administrative fees. These plans are covered in detail in Chapter 18. If you are a solo entrepreneur or another type of small employer, consider these plans before jumping or being pushed into a 401(k) plan.

I have been the co-owner of several small businesses that had 401(k) plans. My businesses paid the administrative fees as an additional benefit to us as owners as well as the other employees, and it helped all our accounts grow faster. The last business I co-owned set up and administered 401(k) plans for small employers, and we strongly recommended that our clients have the business pay the administrative fees.

Small employers are often sold a 401(k) plan instead of an IRA-based plan, when a plan such as a SIMPLE IRA may be much better for both the employer and participants.

Small employers without a retirement plan should seriously consider the IRA-based alternatives because they avoid all this fee complexity and compliance baggage. There are no set-up or administrative fees, and there are no added layers of fees participants must pay. The chapters in Part 6 talk about plans for employers.

The 2021 maximum that may be contributed to an IRA-based plan is $13,500 for employees under age 50 and $16,500 for those over age 50 plus an additional 3-percent-of-pay employer contribution. The 401(k) maximum is $19,500 for employees under age 50 and $26,000 for those over age 50 plus any employer contribution. A 401(k) makes sense when there are employees who want to contribute significantly more than is possible with an IRA-based plan.

Considering Funding Issues

The 401(k) plan set up by your employer gives you choices about how to invest your money. Most 401(k) plans limit these choices to mutual funds. (I talk more about investing in Chapter 13.) What's important to know here is that mutual funds charge an investment fee to pay for the expense of managing the fund. This fee can be very low or pretty high, depending on the type of mutual fund and the share class.

Making a mutual decision

An *actively managed fund*, which most mutual funds are, has a fund manager who constantly buys and sells stocks to try to improve the fund's return. An *index fund*, which buys the stocks included in a specific index such as the S&P 500, doesn't have a fund manager who picks the stocks and bonds for the fund. (I explain index funds and other investments in Chapter 13).

TECHNICAL
STUFF

The annual fee for an actively managed fund is usually in the 0.5 to 1 percent range, compared to 0.2 percent for an index fund. Index funds can even be as low as 0.02 percent. These fees are usually referred to as the fund's *expense ratio*. The fees may also be expressed as basis points (50 to 100 basis points for the managed fund, compared to 20 basis points for the index fund).

Retail mutual funds — those available to the average individual investor — are likely to be more expensive in a 401(k) plan than institutional funds that are geared toward traditional pension plans or other entities with large amounts to invest. Retail mutual funds are preferred by many participants due to brand-name comfort and because the funds can be readily tracked online. You won't find daily performance results of institutional investment managers in the financial section of your paper, but the lower fees may make them a better deal than the higher-cost retail funds. Some large companies use institutional funds to help keep fees, including administrative and investment costs, low. A small employer can select indexed mutual funds with fees as low as those charged by institutional investment managers who are managing a plan with a billion dollars in assets. These funds are listed in financial publications.

An *institutional fund* is one managed by institutional investors — entities that invest a lot of money with a specific investment management firm. This includes large employer pension funds, university endowment funds, and corporations that have a lot of cash to invest.

In the early days of the 401(k), all employers paid administrative fees. This began to change during the mid-1990s with the arrival of what became known as *bundling*, which involves packing all services through one financial entity. Fees are what really got bundled, and now participants pay them.

Unwrapping wrap fees

Sometimes a 401(k) plan provider charges what's known as a *wrap fee,* an additional fee added to the normal fund management fee and the administrative fees. The wrap fee usually provides additional income to the record keeper, investment advisor, and third-party administrator.

Small plans with fewer than 100 participants are most often charged this fee, which is likely to push total fees to between 1.5 and 2.5 percent of the total assets in the plan.

An insurance company, bank, or brokerage firm may charge a wrap fee if it offers funds managed by a number of different mutual fund companies, including ones the provider owns. For example, the provider may offer the well-known Vanguard Fortune 500 Index Fund but add an additional 100-to-150-basis-point annual fee to the standard fee charged by Vanguard.

TECHNICAL STUFF

The wrap fee is another reason why the published return you see for the funds you invest in may be different from what you see on your 401(k) statement or IRA. If the wrap fee is 1.5 percent, for example, your returns will be reduced by 1.5 percent each year, as compared with what's in the newspaper. This may not sound like much, but a 1.5 percent additional wrap fee reduces your 30-year savings by 30 percent!

Prospecting in the prospectus

Looking at a fund's prospectus generally helps you see what investment management fees are charged. The *prospectus* is a document that gives information such as what companies the mutual fund invests in, how often the manager buys and sells stocks within the fund, and what the manager is trying to achieve (the fund *objective*).

The prospectus also tells you the *expense ratio,* which is the fee deducted each year to operate the fund. For example, you pay $100 if you have $10,000 invested in a fund that has a 1 percent expense ratio. You won't get a bill for this expense, and you won't see it deducted from your 401(k) or IRA account. The fee reduces the net return you receive for the fund. The fact that you don't see these deductions is why service providers and investment advisors can easily get away with high fees.

A fund's prospectus doesn't include information about any wrap fee charged by the 401(k) provider. Getting this information is often difficult because providers who charge wrap fees are often reluctant to disclose them. The Department of Labor requires employers to disclose their fees to be in compliance with Section 408(b)(2) 404(a)(5) of ERISA (the Employee Retirement Income Security Act). This notice explains to participants what fees are charged to and paid from their individual account.

Ask the plan provider for the Section 404(a)(5) fee information and get your employer involved. The employer receives a separate disclosure, 408(b)(2), that explains fees applicable to the plan. This information is useful; however, it still may be difficult to understand because organizations with high fees don't want to make it easy for you to see those fees. Get someone familiar with this stuff to help you make sense of the information if necessary.

Many years ago, I helped the Department of Labor address the issue of fee transparency. That resulted in a fee brochure titled "A Look at 401(k) Plan Fees." Enter the title into your browser to find a copy, which also lists many other great resources.

Find out what your plan charges in fees and then tell your employer if you think they're too high. There may be a good reason for the fees charged by your plan (such as extra services), or there may not be.

Knowing What You Can Know

It's not enough for your employer to simply offer a 401(k) plan. You need help understanding how to use and manage it. At a minimum, your employer can and should provide additional support that includes

>> A retirement calculator to help you determine how much you'll need when you retire and how much to invest to reach your goals

>> Information about the various types of mutual funds to help you understand your investments

>> Account statements (at least quarterly) and other tools to help you measure your progress

>> On-site educational seminars about investing, goal setting, and taking advantage of a 401(k)

Additional features can include

>> Internet access to detailed information about your plan investments (including fee information and historical investment results)

>> The ability to make changes at any time, such as moving money from one investment to another or changing your contribution amount

>> Investment advice and financial planning assistance

All of these support services are designed to help participants understand the plan and manage their investments, and they involve additional expenses that must be paid. The added value you receive from these services may warrant higher fees. Chapter 11 tells you where to find advice, education, and retirement calculators if your 401(k) service provider doesn't offer them.

Working to Improve Your Plan

Employers may need to be reminded that the 401(k) helps to attract and retain employees. Armed with information about competitive plans, employers can shape a plan that attracts top-quality employees.

If you don't think your plan is up to snuff, you can try to convince your employer to change it. Don't get your hopes up too high, though. Making a change to a 401(k) plan is complicated for the employer, so there has to be a really good reason for doing so.

For example, many small employers simply can't afford to make a matching contribution. You can petition them until the cows come home, but, for economic reasons, they won't budge.

The top three complaints employees have about their 401(k) plans are

>> Poor investment performance

>> Lack of available information (especially about fees)

>> Not enough funds offered, or not the right types of funds

The next sections look at each complaint in more detail, as well as what you may be able to do about them.

Upgrading investment performance

If you have a caring employer, and if your investments really are performing poorly, you may be able to make a change.

Sometimes participants ask the employer to replace one fund with another that they think is performing better. This change may seem like a no-brainer, but it's not. The employer needs to look not only at the fund's recent performance, but also at long-term returns and other measures. Comparing the fund's performance with that of similar funds is also important. If similar funds are also going through a bad spell, and the fund itself is solid and makes sense as part of the plan, a couple of years of less-than-ideal performance isn't necessarily reason to boot it out of the plan completely.

Most employer-sponsored retirement plans are guided by an Investment Policy Statement. The Investment Policy Statement serves as a road map for selecting, overseeing, adding, and replacing funds. The Investment Policy Statement also identifies the individuals responsible for performing these services. They may be several members of senior management or a committee including a general mix of participants. A plan with $100 million of assets that was a client of mine had an advisory group of participants that provided recommendations to the chief executive officer, chief financial officer, and human resource manager, and these three had the final authority.

Replacing a fund due to poor performance isn't always an easy decision. A fund may be underperforming because the fund manager chose stocks that are likely to do well in the future but that aren't currently in favor. The fund may have performed well for many years and be a favorite of many participants.

Sometimes, even though a fund has good managers and a strong, long-term track record, an Investment Policy Statement requires that it be replaced due to sub-par performance over a two-year span despite the fact that there is a strong possibility the fund will be a top performer in its category again in the future. An employer replacing a fund in this situation runs the risk that the new fund will not perform as well during the coming years.

Style drift is another problem an employer must deal with. *Style drift* means the investment holdings of the fund no longer fit the designated category. This is a common problem for small cap funds, which virtually every 401(k) plan includes. Small cap stocks are companies whose share value is in the $300 million to $2 billion range.

A small cap fund with superior performance attracts a lot of attention, which usually results in a large inflow of new investment money. The fund managers will have a tough time finding enough small companies stocks they're comfortable buying. They may be forced to buy small company stocks they don't really like or to drift into stocks of larger companies, which will ultimately force them out of the small cap category. Employers holding such funds in their 401(k)s will need to replace the fund with a new small cap fund.

Changes of these types often make participants frustrated and unhappy, and make them wonder why the people overseeing their plan can't get it right.

401(k) plans are governed by a law known as ERISA — the Employee Retirement Income Security Act. ERISA lays out minimum standards for 401(k)s and other types of retirement plans. One thing ERISA says is that your employer has a responsibility (known as *fiduciary responsibility*) to make sure that the plan is operated in the best interest of the participants. Anyone else who exercises control over plan assets or management — which may include the plan trustee or the plan provider — is also considered to have fiduciary responsibility. This responsibility covers a number of issues, including what mutual funds you can invest in. Your employer must be able to show that it acted responsibly in choosing funds to offer in the plan. Changing funds every few years on a whim would probably not qualify as responsible. ERISA allows plan participants to sue *fiduciaries* (those who have control over the plan assets) for breaching their responsibilities. (I discuss ERISA in more detail in Chapter 1.)

Searching out information

Timely access to investment information is another big issue employees have with their retirement plans. Managing a retirement account in the best of circumstances is hard, but it's almost impossible when important information isn't available.

Employers are required to provide participants with five pieces of information about their 401(k):

>> **A summary plan description (SPD):** The plan description explains the general terms of the plan — who is eligible and when, the types of contributions permitted, vesting, withdrawal rules, and so on. Although it's useful when you need to know your plan's rules, the information about plan investments is typically limited to generic fund descriptions. Some SPDs don't even give fund descriptions; they say only that participants can split their contributions among various funds selected by the employer.

>> **A summary annual report (SAR):** The annual report isn't exactly what you'd call useful, up-to-date information. The SAR is pulled from a form that your employer has to file with the Department of Labor within seven months after the plan year ends. But the information on the form is for the previous year, ending December 31 (if the plan year ends on December 31), so the information is dated by the time you receive it. The summary annual report lists general financial results for the year for the entire plan, including total contributions, interest, dividends, realized and unrealized gains, and benefit distributions. None of this information helps you decide how to invest your money.

>> **An annual statement of their account:** This statement doesn't have to include detailed information on the actual return and expenses for each participant's investments. It may be limited to the beginning balance, contributions, withdrawals, investment gains or losses, and ending balance. The service provider for your plan may also include each participant's specific *rate of return* (the percentage by which your own investments grew, or shrank, over the year).

>> **Fee disclosure in compliance with Sections 408(b)(2) and 404(a)(5) of ERISA:** You're supposed to receive a copy of the fee disclosure form when you join your plan. Request it from your service provider or employer if you don't have one.

The Department of Labor (DoL) provides the 401(k) Plan Disclosure Form that service providers can use to satisfy the Section 408(b)(2) disclosure requirements.

The information provided isn't easy to understand. Get help from the financial advisor for your plan or someone else who is familiar with this stuff if you don't understand the info. The person at your employer who administers your plan may be able to help.

>> **Potential annuity income:** The Secure Act contains a provision requiring 401(k) service providers to inform each participant how much monthly income would be provided if the participant's account balance were used to buy a lifetime income annuity with payments starting at age 67.

Some service providers currently provide lifetime annuity income projections often also showing a projected monthly annuity income if you continue your current rate of contributions until retirement.

REMEMBER

Some funds offered by 401(k) plans are special funds created by the provider, and they aren't available to the general public. In this case, you need to ask the provider or your employer for information about the fund. Written requests are usually the most effective.

Here's a sample letter asking for more information about plan fees:

> Dear 401(k) Plan Representative:
>
> Planning for my retirement is a serious matter. I want to do everything I can to be sure that I have an adequate income during my retirement years.
>
> Unfortunately, I haven't been able to make informed investment decisions because I can't get adequate information about the fees that I pay. I called the service center at the Outback Investment Company, and their representative told me that I don't pay any fees. Perhaps I should consider this wonderful news, but I'm not dumb enough to believe that it's true.
>
> As a result, I'm requesting a written explanation of all the fees that I pay, including the ones deducted from plan assets by the organizations that invest and manage the plan, and that reduce the net investment return I receive.
>
> Sincerely,
>
> 401(k) Plan Participant

Questioning investment strategy

You may be convinced that your plan needs to offer more or better mutual funds. In some cases, you may be right; in others, you may not be. In any case, you have a better chance of getting your plan sponsor to listen and take action if you submit detailed written complaints. Generic complaints that simply state that a plan's investment options stink aren't very useful. It's best to explain why, specifically, you're dissatisfied. It may be the fact that a particular type of fund isn't offered, or it may be generally due to high fees or poor performance.

Here's a sample letter that may get the attention of a plan sponsor:

> Dear 401(k) Plan Representative:
>
> I take 401(k) investing very seriously, because I want to do everything I can to be sure that I have an adequate income when I retire. As you know, investment return has a major impact on the savings that I, and other participants, will accumulate.
>
> I am very dissatisfied with the return of our large-cap stock fund, the Outback Super Stock Fund. In the past year, the return for this fund was 2.4 percent less than the S&P 500 index. During the last three years, the fund returned an average of 2.6 percent less than the S&P. This fund has also ranked in the bottom quartile for three years, and it only has a two-star Morningstar rating.
>
> It would clearly be in the best interest of all participants to replace this fund with a similar fund that has a better track record and rating.
>
> Sincerely,
>
> 401(k) Plan Participant

This letter contains specific reasons for the dissatisfaction of the fund. The reasons are supported by Morningstar ratings, an independent source. The letter also properly identifies the type of fund and compares its performance with the S&P index, an appropriate benchmark for this type of fund. (Chapter 13 has more information about S&P and other indexes.) Gathering this information may appear to be very difficult, but it isn't. The Morningstar.com website (or other similar fund resources we mention in Chapter 13) provides all of this information.

TIP

Consider your company culture before you attack the 401(k). You don't want to be labeled a troublemaker if this is how your employer views people who complain. At your company, a casual remark at the water cooler followed up by an email with "just the facts" may be enough to spur someone in a position of authority to consider a change.

If you fail to get the information you need, consider writing to the United States Department of Labor. Explain what efforts you've made to get the information and the responses you received. Letters should be addressed to: The Assistant Secretary of Labor, Pension and Welfare Benefits Administration, 200 Constitution Ave., N.W., Washington, D.C. 20210-1111. You can go to the United States Department of Labor's Pension and Welfare Benefits Administration website at http://askpwba.dol.gov and click on Postal Mail/National Office for up-to-date information.

In the end, as you evaluate your 401(k) plan, you're really evaluating the corporate citizenship of your employer. If your employer realizes the importance of having a strong 401(k) plan, that's a good sign.

RECALLING THE NOT-SO-GOOD OLD DAYS

401(k) plans today may have problems, but they've come a long way, baby.

In the early days, all administrative activity was paper-based, labor-intensive, and slow. Participant accounts were generally updated on specific *valuation dates* (dates when the value of the account was calculated and recorded) only once or twice a year. The really advanced plans updated participant accounts quarterly — four times a year. If you wanted to change your investments or take a distribution (withdrawal), you can do so only on these valuation dates. Because of cumbersome administration, you usually had to wait six to eight weeks *after* the valuation date for the transaction to be completed.

Today, the administration of 401(k)s has moved from cumbersome paper-based processing to electronic processing. Participants can get information about their accounts and investments all day and every day, from anywhere in the world. You should be able to change investments and make other transactions just as easily.

Participant education didn't even exist in the early days of 401(k) plans. Now, more and more employers offer good education programs, although unfortunately not all of them do. Individuals can also find investment education in special retirement planning sections of many financial institutions, including the one that services your plan.

Chapter **7**

Weighing Your Options When You Leave Your Employer

hen you stop working at the employer that sponsors your 401(k) plan, some restrictions on your money magically drop away. Except in a few extreme cases, you're allowed to withdraw your money for any reason at all (it doesn't have to be a hardship), although you still have to pay applicable taxes and penalties.

This newfound freedom makes about a third of 401(k) participants giddy enough to do something silly — that is, take the money and run. That's a bad idea, and I tell you why later in the chapter. Fortunately, there's an easy way to avoid pillaging your 401(k) — do a *rollover*. You can transfer your 401(k) money directly from your former employer to an individual retirement arrangement (IRA) — also referred to as an individual retirement account — or to your new employer's retirement plan (if it allows rollovers), without owing tax. In the new account, the money continues to grow tax-deferred, with no income tax on annual earnings.

If you don't do a rollover right away, you can most likely leave the 401(k) money in your old employer's plan while you consider your options. This chapter explains how to preserve your 401(k) tax advantage when you change jobs and how to avoid costly mistakes with your retirement money.

Your employer is required to give you a detailed written explanation of your options when you leave a job. Chapter 17 explains your options when you retire, which may be slightly different.

Taking Your Savings with You

When you change jobs, you can take your 401(k) money with you — and keep the tax advantages — by putting it into your new employer's 401(k), 403(b), or 457 plan, or into an IRA.

Transferring your money to a new employer's plan or an IRA is known as a *rollover* or *trustee-to-trustee transfer*. See Chapter 10 for more on rolling your money into an IRA.

Many employers require you to work for a minimum number of years before the employer contributions are yours to keep (known as *vesting*). Your contributions are always yours.

REMEMBER

Because your 401(k) is *portable*, or transferable, you can build up a retirement nest egg even if you change jobs frequently. This beats the traditional defined-benefit pension plan (in which you receive a set amount from your employer each month in retirement, if you qualify). With those plans, you can lose *all* retirement benefits if you don't work at the company for the minimum vesting period — this can be at least five years, or even longer at some companies.

A Rolling 401(k) Gathers No Taxes

When you leave your job, one of the many forms that you'll likely have to fill out is a 401(k) *distribution election form. Distribution* is employee-benefit-speak for the payment to you of your vested 401(k) money.

The most sensible thing to do with your 401(k) from a tax-management point of view is a *direct rollover* (also known as a *trustee-to-trustee transfer*) of the money. With this type of rollover, your old service provider writes a check directly to the financial institution where your new account is. The money goes directly from your 401(k) plan into another tax-deferred account — an IRA or your new employer's 401(k) plan, 403(b) plan, or 457(b) plan. 403(b) plans are offered by many nonprofit organizations and 457(b) plans are offered by state and local governments. By doing a direct rollover, you don't have to pay any tax on the money when it comes out of your old employer's 401(k). The money also continues to grow tax-deferred in the new account.

Many participants wonder whether it's better to roll their 401(k) into an IRA or into another employer's plan. It really depends on your situation. Check Chapter 10 for rollover info.

Instead of transferring the money directly to the new plan or IRA, the service provider may write you a check for the 401(k) balance, which complicates things for you.

WARNING

If the check is payable to you, the service provider is required to withhold 20 percent of the account value as federal withholding tax. So, if you have $10,000 vested in your account, you'll receive a check for only $8,000.

In order to avoid paying income tax and an early withdrawal penalty, you have to deposit the $8,000 check plus $2,000 of your own money into an IRA or your new employer's plan within 60 days of receiving the distribution. (The IRS will return the $2,000 to you when you file your tax return if you do the rollover correctly.) The amount that you don't deposit in the new account will be considered a cash distribution on which you'll owe applicable tax and penalties. The IRS is firm on this 60-day limit. The only leeway is in the case of a national disaster when the IRS can decide to extend the 60-day period.

Your employer may also require your spouse to sign if you're married because you have the right to name a beneficiary other than your spouse if the money is transferred to an IRA. If so, the spouse's written consent is usually required on the election form, and it must be notarized or approved by a plan representative.

Realizing that account size matters

If your account balance is less than $5,000, you may be forced to take the money out of your employer's 401(k) plan when you leave. If it's more than $1,000 (and less than $5,000) and you don't tell your employer what you want to do with the money, your employer can automatically roll the money into an IRA on your behalf. If the balance is $1,000 or less, your employer can simply issue a check to you for the entire amount without giving you any alternatives, but you'll owe tax and penalties on the money.

TIP

Let your employer know right away that you want to do a rollover if your balance is less than $1,000 to prevent paying taxes and penalties.

If your vested 401(k) balance is $5,000 or more, and you're younger than the normal retirement age specified in the plan document (usually 65), your employer is required to let you leave your money in the 401(k) if you want to. Leaving your money in the plan can be a useful strategy, at least as a temporary measure. See the section "Leaving Money with Your Old Employer" later in this chapter for details.

Moving your money to your new employer's plan

You may be able to roll the money over into your new employer's plan. You may decide to do this for a number of reasons, including the following:

>> Your new employer has a terrific plan with great funds and low expenses.

>> You want to consolidate all your retirement savings in one place for ease of management.

>> You think you may want to take a loan someday (remember, you can't take a loan from an IRA).

WARNING

Before you decide to roll over your 401(k) into the new employer's plan, make sure you get a copy of the new plan's summary plan description to find out all the rules your money will be subject to. After the money is in the 401(k) plan, you may not be able to withdraw it and move it into an IRA unless you leave your job, so be certain about the rollover before you do it.

TIP

You also need to find out whether your new employer's plan accepts rollovers. In theory, you're allowed to roll a 401(k) plan into another 401(k) plan or into a 403(b) plan or 457(b) plan. In practice, though, not all employer plans accept rollovers. If yours doesn't, you can leave your money in your old 401(k) or roll it into an IRA to preserve the tax advantage. (See "Leaving Money with Your Old Employer," later in this chapter and Chapter 10 on rollovers.)

Your new plan may require you to wait until you're eligible to participate before accepting a rollover from your old 401(k). Although many employers allow you to roll money into the plan before becoming eligible to contribute, some employers restrict the availability of rollovers until you actually become eligible for the plan. For example, if your new employer has a waiting period of one year before you can contribute to the 401(k), you have to wait one year to roll the money into the 401(k). In that case, you can either leave your money in your former employer's plan or move it to a rollover IRA, ready to be transferred into the new 401(k) when the time comes.

Waiting for the money to transfer

After you decide to roll over your 401(k) money into an IRA or a new employer's plan, the transaction may take a while to happen. I've heard from participants who've had to wait months before their former employer released their money.

Your plan is allowed to retain your money as long as it wants, but no longer than the "normal retirement age" specified in the plan document. Some companies restrict money in this way for up to five years after an employee leaves. One reason that an employer may set up a plan this way is to help retain good employees. Delaying distributions prevents an employee from quitting simply to access 401(k) money. Employees in this situation usually ask me whether their former employers can legally hold on to the money. The answer is "yes." Amazingly (and somewhat frighteningly), under federal law, a plan is only required to distribute your money when you reach retirement age. (More specifically, it must be paid no later than 60 days after the end of the plan year when you reach the plan's normal retirement age, which is often 65.)

Benefit distributions may be delayed for administrative reasons. Employers that make profit-sharing contributions typically do so just before filing their corporate tax return, which can be 9½ months after the end of the year.

The good news is that most employers want to get rid of the responsibility of administering an account for someone who's no longer an employee, so most plans provide for immediate distribution of your money.

Another rule that the employer has to follow is to treat employees in a uniform and nondiscriminatory manner. In other words, your former employer has to handle your benefit distribution the same way it handled those of other employees who left under similar circumstances.

Leaving Money with Your Old Employer

Leaving your money in your old 401(k) plan may be a good temporary solution while you figure out your next step, but it's probably not the best long-term solution.

Leaving the money in the 401(k) may have advantages for some investors because

>> Some people don't want to make new investment decisions. If you're satisfied with your 401(k) investments, this strategy is fine. However, be aware that an employer can change the investments offered by the plan at any time. If your

money is in your former employer's 401(k), you have to go along with the change. During the switchover period, which can take several weeks or months, you won't be able to access your account.

>> Money in a 401(k) generally has more protection from creditors than that in an IRA should you declare personal bankruptcy.

WARNING

Consider some of the drawbacks to leaving your money in your former employer's 401(k):

>> After you leave a company and are no longer an employee, you'll be low in the pecking order for service if you request a distribution from the 401(k) plan or if you have questions or complaints. Companies can change a lot over time, including being acquired, restructured, or even going out of business. The level of support you receive as an ex-employee usually drops dramatically if this happens.

>> While the money is in a former employer's 401(k) plan, you can't take a loan. (You have to pay back such a loan through payroll deductions.)

>> You can no longer contribute to the old 401(k) plan, but you can rebalance the investments.

So, think long and hard before leaving your money when you change jobs.

Taking a Lump Sum

I would never advise this, but just so you know all your options, when you leave your employer, you can withdraw all the money in your 401(k) account in what's called a *lump-sum withdrawal*. Surveys show that about one-third of participants who change jobs withdraw all the money in their 401(k) accounts. Often, they have small account balances and probably figure that it's just not worth it to bother with a rollover.

WARNING

Unless you have a serious financial need, cashing out the money and spending it is something you should avoid. Even if your account balance is small, it's worth leaving the money alone. If you take cash, you'll have to pay income tax on it. You'll also owe the 10 percent early withdrawal penalty if you're under 59½ when you leave your employer unless you qualify for one of very few exceptions.

MOVING OUT OF THE COUNTRY

I used to receive questions from non–U.S. citizens who work for a time in the United States, build up a 401(k) balance, and then wonder whether they can transfer it overseas and preserve the tax advantage.

You should consult an international tax expert for details about your specific situation, because the answer may depend on tax treaties between the United States and the country where you want to transfer your money.

But even if you can't do the equivalent of a rollover when you depart the United States, it may still be worthwhile to save in a 401(k) while you have the chance, particularly if you will get an employer matching contribution. When you leave your employer, you can leave the money in the 401(k) or (better yet) transfer it into an IRA to preserve the tax advantage. When you reach age 59½, you can withdraw the money without a 10 percent penalty, either all at once or little by little. (If you were at least 55 when you left your employer, you don't have to pay the penalty.) In any case, you'll still owe U.S. income tax, so you should try to withdraw the money in a year, or years, when you have no other taxable U.S. income and your tax rate is lower.

REMEMBER

Some people take a cash distribution and spend the money, figuring it's such a small amount that it won't matter. This is a mistake. An amount as small as $5,000 when you're 25 can grow to $157,047 by the time you're 65, assuming a 9 percent rate of return. That additional income can mean puttin' up at the Ritz rather than puttin' up a tent during your retirement travels.

What's more, you wouldn't even get the full $5,000. You'd get just $4,000 because your employer must withhold 20 percent for taxes.

While you're still with your employer, the magic age for withdrawing money from the plan without a 10 percent early withdrawal penalty is 59½. This is also the magic age if you have an IRA. However, the IRS lets you avoid the penalty if you're at least 55 when you leave your job (the job with the employer who sponsors your 401(k) plan). The reasoning is that if you lose your job at age 55 or older, it can be particularly hard to find a new one, so you may need the money. Imagine that — for once, the IRS gives you a break.

Taking Stock into Account

If you have stock in your employer's company in your 401(k), you need to know a few things about taxation before you decide what to do with it.

One option is to convert the stock to cash and then transfer it along with your other 401(k) money into an IRA. This gives you an opportunity to diversify your investments by selling the stock (a single investment) and using the proceeds to buy a variety of investments. That's good. However, if you're willing to take on the increased risk of holding company stock outside your IRA, you can get an additional tax break on the company stock.

Here's how this option works: If you take a distribution of the company stock from your 401(k) but you don't roll it over into an IRA, you pay tax on the value of the stock at the time you acquired it — not at the time you withdraw it from the plan. This special provision of the tax law provides your first tax break, because the stock is most likely worth more now than when you received it. (Your employer is responsible for letting you know the total taxable value of the stock when you receive the distribution.)

Assume that you have $50,000 worth of company stock in your 401(k) when you take a distribution, but it was valued at $20,000 when you received it. At the time of your distribution, you receive $50,000 worth of stock but pay tax on only $20,000 of it. Later, when you sell the stock, your investment gain (whatever the stock is worth over $20,000) is taxed as a capital gain, a lower rate than the income tax rate. Another advantage is the fact that you don't have to hold the stock for a one-year period in order for the gain to be taxed as a capital gain. If you don't want the risk of holding onto the stock, sell it as soon as you want after receiving it.

If you hang on to the stock for a long time and still own it at the time of your death, your heirs will benefit. They'll have to pay tax only on the gain that occurs after they receive the stock. Say it's worth $100,000 when they get it, and they sell it at $110,000. They pay tax only on $10,000 — the difference between the value when they received it and the sale price. They never pay income tax or capital gains tax on the $50,000 gained while you held the stock.

This is a big tax break, but it's only useful if you don't need the money during your retirement years. You must also be willing to take on the higher investment risk of having a chunk of money invested in a single stock for a number of years.

There's a high probability that the value of the stock will drop by 50 percent or more over a 20- to 30-year period regardless of how great a company it is. Committing to sell at some predetermined price — when the stock drops by 10 percent or more, for example — can provide some downside protection if you stick with that plan.

3

Here Come the IRAs

Deciding on a place to open an individual retirement arrangement account, or IRA, and watching your money grow tax free.

Checking the upsides and downsides of Roth IRAs. You pay tax up-front when you invest your money, but you can take money out when you want to with few or no penalties.

Moving money from one retirement account to another is called rolling it over. It's not very tricky to take your money from a 401(k) and move it to an IRA — you just have to know how to make the move safely for your tax health.

Chapter **8**

Investing in an IRA

ndividual retirement arrangements (also known as individual retirement accounts), or IRAs, came into being through provisions added to the internal revenue code (IRC) in 1978. These provisions encourage you and every other American worker to save money for retirement. Tax advantages sweeten the pot, and automatic deductions can make saving nearly painless.

This chapter clues you in to the types of IRAs available, finding the place to put your funds, keeping track of your money, and moving it if necessary.

Looking at the Basics of Your IRA

An IRA is a special type of savings and investment account that helps you save for retirement by providing specific tax advantages. (I talk about the tax issues covering retirement accounts in Chapter 2.)

Federal law limits the amount you can contribute during 2021 to an IRA (or to all your IRAs combined, if you have several) to $6,000 in a single year plus a $1,000 catch-up contribution if you're at least age 50. The IRS reviews the limits annually and may update them. (Chapter 15 offers details on contributions.) Your contributions are invested and grow tax-free until you withdraw them. All the money you withdraw is taxable except for a Roth IRA. Withdrawals from a Roth IRA aren't taxable if you follow the rules.

REMEMBER

The primary reason for tax advantages that accompany IRAs is to encourage you to save for retirement, so taking funds out before then can be financially painful. If you withdraw funds from your traditional pre-tax IRA before you're 59½ for any other than a few approved expenses, you pay a 10 percent penalty. The details of early withdrawals are covered in Chapter 16.

As well as saving for retirement, you can use IRA savings for select other purposes — buying your first home or adding a child to your family, for example. If you withdraw money for a specific, approved reason, you must pay tax on the amount you withdraw from a traditional IRA but you don't have to pay a penalty tax. If you take money out for other than approved purposes, you're liable for taxes and penalties.

The financial bite for taking money from a Roth IRA isn't as harsh as from a traditional IRA, although you are liable for taxes on the portion of the investment gains you must withdraw if your Roth IRA is less than five years old. A pro-rata portion of the investment gains must be withdrawn and will be taxable if the Roth IRA is less than five years old but there isn't an early withdrawal tax penalty. Read on for information on the different types of IRAs, and see Chapter 9 for detailed information about Roth IRAs.

Historically, IRAs haven't been connected to employers, but that's changing. Some states are requiring employers that don't offer a retirement plan to start offering one. Most states have or will have state-run payroll-deduction IRA plans to make it easier for employers to meet these mandates. Oregon has what's known as the OregonSaves state-run payroll-deduction IRA plan, and a growing number of employees are enrolled in this plan.

Small employers including solo entrepreneurs, family businesses, and gig workers have a number of IRA options that I explain in Chapter 18. These include the SEP IRA and SIMPLE IRA, which are two types of employer-sponsored plans — and self-employment plans.

For more information about IRAs, take a look at IRS Publication 590, Individual Retirement Arrangements, which you can download for free from the IRS website at www.irs.gov/pub/irs-pdf/p590.pdf. (The IRS home page is www.irs.gov.)

Staying traditional

Most IRA holders have traditional IRAs because (as their name suggests) they've been around for a while — since 1974.

You can make two types of contributions to a traditional IRA:

>> **Deductible:** You can deduct your contributions from your income for tax purposes.

>> **Nondeductible:** You guessed it — you *can't* deduct your contributions. (Who said this financial stuff was complicated?)

With both types of contributions, you don't pay income tax on your earnings until you withdraw money from the account. You owe income tax when you withdraw the untaxed portion at retirement. With deductible contributions, you owe tax on the contributions plus the earnings. With nondeductible contributions, you owe tax only on the earnings. As you can imagine, if you make both types of contributions to an IRA, you need to keep meticulous records in order to know what's what when you start withdrawing the money, which can be many years from now.

The deductible IRA is a better deal because you get the extra tax break of being able to deduct your contributions from your taxable income. The catch is that if you have a 401(k) or any other employer-sponsored tax-qualified plan, you can deduct your contributions to an IRA only if your income is below certain limits set out in Chapter 2. (*Income* means modified adjusted gross income (MAGI), which is your gross income minus certain deductions as defined in detail in IRS Publication 590.) Check Chapter 2 for more info on tax issues.

REMEMBER

Even if you participate in a 401(k) plan, you're allowed to use earned income to contribute to an IRA — earned income is the only acceptable source for IRA contributions. Your spouse can contribute as well even if they don't work. The only question is whether your contributions will be deductible.

A traditional IRA is typically used for making pre-tax contributions. After-tax contributions to this type of IRA are unusual and are usually made by high-income earners who aren't eligible to make Roth IRA contributions. Individuals who aren't covered by an employer-sponsored retirement plan can reduce their taxes by making pre-tax contributions.

Touching on Roth IRAs

You can't deduct your contributions to a Roth IRA, so in that sense, it's like a nondeductible traditional IRA. The advantage of a Roth is that the amount you contribute grows without being taxed, and you don't pay tax on your investment earnings — ever.

As long as you follow all applicable rules, your money grows tax-deferred in the account, and you can withdraw it tax-free at retirement.

You may wonder why anyone would bother with nondeductible contributions to a traditional IRA, where you have to pay tax on withdrawals, when they can have a Roth IRA. Good question. The answer is that you can't contribute to a Roth IRA if your income is over a certain limit. I go into detail about Roth IRAs in Chapter 9.

Benefiting from a spousal IRA

A spousal IRA is available to a spouse who doesn't work for pay and who checks the "married, filing jointly" box on their tax form. The togetherness doesn't hold for the actual IRA, though: The spousal IRA must belong solely to the spouse and cannot be in a jointly held account.

If neither spouse is covered by an employer-sponsored retirement plan, a couple can double the amount of their tax-deductible IRA contributions. If you fit this category, you can contribute between $12,000 and $14,000 to an IRA depending on your age and the age of your spouse. The $6,000 regular and the $1,000 catch-up contribution limits apply to each spouse. A spouse under age 55 can contribute $6,000 and a spouse 55 or older can put in $7,000. One spouse under and one over age 55 results in a $13,000 combined limit.

The money contributed to the spousal IRA can come from any source — the employed spouse's income, other savings, and so on. However, the contribution can't exceed the employed spouse's earned income.

It may also be possible to have a spousal IRA if one of the spouses is covered by an employer-sponsored retirement plan if their combined modified adjusted income is less than $198,000 during 2021. The limit is usually adjusted annually. Check Chapter 2 for more details.

Starting an IRA for a child

You can set up a traditional or Roth IRA for a child or grandchild provided the child has earned income — so, one thing toddlers can't charm their way into. A parent or other adult can open a custodial traditional or Roth IRA account for a child anywhere IRAs are offered.

REMEMBER

Contributions to an IRA that benefits a child can't exceed the amount of income the child earns.

If you open an IRA account to benefit a child, you have control of the account, including how it is invested and administered, until the child becomes an adult at age 18 or 21, depending on the state. Anyone can contribute to the account. For example, you can contribute to your favorite niece's account and so can her parents. Just check to make sure that total contributions don't amount to more than she earned.

WARNING

You can withdraw funds but only for the benefit of the child. And if you take money out of the IRA, you may create taxable income for the child.

TIP

A Roth IRA is the way to go for a custodial IRA for a child if the child doesn't pay any income tax or is taxed at the lowest tax rate. Also investing aggressively in an attempt to achieve a higher investment return makes sense assuming the time horizon is at least 10 to 20 years. Having funds growing for 50 or more years without any withdrawals would be even better. The potential for early withdrawals also makes a Roth IRA a good option because you can take money out of it for any reason any time after the account is five years old. If the child is over age 59½ when the funds are withdrawn, neither the principal *or* the earnings are taxable.

Keep in mind that an early withdrawal from a Roth IRA isn't totally painless because a pro-rata portion of the investment earnings are taxable, and an early withdrawal penalty tax will apply unless the withdrawal is for one of the reasons that qualifies as an exception.

Offering to open and contribute to such an account may encourage a child to earn some income and can also help a young adult discover how to save and invest.

Setting Up Your IRA

Your first step in starting an IRA is selecting a financial institution where your contributions will be deposited and invested. To qualify for the tax advantages, your IRA must be held by a qualified custodian or trustee. The number of possibilities is almost endless because banks, insurance companies, credit unions, mutual fund companies, brokerage firms, and some other entities are considered qualified to offer IRAs.

In choosing the institution in which to invest your IRA money, you need to decide how much investment choice and what level of service you want.

With virtually all major financial institutions offering IRAs, you can invest IRA funds in any legal, traditional investment vehicle. *Traditional* means stocks, bonds, certificates of deposit (CDs), exchange-traded funds (ETFs), and other publicly traded securities.

Along with brokerage firms, just about any financial organization can now sell you stocks and bonds, including banks and insurance companies. If you buy a mutual fund from a bank, keep in mind that it's not guaranteed or insured like other more traditional bank investments, such as certificates of deposit (CDs) or plain old savings accounts.

Nontraditional investments include everything else you can legally invest in, including real estate; gold, silver, and other precious metals; and crypto currencies. You need to find a special custodian for nontraditional investments and open a separate account. Investment details are covered in Chapter 13.

I strongly recommend having all your IRA investments in a single traditional or Roth IRA to make it easier to track and manage them.

Deciding where to invest your money

Seeking help from someone you respect is a good idea if you have little-to-no investment experience. Check with family members or friends who have experience and are people you can trust. Asking an accountant, an investment advisor, or another individual you respect are other possibilities.

All entities that offer IRAs are tightly regulated. You don't invest in the actual entity where you open your IRA unless you're investing in CDs and/or some annuity products.

Your major consideration is how you want to invest your IRA savings, which is a difficult question if you're not an experienced investor.

Please note that one type of financial organization isn't safer than another. Some IRA investors think they receive FDIC (federal deposit insurance corporation) protection when they use a bank to house their IRA account. This is true only when you buy the bank's CDs. You don't get FDIC protection when you open your IRA at a bank and invest in mutual funds. Other investment firms such as Vanguard, Fidelity, and Charles Schwab also offer FDIC-backed CDs.

I heard from a 48-year-old woman who'd taken her bank's advice and invested in two mutual funds. The investments dropped in value by more than 35 percent during the 2008 meltdown, and she was deeply troubled by this because she thought banks were a safe place to invest. She didn't realize that the mutual funds weren't guaranteed investments. Keep in mind that stocks, bonds, and mutual funds involve the same level of risk whether you buy them from a bank, stock-broker, or other financial institution.

TIP

Spend time getting familiar with the organization you're considering before you open an account:

>> Visit websites to see how easily you can find useful information about the type of account you want to open and get basic investment information.

>> Call the technical support number a couple of times to test the quality of support they provide.

I recommend setting up your account where you have access to a broad range of investments. You want a range that includes both low-risk investments and those with growth potential. Having a wide range of investments available gives you the ability to stick with the institution you select for the long term.

Consider one of the top-brand mutual fund companies such as Vanguard, Fidelity, and T. Rowe Price. Charles Schwab and other discount brokerage firms are also a good option. These entities give you access to their own brand of mutual funds plus the option to utilize a brokerage account.

A brokerage account enables you to buy stocks, bonds, CDs, ETFs, and so on. Go to Chapter 13 for more about investing.

WARNING

Don't invest your contributions where you pay a front-end fee or a back-end surrender charge. Avoiding these types of investments enables you to move your IRA to another organization if you feel the need.

Opening your account

The easiest way to open your account is online unless you're dealing with a local institution. You must decide which type of account you want to open — a traditional or Roth IRA — and you will be required to name your beneficiaries. See Chapter 3 for more information about beneficiaries.

You can send money to be invested once the account is open.

Starting with lower-risk investments isn't a bad idea until you accumulate a meaningful account balance, such as $10,000. At that point you are in a better position to invest more broadly following what I suggest in Chapter 14.

REMEMBER

A huge advantage 401(k)s offer is to take money out of your paycheck each pay period. For most workers, having semi-forced savings is an easy way to become successful long-term savers. You can do the same thing with a personal IRA by having money transferred directly from your bank account to your IRA each pay period or every month.

Maintaining Your IRA

You don't need to follow any specific requirements to keep your IRA ticking along. However, paying attention to a few issues makes sense:

>> Keep your beneficiaries up to date. This may be easy to forget when an important life change occurs.

>> Track your investments and the value of your account. Don't hover over your investments — you don't want to overreact to the daily ups and downs of the investment markets; you just want to keep an eye on them from afar. Your account should contain investments you're comfortable holding for the long haul, but there are times when a change may be advisable.

Chapter 13 covers investments in a lot more detail.

When you reach your late 30s/early 40s, you need to start devoting more time to overseeing your retirement savings. You want to pay closer attention to the quality of your investment options; the fees you pay; your current and possible future tax situation; and how much access you have to your money, especially without a tax penalty. You need to also be realistic about your ability to

>> Save each paycheck or month without it being taken off the top each pay period

>> Keep your sticky hands off the money each time an emergency happens

I used to spend time at the end of each year reviewing my retirement accounts. It's easier to do this if you have only one account or have multiple accounts at the same place — a traditional and Roth IRA, for example.

Moving Your IRA

You may want to move your IRA to a different financial organization at some point for any number of reasons. Perhaps the investment results have been okay, but you aren't satisfied with the service you receive. You may have made a bad decision when you picked your financial organization initially, or the size of your account may have grown to a point where you want to make investments that aren't offered by your current financial institution.

Changing to a new financial organization isn't hard, but it requires some time. You need to open an account with the new entity and then provide the transfer instructions to the old entity. You can probably retain most of your current investments even if you transfer to another financial organization, although this isn't always the case. For example, if you want to move your IRA to Fidelity and keep your current Vanguard fund investments, you may not be able to do so.

TIP

The transfer must occur via a direct transfer from the old entity to the new one. Ask your agent at the new entity if they can manage the transfer process. The major financial organizations are all able to offer a broad range of investments, but they may not have all the ones that you want. Check before you start the transfer process.

Chapter **9**

To Roth or Not to Roth

A *Roth IRA* is a savings and investment account like a traditional IRA, except you pay taxes on the amount you put in, the money grows tax-free, and, if you follow the rules, you don't pay any taxes on the investment gains when you withdraw funds.

Perhaps I should note up front that it doesn't make any difference to me which type of IRA you choose. My sole objective is to give you information to help you make a decision.

Even if you don't pay any federal income tax now, so that your future tax rate is bound to be higher and a Roth IRA seems a sure bet, review this chapter before you conclude that you want to go with a Roth IRA. Life's uncertainties are one reason I recommend taking advantage of pre-tax opportunities to save for retirement via your 401(k) or a traditional IRA rather than after-tax Roth savings. Roth IRAs have some definite advantages; however, they are oversold as a huge tax break.

When I mention Roth contributions in this chapter, that includes Roth IRAs and Roth 401(k) contributions. When I mention pre-tax savings, that includes both a traditional IRA and 401(k) pre-tax contributions.

Predicting Future Tax Rates

It amazes me that some of the most popular financial gurus ask the question: "Do you expect tax rates to be lower or higher when you retire?" These advisors act as if the future tax rate is the only thing that matters when deciding whether to utilize an after-tax Roth IRA rather than a traditional pre-tax IRA. Most people expect tax rates to be higher in future years than currently, but they may or may not be right.

You need to answer many questions about the future, other than unknowable future tax rates when deciding whether to use pre-tax or after-tax contributions when saving for retirement.

Many states have legislation requiring employers that don't have retirement plans to start one. Most of these states are setting up state-run plans for employers to adopt, making it easier for them to comply. Some state-run plans offer only Roth IRAs, which adds to the perception that these must be better than pre-tax IRAs. States certainly aren't unbiased because those in office prefer collecting tax revenue now rather than later. The same is also true at the federal level. Governmental entities would rather get your taxes now than many years from now.

Calculating accurately

Many examples that show a Roth IRA having a big advantage usually compare $6,000 deposited each year into both a traditional pre-tax IRA and a Roth IRA. Such examples ignore the fact that you must pay taxes up front on what you contribute to a Roth IRA.

Assume you have $6,000 of income you want to save for retirement. With Roth contributions, you have to pay income tax on that amount. For the purpose of this example, say your marginal tax rate is 22 percent. You also have to pay state income and local wage taxes. Assume the combined state income and local wage taxes are 8 percent (your rate may be much higher). Because your state and local taxes reduce your federal taxes a bit, your combined effective tax rate is approximately 29 percent.

After paying 29 percent of the $6,000 in taxes, you actually have only $4,260 to put into your Roth IRA account. If both the $6,000 and the $4,260 receive the same investment return, the $6,000 invested each year will be 29 percent more than the $4,260 at the end of the investment period, which is probably your retirement.

Applying a 29 percent tax rate at the time of withdrawal to the larger $6,000 accumulation results in the same after-tax amount as the $4,260 with the Roth contributions. You will have the same amount left after paying tax during your retirement years as you would if you made after-tax Roth contributions during all the years you were saving for retirement.

REMEMBER

The best way to build your nest egg is by contributing $6,000 per year to a pre-tax IRA rather than $4,260 to a Roth IRA. For sure your nest egg will be growing 29 percent faster each year in this example. The difference is even bigger for those who are in a higher tax bracket. This puts you in a much better position if your intended plans are disrupted.

Solo entrepreneurs and other self-employed individuals can get an even bigger tax break by setting up an employer-funded plan. Check out more about retirement plans for the self-employed in Chapter 18.

Talking tax breaks

If you don't pay any federal income taxes, you have nothing to lose at the federal level by making Roth contributions; however, your state wage taxes may be high enough that you need to take that into account.

WARNING

There is a widely held perception that a Roth IRA provides a huge tax break because you never have to pay taxes on the investment gains. The reality is that you get a federal income tax break only if your marginal tax rate is higher when you take your money out of the IRA than your marginal tax rate when you put the money in. So, if your tax bracket is lower when you withdraw your money, then you've lost. Making Roth contributions results in less taxes only if you have a higher marginal tax rate after you retire than before you retire.

TIP

If you start with Roth contributions, you may want to consider changing to pre-tax IRA contributions if your income increases and pushes you into a higher tax bracket.

Inflation, when prices go up, is another point to consider because inflation decreases the value of money. You can't buy as much when prices increase; therefore, $1 of tax savings now is worth much more than $1 of taxes paid 30 years from now unless the economy experiences deflation rather than inflation.

REMEMBER

Unless you don't pay any federal income taxes now or you expect to accumulate millions of dollars in pre-tax savings by the time you retire, Roth IRA or Roth 401(k) contributions may not be your best option. The one exception is if you're expecting a large inheritance — or planning to win the lottery. A large chunk of money may push you into a higher tax bracket then and make a lower tax payment now a no-brainer.

The "Or Not to Roth" Section

I always take any tax break I can get now rather than worrying about future tax rates because the future is too unpredictable. Your personal situation can change in so many ways over a 20-plus-year period including your marital status, health, employment, and so on. Expecting things to continue over a 20-to-30-year period without any disrupting events isn't a good idea. I strongly recommend building your nest egg faster rather than slower because life is so unpredictable.

WARNING

There's no guarantee the Roth tax exemption will still be available when you retire. It's certainly possible that Congressional members will decide at some point that they gave too big a tax break with the Roth IRA and levy taxes on the currently untaxed portion.

Social Security is a good example of changing tax rules. Social Security benefits weren't taxable until 1984. Today, you can pay tax on up to 85 percent of your Social Security benefit — even though you pay federal income taxes on the amount you contribute to Social Security during all the years you work.

This comment used to get people attending my speaking engagements turning their heads, so let me explain: Both your federal income tax and Social Security taxes are computed as part of your gross income. This means you pay federal income tax on your Social Security taxes when you are working and paying them in. You also may have to pay taxes on 85 percent of your Social Security benefits after you retire. Not what I call fair.

Matching employer contributions are another factor if you're fortunate enough to get them. For example, if your employer matches the first 6 percent of your pay, it's easier to contribute this amount through your pre-tax 401(k) deferral than with 401(k) Roth contributions. You give up money from your employer when you don't contribute the maximum amount that is matched.

REMEMBER

It's highly unlikely that tax rates will increase to a point where your tax rate on the substantially lower amount of taxable income you have after you retire will be higher than your current tax rate.

Taking Money Out of Your Roth IRA

You have reasons for saving other than retirement. Legislators realize that, which is why they added terms for withdrawing funds from a 401(k) in 1987. Roth contributions have an advantage if you need to withdraw them early in that your Roth contributions aren't taxable when you withdraw them. Find more information on preretirement withdrawals in Chapter 16.

REMEMBER

Roth contributions to a 401(k) may be withdrawn at any time if your plan permits.

The contributions you made to the Roth IRA aren't taxable when you withdraw them. That said, you must also withdraw a pro-rata portion of your investment gains when you withdraw any portion of your Roth contributions. So, say you have $8,000 of Roth contributions to your 401(k) and those contributions have earned $2,000. Now you want to withdraw $6,000 to buy your first home. You're withdrawing 60 percent of the $10,000 total. For tax purposes, the withdrawal equals 60 percent of your $8,000 contributions, or $4,800, and 60 percent of the $2,000 of investment gains, which is $1,200. The $4,800 isn't taxable but the $1,200 is.

You also have to pay a 10 percent penalty tax on the $1,200 unless it is a qualified withdrawal. To be qualified you must have been making Roth contributions for at least five years and be over age 59½. This means if you're 30 years old, you pay tax on the $1,200 plus a 10 percent penalty tax.

The way to minimize the tax impact when you take money out of a 401(k) for a first-time home purchase is to withdraw the money at the beginning of a year and to complete the home purchase shortly thereafter. The tax deduction for mortgage interest, state, and local taxes should more than offset the taxes triggered by the 401(k) withdrawal. Even better, your employer may have added to your 401(k) account via matching contributions, putting you much farther ahead by participating in the 401(k) rather than waiting until after you've saved enough outside the plan to buy the home.

Different rules apply to first-time homebuyers when withdrawing money from a traditional or Roth IRA. With a traditional IRA you (and your spouse, if you have one) may withdraw up to $10,000 for your first primary residence without having to pay the 10 percent penalty tax. You still have to pay tax on the amount withdrawn, but you don't have to pay a penalty.

For IRA purposes, you're considered a first-time homebuyer if you (and your spouse) haven't owned a home during the preceding two years. You may qualify as a first-time buyer even if you own a vacation home or have an interest in a time-share. You can also withdraw money to help a child, grandchild, or parent buy their first home even if you own a home.

The five-year rule applies to a Roth IRA: You can withdraw all your contributions and up to $10,000 of the investment gains without paying any tax if your account is at least five years old. If your account is less than five years old, the investment gains you withdraw are taxable; however, the 10 percent penalty tax will not apply.

Converting to Roth

You can convert pre-tax 401(k) contributions, including any employer contributions and pre-tax money in a traditional IRA, into a Roth IRA. Conversions within a 401(k) are possible only if your plan permits you to do so.

You will be able to do so after you leave your employer or after you reach age 59½ if the plan permits you to withdraw your money after reaching that age, which most plans do.

WARNING

In withdrawing money from a traditional IRA to put it into a Roth IRA, the entire amount you convert is taxable.

Converting to Roth probably doesn't make sense while you're still earning your normal income because doing so adds to your current taxable income. As a result, you will probably pay more taxes than if you wait until after you retire. Converting while you're still working also reduces the size of your retirement nest egg by the amount of the taxes you pay.

Investment advisors often suggest converting to Roth after the value of your investments drops substantially. This enables you to avoid paying taxes on the investment gains after the market recovers. This is worth considering; however, seeing your retirement account drop by 50 percent is hard to accept. Eating further into your savings by paying tax on the balance you transfer to a Roth IRA makes it even more unpleasant.

If your $100,000 in your IRA becomes just $50,000, you may think investing in a Roth IRA will help mitigate your losses. The tax would be $11,000 assuming a 22 percent tax rate, leaving you with $39,000. It would take a 250 percent increase to get back to $100,000. This may not be a bad idea, but it takes some guts to pay the taxes a conversion requires.

Your employer may permit you to convert pre-tax money in your 401(k) account to Roth money. This would be a Roth conversion inside the 401(k) because the money stays in the 401(k) after the conversion. If so, you must pay taxes on the amount converted even though the money stays in the plan, and you can't use money in the account to pay those taxes — you need to use money from outside the plan. So, if you convert $10,000 of the pre-tax money in your account to Roth, you pay tax on the whole $10,000.

However, if you're over age 59½, you can withdraw money from your 401(k) unless your plan doesn't permit this. In this instance, you can use a portion of the amount withdrawn to pay the taxes resulting from the conversion.

The best way to do a Roth conversion when you withdraw money from a 401(k) is via a *trustee-to-custodian* transfer directly into your Roth IRA. This means the money goes directly from your plan account to the custodian of your IRA. Use an existing Roth IRA if you have one because this eliminates the need to wait at least five years before you're able to withdraw money from the account without a tax penalty.

TIP

You can make any number of Roth conversions, so you can convert smaller amounts over several tax years rather than doing a one-shot conversion.

You can make only one rollover from an IRA to another (or the same) IRA in any 12-month period regardless of the number of IRAs you own, with a few exceptions. See Chapter 10 for more details on rollovers.

 If you're thinking of doing more than a standard rollover or conversion, talk to a financial advisor or check the IRS resource guide at www.irs.gov/retirement-plans/ira-online-resource-guide to make sure what you plan to do is permitted. You may have to pay a big penalty if you mess up.

Chapter **10**

Rolling Over an IRA

A *rollover* is IRA-speak for transferring funds without penalty or tax liability. When you leave a job or take a new job, a rollover makes sure your retirement funds go where you want them.

In this chapter, I cover several rollover tricks: gathering the information you need, being aware of Roth oddities, and staying aware of tax issues. I also mention what happens if you want to take money out of your 401(k).

Rolling-Over Basics (How to Shake Is Next)

A job change may be the most common reason to roll over retirement funds into an IRA, but it is by no means the only one. The following list includes every reason I can think of that may prompt you to do a rollover:

» You have a new job with an employer that doesn't offer a 401(k) plan.

» You have a new job and want to transfer the money to the new employer's plan.

» You're now 59½ and want greater flexibility than your 401(k) offers.

» Your employer terminates the retirement plan you participated in.

» Your account balance is less than $1,000.

Transferring money from one 401(k) to another can be accomplished by either a direct plan-to-plan transfer or by using a conduit IRA. Take my word for it, a direct transfer is better as I explain in the upcoming "Rolling through a conduit" section. You can also transfer funds held in a traditional IRA into a 401(k) if the plan permits. You won't have as much investment flexibility, and the fees may be higher. On the positive side, you will have access to the fund at age 55 without a tax penalty if you leave the employer after age 55, and you may be able to borrow from the plan. You will have greater protection from creditors; however, your spouse will be the primary beneficiary unless your spouse signs a spousal waiver.

IRAs have different rules from 401(k)s. Be aware of the following before you do a rollover:

>> You aren't allowed to take a loan from an IRA. If you roll your 401(k) into an IRA, you won't be able to take a loan as you may be able to with a 401(k). However, you most likely will not be able to borrow from your 401(k) after leaving your employer anyway. If you roll over a 401(k) from one employer to the next, you retain borrowing possibilities as long as the new employer permits loans in its 401(k) plan. Rolling over an existing loan is possible only if both plans permit loans and if the new employer is willing to accept a rolled-over loan.

>> You can withdraw your money from an IRA at any time subject to the early withdrawal tax penalty.

WARNING

You can make only one rollover from an IRA to another (or the same) IRA in any 12-month period, regardless of the number of IRAs you own. The limit encompasses all your IRAs, including SEP and SIMPLE IRAs as well as traditional and Roth IRAs, effectively treating them as one IRA for purposes of the limit. While I'm talking about limits, let me mention no-limit exceptions:

>> Trustee-to-trustee transfers between IRAs are not limited.

>> Rollovers from a traditional IRA to a Roth IRA, which is called a *conversion,* are not limited.

Okay, this limits/no limits stuff sure is confusing, so let me add some detail. You can make only one Roth-to-Roth IRA transfer within a 12-month period, but there are no limits on how often you can do a Roth conversion. The government is glad to have you do as many Roth conversions as you want as often as you want because you pay taxes on each conversion.

Employers are permitted to force you to take your money out of a 401(k) when you resign if your account balance is less than $1,000. You can prevent this by doing a direct transfer into an IRA or a rollover into an IRA.

Finding a financial organization that doesn't have at least a $1,000 minimum for setting up an IRA is challenging. Charles Schwab and TIAA are two I am aware of at the present time.

If you already have a traditional IRA, you can roll your 401(k) money into that account. However, it's probably a better idea to open a separate IRA just for your rollover money. This makes keeping track of the funds easier. This type of account is often referred to as a *conduit IRA*, because it can act as a conduit between your old 401(k) and a new employer's plan. See the upcoming section, "Rolling through a conduit" for more details.

REMEMBER

Money in an IRA can come from two sources: your own contributions made directly to the IRA, or a rollover of money in a 401(k) or similar plan from a former employer. You can also roll money in the other direction — from an IRA into a 401(k) or another employer plan.

Rolling through the Process

You've found your next, best job, and you're taking your talents and your retirement fund with you. Your former employer is required to provide detailed information about your options after you leave your job — probably shortly after your last day.

Your former employer can't force you to take the money out of the plan if you have more than $5,000 in your account. Both you and your former employer have options:

>> You can leave your money parked in your old employer's plan until you're eligible to transfer it into your new employer's plan.

>> Your former employer has the right to transfer your entire account into an IRA if your account balance is between $1,000 and $5,000. The employer picks where the IRA will be established, but you have the right to transfer it to another financial entity without penalty.

>> Your former employer can force you to take the money in a lump sum if it is less than $1,000.

You must act promptly after receiving information about your options to avoid an automatic distribution.

Rolling over to a new account requires all the same information you need to provide to open any financial account:

>> Your name

>> Your address

>> Your birthdate

>> Your phone number

>> Your Social Security number

You also need to provide details specific to the rollover including

>> The effective date

>> Where the money is going

- Name of the institution

- Routing number

- Account number

- Contact information

>> The type of rollover

- A direct transfer to a different 401(k)

- A direct transfer to an IRA

- A transfer to a conduit IRA

>> The amount

When you initiate a rollover, you get a form that prompts you for this information. You may want to consult your financial advisor or someone from the financial organization where the money is going at the beginning of the process so that they can help you with some of the decisions and information. The financial organization and the financial advisor are interested in having you keep the money where it is if the amount is significant. Otherwise, they generally prefer having you transfer the money because small accounts aren't profitable.

Have a representative from the financial organization take control of the transfer process after you open a rollover IRA account.

A rollover into an IRA or another plan must be made within 60 days after your account is distributed to you.

Rolling through a conduit

A rollover IRA is sometimes called a conduit IRA. The money from your 401(k) account is transferred into the conduit IRA without any tax penalty. It continues to grow tax deferred and can be transferred to another 401(k), 403(b), or 457 plan maintained by a different employer.

You can open a conduit IRA at any financial institution that offers traditional and Roth IRAs. The financial organization you choose will help you set up the account. The first step is to complete the paperwork needed to open the account.

You need to give the person handling your rollover enough information to complete the transfer. That information should appear in the notice you receive from your former employer about your options.

I recommend a direct plan-to-plan transfer rather than a conduit IRA because a direct transfer gets the money where you want it to go in one step. Using a conduit IRA takes two steps:

>> A transfer first into the conduit IRA

>> A second transfer into the next employer's plan

Your new employer may not allow you to rollover your funds until you're eligible to join the plan at your new job. Employers aren't required to permit rollovers, but most do. In this instance rolling your money into a conduit IRA is a good idea. The conduit IRA holds your money and lets it grow. You may be able to transfer the money into a plan sometime in the future.

TECHNICAL STUFF

Conduit IRAs seemed to become less important in 2002 when Congress eased the rules to allow you to roll *any* traditional IRA money into a 401(k), whether it comes from a former employer's 401(k), 403(b), or 457(b) plan, or from your own contributions. The problem is you never know what those guys and gals in Congress are going to do next. The rules can change in any session.

The other issue is that employers have the option to designate what rollovers are acceptable. Although most plans currently accept rollovers from all allowable IRAs, your new plan may limit the rollover, and a conduit IRA assures your new employer that the only money in that IRA came from a qualified plan.

Rolling partially over

When rolling over into an IRA, you can do a *partial rollover*, rolling over only part of your 401(k) while leaving the rest in your 401(k) account or cashing it out. For example, you may not want to roll over employer stock if you receive shares as part of your distribution. Or, you may withdraw some of your 401(k) money right away to pay for an expense, but roll the remainder into an IRA to keep it working for your retirement. Likewise, you can do a partial conversion of a traditional IRA into a Roth — leaving some of the traditional IRA intact. (Because you pay income tax on the converted amount, reducing the amount you convert lowers the tax you pay for the conversion.)

Rolling Roths with care

Make sure to transfer any Roth contributions you made to the 401(k) into a Roth IRA or your next employer's 401(k) plan as Roth money. You've already paid tax on your Roth contributions and don't want to pay tax on them again, so you need to preserve them as Roth contributions.

REMEMBER

You must wait at least five years after you open a Roth IRA before you can make withdrawals without paying a tax penalty. The five-year period is measured from the date you opened your Roth IRA if you roll the money into an existing Roth IRA. It begins with the date you open the Roth IRA if you open a new account.

Rolling your 401(k) Roth contributions into your next employer's plan is another option to consider if you are permitted to do so. This doesn't trigger a new start date for a five-year period, but you need to give your new employer the applicable information to prevent it. Your new employer will need to know the date of your initial deposit into the Roth account so they can continue counting the five years. You will also have to give your new employer the breakdown between your Roth contributions and the investment gains. The holder of your 401(k) account should provide this information.

You can also convert the pre-tax portion (your pre-tax contributions, employer contributions, and investment income on these contributions) into a Roth IRA. You can do this at the time the money is being transferred, or you can transfer it into a traditional IRA and do the conversion into a Roth after doing the rollover.

Calling a Roth Conversion: No, It's Not a New Football Play

If you have money in a traditional IRA, and you'd rather have it in a Roth, you can do what's called a *conversion* of the traditional IRA to a Roth IRA.

A conversion is kind of like a rollover, except you have to pay tax on the amount you convert. You can either have your IRA custodian (the bank or other financial institution where you have your IRA) make a check out to you, which you deposit in the Roth within 60 days, or do a direct transfer of the money to the new Roth IRA custodian. If you're keeping the Roth IRA at the same institution as your traditional IRA, the process is even simpler — the institution can simply transfer part or all of the traditional IRA balance into a Roth IRA. You have to pay income tax on the amount transferred, but there's no early withdrawal penalty.

TIP

Some investors do a Roth conversion because they like the idea of having tax-free income at retirement. But you take a big tax hit in the year you do the conversion. One strategy is to do a conversion in a year your IRA investments haven't done too well: The value is down, so you pay tax on a lower amount.

REMEMBER

If you're required to take a required minimum distribution (RMD), you must take it before doing a Roth conversion. (Chapter 17 explains the when and how much of RMDs.)

A traditional IRA direct, trustee-to-trustee transfer or a Roth-to-Roth IRA direct, trustee-to-trustee transfer usually involves moving the money from one financial organization to another one. Even though this is obviously a transfer, it isn't counted as such with respect to the "one transfer per year" rule. You'd pay a tax penalty if this exception didn't apply.

Paying 20 Percent

If you want to take money from a 401(k), a rollover isn't required. You take the cash less the 20 percent withheld for taxes and do whatever you want with it.

The amount you roll over isn't taxable. However, if you choose not to rollover your entire retirement fund, the amount you don't roll over is taxable, plus you generally pay a 10 percent early distribution tax penalty unless you left your employer after attaining age 55 or you're 59½ and are still an active employee. You can withdraw funds penalty free in a few other situations that I describe in Chapter 16.

Your former employer is required to withhold 20 percent of your account if it is paid to you directly. So, if you have $10,000 in your former employer's account, you will receive $8,000 because $2,000 will be withheld for taxes.

As a result, you have to make up this amount from other funds if you want to do a 100 percent rollover. You can then roll over any portion of the $10,000 total you want into a conduit IRA or directly into another employer's plan.

4

Saving and Investing

Making saving more than a concept is the first benefit of starting a retirement account. Mapping out a savings plan will help you down the road to your retirement destination.

Figuring out how to save quickly segues into how much you need to save. Beating inflation while weathering the ups and downs of the market is an achievable goal.

Choosing what to invest in and in what proportions can be nerve-wracking but is certainly necessary. You may have limited choices through your employer's plan or have a wide field to pick from for your personal IRA.

Setting your best investment strategy is something you'll undoubtedly need to do more than once. As you get closer to your retirement, switching ratios of growth and income investments makes sense.

No risk, no reward. Knowing that a reasonable amount of risk is included in making investment choices is necessary to keep you on track with your plan. Ups and downs will happen through the years; you just need to find a comfortable level of risk.

Chapter 11

Setting Up Your Savings Plan

Spontaneity can be a lot of fun. But it's the last thing you want when you're planning for retirement. Saving for retirement involves delayed gratification, planning, and discipline, but today's sound-bite society may find this news hard to swallow. Luckily, tools like a 401(k) and IRAs can help make the process less painful, because a lot of the saving is automatic after you set up the plan.

If you're young, you may think it's too soon to plan for something that's 30 or 40 years away. The truth is that the earlier you start, the better, because your savings will have more time to build up through compounding (as the earnings on money in your account continue to earn even more money). Starting to save early will give you more freedom later to decide what you want to do.

On the other hand, if you're already in your 40s or older, you may wonder whether it's too late for you to plan. The bottom line is that it's never too late. But you may find that you need to scale back some of your goals or increase the amount you save each year if you're getting a late start. This chapter aims to help you set and meet retirement goals and develop a detailed plan for achieving them. It walks you through the steps of deciding on a target date to retire, calculating how much income you'll need in retirement, developing a savings plan to achieve that amount of income, and tracking your progress as you save over the years.

Targeting Your Retirement Date

The first step in planning for retirement is deciding when you want to retire. This can be trickier than it sounds. Attitudes about what retirement means and when it should happen have been changing over the last decade or two.

In choosing a target date for retirement, you need to consider several factors, including

>> When you can access your various sources of retirement income

>> What you'll do when you retire

>> Whether living to the age of 100 runs in your family

It used to be clear-cut — you worked until you were 65 (or maybe 62), and then you were forced to retire with a gold watch and a pension. Social Security checks started arriving in the mail soon after your 65th birthday. Nowadays, things are different. There's no standard retirement age that applies to everyone and every type of account. Check some of the options:

>> You're *allowed* to withdraw money from your 401(k) or IRA without penalty at age 59½ (or age 55 if you leave your employer).

>> You're *required* to start withdrawing money from your 401(k) when you're 72 — unless, that is, you're still working for the company sponsoring the 401(k). Then you can wait until you retire to take out your money, unless you own more than 5 percent of the business.

>> You're *allowed* to withdraw money from a traditional IRA without penalty at age 59½.

>> You're *required* to start withdrawing money from a traditional IRA when you're 72. It used to be age 70½, but Congress changed that with the SECURE act in 2019.

>> You're *allowed* to start withdrawing money from a Roth IRA anytime without penalty if the account has been open for at least five years.

>> You're *never* required to withdraw money from a Roth IRA during your lifetime.

Whew! With all those different ages, how can you know when to retire?

REMEMBER

For planning purposes, you need to estimate when you'll have to start withdrawing the money in your retirement accounts and whether that money will be supporting you entirely or whether you'll have other sources of income.

Choosing an age now can help you plan how much you need to save and how much time you have in which to save it (your *time horizon,* in financial planning lingo). The advantage of estimating a retirement age now is that you can see whether that goal is reasonable. If it's not, you may have to rethink it. The key is to remain flexible.

Getting Your Hands on Your Money

When you retire and no longer earn a paycheck, you'll need to get income from somewhere. If you plan well, that income should be available from several sources.

Drawing on your Social Security

If you are at least age 62, the first source of income you'll have during retirement is *Social Security,* the federal government's social insurance program that includes monthly benefit payments to retirees.

How Social Security works

You earn Social Security credits by working and paying Social Security taxes. You can accumulate up to four credits every year. You need a minimum of 40 credits to collect Social Security, so if you work for ten years, you can look forward to getting some money when you're older.

REMEMBER

Your Social Security benefits are based on your income throughout your working life, so the more you make, the more you reap in retirement.

Your earnings are adjusted or indexed to account for changes in average wages since the year you earned the money. Your average indexed monthly earnings (AIME) are calculated using the 35 years when you earned the most money. The Social Security number crunchers apply a formula to the AIME to compute your primary insurance amount. The formula breaks down your AIME into three parts, which for 2021 are as follows:

>> 90 percent of the first $996 of your AIME

>> Plus 32 percent of any amount over $996 up to $6,002

>> Plus 15 percent of any amount over $6,002

This formula results in your primary insurance amount (PIA), which is the amount of your monthly benefit.

The ratio is different depending on your income though. Lower-paid workers get a larger percentage of their income from Social Security than higher paid workers. For example, if you're retiring at 66

>> Earning $30,000, you can expect to receive approximately 45 percent of your earnings, or $13,500 per year.

>> Earning $100,000, you can expect to get approximately 25 percent of this amount, or $25,000 per year.

So, if you earn more, you get more, but you get a smaller percentage of your earnings.

How to access your Social Security benefits

You can access your full Social Security benefits sometime after you turn 66, depending on when you were born. Table 11-1 shows the age you're eligible for full benefits. Again, Congress can change the full Social Security age in the future.

TABLE 11-1   **Retirement Age by Birth Year**

Birth Year	Full Retirement Age
1943–1954	66
1955	66 and 2 months
1956	66 and 4 months
1957	66 and 6 months
1958	66 and 8 months
1959	66 and 10 months
1960 and later	67

Source: Social Security Administration website (www.ssa.gov).

If you were born on the first day of a month, special rules apply to you:

>> If your birthday is January 1, the Social Security Administration (SSA) considers you born in the previous year.

>> If your birthday is the first of any month, the SSA treats you as if you were born the previous month.

When your Social Security money appears in your bank account depends on where your birthday falls in the month — and it will appear there the month after you qualify.

If you're a surviving spouse, the maximum benefit you receive is 50 percent of the benefit your spouse would receive at full retirement age. If you opt for early payments of a reduced benefit, the percentage reduction is applied after the automatic 50 percent reduction.

You can start receiving reduced benefits when you reach age 62 and have been 62 for an entire month. Reduced is the operative word: If you choose to start tapping into your Social Security benefits before your full retirement age, you receive at least 25 percent less than if you'd waited. Table 11-2 shows how much your benefits are reduced if you decide to take your money early.

TABLE 11-2 **Reduced Social Security Benefits**

Birth Year	Months between 62 and full retirement age	$1,000 benefit reduced to	Percentage of reduction (approximate)
1943–1954	48	$750	25.00%
1955	50	$741	25.83%
1956	52	$733	26.67%
1957	54	$725	27.50%
1958	56	$716	28.33%
1959	58	$708	29.17%
1960 and later	60	$700	30.00%

Source: Social Security Administration website (www.ssa.gov).

You can delay taking your Social Security benefits until you turn 70. Your benefits increase if you wait until then but don't increase after that. Table 11-3 shows how much your benefits increase if you wait to collect them.

REMEMBER

Once you tap into your Social Security benefits, your monthly payment remains the same, barring any adjustments Congress may make — a cost-of-living adjustment (COLA), for example. So, before you decide to take the money and run when you hit 62, think about how much you may miss out on.

TABLE 11-3

Enhanced Social Security Benefits

Birth Year	Percentage increase (approximate)	$1,000 benefit increased to
1943–1954	132	$1,132.00
1955	130.66	$1,130.66
1956	129.33	$1,129.33
1957	128	$1,128.00
1958	126.66	$1,126.66
1959	125.33	$1,125.33
1960 and later	124	$1,124.00

Source: Social Security Administration website (www.ssa.gov).

In sum, you can't expect to receive any retirement benefits from Social Security before age 62, and you can increase the amount you receive if you wait until you're 66 or 67. If you wait past your "normal retirement age" until you're 70, your benefits are even higher.

How to estimate your Social Security benefits

TIP

You can find a variety of opinions about when you should start taking your Social Security benefits. The monthly amount will be larger if you delay taking your benefits; however, you must live for a significant number of years before the increased monthly benefit will have replaced the benefits you would have received if you started taking benefits earlier. If you don't need the income, take your health and your gene pool into consideration before deciding to delay the benefits. Political risk is another factor to consider. The fact that future benefits may be reduced was one of the reasons I started taking my benefits when they wouldn't be reduced because I still had earned income.

If you continue working while you're drawing Social Security benefits, your benefits may be reduced. If you opt for early, reduced benefits, your reduction is $1 for each $2 of wages in excess of $18,960 during 2021. The wage limit increases each year. This reduction applies to each year until you reach your full benefit age. The year you reach your full benefit age, your benefits will be reduced by $1 for every $3 you earn in excess of $50,520. This limit also increases each year. Take these reductions into consideration if you are phasing into retirement from your current job or are planning on other earned income-generating work after leaving your current job.

Starting the year after you reach your full retirement age, you keep all your benefits regardless of how much you earn.

SOCIAL INSECURITY?

Social Security is what's known as a "pay-as-you-go" system. When you pay Social Security taxes out of your paycheck, the taxes don't go into an "account" in your name. The taxes go to pay the benefits of today's retired folks. In the same way, today's toddlers and teenagers will be supporting you one day — hopefully. But as the 76-million-strong Baby Boom generation started turning 65 in 2011 (and doesn't stop until 2029), a tremendous strain is being placed on the system. The COVID-19 pandemic has worsened the situation due to fewer workers and a larger than normal number of retirees.

In 1945, there were an estimated 41.9 workers for every retiree. By 1999, the ratio dropped to an estimated 3.4 workers for every retiree. By about 2030, the ratio is expected to drop to two workers for every retiree. Clearly, something will have to give.

The Social Security program is probably currently running at a deficit with benefits being paid exceeding taxes being collected.

The Social Security Administration mails annual statements to workers who are over 25 years old. These statements estimate how much money you'd receive monthly at age 62, at full retirement age, and at age 70, based on your income to date. If you threw yours away or can't find it, you can create a My Social Security account online and download or print a new one at www.ssa.gov/mystatement/. Or if you prefer not to send personal information over the internet, you can download a form that you mail in to request the statement. You can also request the form by telephone, at 1-800-772-1213, or by appearing in person at your local Social Security office.

You can factor the estimated benefit amount into your planned retirement income, but remember that Social Security was never meant to be your only source of retirement income. What's more, the future of Social Security is somewhat uncertain. Although Social Security benefits may not disappear completely during the next 20 to 30 years, they may be reduced.

Tapping into other sources

Managing your retirement savings to last the rest of your life is challenging if the only fixed monthly income you have is Social Security. You likely need other sources of income during retirement. The following list highlights possible retirement resources above and beyond Social Security:

>> **401(k):** As long as you're working for the employer that sponsors the plan, you generally can't take money out before you're 59½ other than for hardship

withdrawals. Taking a hardship withdrawal prior to age 59½ means you pay income tax and a 10 percent penalty tax unless the withdrawal is for a reason that is exempt from the penalty tax. (Check Chapter 16 for a list of exempt withdrawals.)

If your plan permits you to withdraw money after age 59½, you'll have to pay taxes on the money you take out, but you don't pay an early withdrawal tax penalty.

If you leave your job at age 55 or older, you can withdraw the money without any penalty tax, but you still have to pay income tax.

TIP

You can withdraw the money as an income stream provided your 401(k) plan permits installment withdrawals. The amount you withdraw each year will be taxable but without any penalty.

You can also roll it over into an IRA, but that won't be a good idea if you want to withdraw money prior to age 59½ because the early withdrawal penalty will apply.

>> **Other tax-favored retirement accounts:** Accounts similar to a 401(k), such as a 403(b) or IRA, have rules similar to those of 401(k)s. Generally, you shouldn't count on having easy access to your money before age 59½, or possibly age 55. There aren't any early withdrawal penalties for 457 deferred comp plans.

>> **Annuity:** Consider converting at least 50 percent of your retirement savings (401(k), IRA or other) into a lifetime income stream by purchasing an annuity that provides a guaranteed monthly income. There are many types of annuities on the market, but the only type I recommend is one that provides a monthly income.

>> **Traditional defined-benefit pension plan:** If your employer offers one of these plans, your human resources or benefits representative should be able to tell you what your expected payment will be if you qualify to receive benefits.

>> **Life insurance:** Some people buy a type of life insurance policy that allows them to build up a cash account (a *cash value* policy) rather than buy term life insurance, which is worth nothing after you stop making payments. If you have a cash value policy (such as whole life or variable life), it should have a cash account that you can tap at retirement.

>> **Regular taxable savings:** A taxable account is any kind of account (such as a bank account, mutual fund account, or stock brokerage account) that doesn't have special tax advantages.

>> **Part-time work:** No matter when you retire, you may want to take a part-time job that will keep you active and give you extra income.

>> **Inherited wealth:** You shouldn't count on any inheritance until you actually receive it. But if you do inherit a substantial amount of money, integrate at least part of it into your overall financial plan to give yourself a higher retirement income.

Rental property is another type of investment to consider as you approach your retirement years. My wife and I bought a small farm as an investment property during our late 50s. It has two houses that we rented. The same tenant was in the larger house for 14 years. We remodeled it, sold our other house, and moved three years ago. We have great tenants in the other house and a couple of horses to board that still provide rental income.

TIP

You can take the first step toward figuring out when you can feasibly retire by writing down your sources of income and when you can access them.

Living the retirement life

Assume that your retirement begins tomorrow. What will your life be like? This is the necessary question that retirement calculators don't ask. Most importantly, what will you do six months after the novelty of retirement wears off, when you're tired of golfing, shopping, traveling, or just being a couch potato? Many people find it difficult to go straight from full-time work to full retirement — particularly when they haven't developed interests outside of work. A recent RAND corporation survey shows that up to 40 percent of retirees are eventually returning to work full-time or part-time. Seventeen percent of those between 70 and 74 are working at least ten hours per week according to a Stanford University study. Some work because they enjoy it and want to stay involved. Others continue working to keep medical or other benefits. Many continue working because they need the income.

Having an idea of what you'll do in retirement is important so that you can avoid these common mistakes:

>> Retiring too early, realizing that your money isn't going to last, and being forced to go back to work. In the meantime, you've lost out on contributing more to your 401(k) — and possible employer contributions, as well.

>> Retiring, becoming totally bored within six months, and begging for your old job back.

Imagining your retired life can be both fun and motivating.

Testing the waters in your gene pool

When you think about your retirement age and how long you'll need to finance your retirement, keep your genes in mind. If your family has a history of longevity, you should plan financially to live until 100. (If you're the cautious type, you may want to do this anyway, even if you don't think there's a chance you'll live that long.)

Developing Your Retirement Savings Plan

After you recover from the shock of how much you'll need in your retirement account, your first thought will probably be, "How on earth do I accumulate ten times my annual income — and then some — by the time I retire?"

REMEMBER

The key is to start as early as you can, because the earlier you start saving, the longer your money has to benefit from compounding, even if you start by putting away small amounts. See the benefits of compounding in the upcoming section "Counting on compounding."

Cutting down on your expenses

I realize that many workers barely earn enough to pay for basic necessities and can't eke out anything extra for a 401(k) plan or IRA contribution. But it's important to try. Or you may be in your 40s and want to save more to catch up, but you can't figure out where to find the money. You may be surprised at some of the places you can save money. Often, a few minor spending adjustments can free up money for savings.

Like most everything, it all boils down to making choices. Table 11-4 lists suggestions for cutting your spending. None of the expenses listed are necessities — and cutting out one or two, or reducing the cost of a few, can help begin your savings program.

You're probably wondering whether all this nickel-and-diming is really worth it, but it can add up. I'm not suggesting that you give up *everything* on the list — only that you look at what you spend to see if you can cut some costs without feeling too much pain. Giving up a few nonessential items today is far better than struggling *without necessities* during your retirement years.

TABLE 11-4   **Ten Tips for Saving Money**

Expense	How to Save
$1 each day or week for a lottery ticket	If you buy one ticket daily, cut back to one a week. If you buy one a week, cut back to one a month.
$25 a year for apps you don't use anymore	If you pay for updates or upkeep on several apps, review to see which ones you really use and cancel the others.
$18 or more a month for streaming services	Have watch parties. Trade with friends and go to their house for the Hulu series you're both into and have them to your house for the Apple TV show you can't miss. Limit your streaming services to one or two must-haves.
$40 for a movie and popcorn for two at a cinema	Check out a disc from your local library for free or tap into your streaming options. Pop some popcorn yourself — it'll probably taste better, anyway.
$10 a day for a drink after work	Instead of going out every night with your friends, cut back to just weekends.
$5 a day for various other beverages of choice (bottled water, soda, coffee, and so on)	Drink what's provided at your office, or buy in bulk and bring it to work.
$10 to $15 a day for lunch	Pack your own lunch a few times a week.
A $500 monthly car payment versus a $350 payment	Do you really need an SUV with leather seats and all the goodies?
A $350,000 home versus a $200,000 home	This depends on where you live. In California, add $400,000 to each price.
A $1,000 vacation versus a $2,000 vacation	Visit attractions close to home to avoid plane fares. Go to places that people would go if they were visiting you.

REMEMBER

I've never met a 401(k) participant who claimed to have saved too much. I've never heard participants say that they wished they'd spent more money earlier. Instead, what many older participants tell me is that they wish they had started saving sooner.

This may be difficult to believe, but the important thing about money is *not* how much you earn. It's how you manage what you have. Spenders will always spend what they have or more, regardless of how much they earn. Spenders who get a substantial increase in income will adjust their spending habits to the new level within a very short period of time.

TIP

If you have a tendency to spend, automatically take a portion of any pay increase and put it into a 401(k) or similar forced savings vehicle before you get used to having it in your hot little hands. Otherwise, you may never break your spending cycle.

Picturing your progress

After you start saving, you have to keep checking to make sure that you're on track. Benchmarks can generally help you gauge where you should be.

The savings goals in this section are designed for 25-year-olds just starting their savings programs. If you're over age 25, these benchmarks can still tell you if you're on target with your retirement planning. If you're significantly behind these benchmarks, you're certainly not alone.

Remember that these are ideals; they're not here to make anyone feel defeated. Instead, the intention is to motivate you to sit down and develop a workable plan for catching up. This may mean that you have to work longer than you'd like or substantially increase your savings rate. If you feel depressed looking at these, just be glad you're starting now. If you'd waited, imagine how much more catching up you would have to do!

If you don't have a 401(k) or other employer-sponsored retirement savings plan, use an IRA to hit the numbers I use in the examples in the following sections.

Savings equal to your annual income by the time you're 35

You need to shoot to accumulate the amount of your annual income by age 35. Table 11-5 shows what you need to do to accomplish this goal.

The numbers in the table are based on the following assumptions:

>> Annual pay increases of 4 percent

>> Employee contributions of 4 percent of pay the first year, 5 percent the second year, and 6 percent in subsequent years

>> Employer matching contribution of 50 cents on the dollar, limited to the first 6 percent of pay that the employee contributes

>> An average investment return of 9 percent

REMEMBER

The 50 percent employer matching contribution is a big help. You have to adjust your contributions if you're in a plan that has a lower employer contribution or none at all.

TABLE 11-5   **How to Accumulate One Times Your Pre-Retirement Income by Age 35**

Age	Your Pay	Your Contribution	Employer's Contribution	Total Return	Year-End Value
25	$25,000	$1,000	$500	$68	$1,568
26	$26,000	$1,300	$650	$229	$3,747
27	$27,040	$1,622	$811	$446	$6,626
28	$28,122	$1,687	$844	$710	$9,867
29	$29,246	$1,755	$878	$1,006	$13,506
30	$30,416	$1,825	$912	$1,339	$17,582
31	$31,633	$1,898	$949	$1,710	$22,139
32	$32,898	$1,974	$987	$2,126	$27,226
33	$34,214	$2,053	$1,026	$2,588	$32,893
34	$35,583	$2,135	$1,067	$3,104	$39,199

Tripling your nest egg by 45

Assume that in the next ten years you increase your contribution rate to 10 percent. You continue to receive a 50 percent match (equivalent to a 3 percent of pay contribution from your employer), your annual pay continues to increase by 4 percent per year, and your investment return is 9 percent per year. Table 11-6 shows the results.

By age 45, you'd be ahead of schedule with an accumulation of more than 3.5 times your annual pay.

Getting conservative when you hit 55 — financially, anyway

Assume that everything stays the same for the next ten years — except that you increase your contribution rate from 10 percent to 15 percent at age 50, your annual salary increases by 4 percent per year, and your investment return continues at 9 percent until age 50. The return then drops to 8 percent from age 50 to 55, because you sell some of your more risky stock investments in favor of investments that provide a more stable, but lower, return. Table 11-7 shows the result.

At this point, you will have accumulated 7.2 times your annual pay. As you near retirement, your goal is within reach.

TABLE 11-6 How to Accumulate Three Times Your Pre-Retirement Income by Age 45

Age	Your Pay	Your Investment	Employer's Contribution	Total Return	Year-End Value
35	$37,006	$3,700	$1,110	$3,744	$47,753
36	$38,487	$3,849	$1,154	$4,523	$57,279
37	$40,026	$4,003	$1,201	$5,389	$67,872
38	$41,627	$4,163	$1,249	$6,351	$79,635
39	$43,292	$4,329	$1,299	$7,420	$92,683
40	$45,024	$4,502	$1,350	$8,604	$107,139
41	$46,825	$4,683	$1,405	$9,917	$123,144
42	$48,698	$4,870	$1,461	$11,368	$140,843
43	$50,646	$5,065	$1,519	$12,973	$160,400
44	$52,672	$5,267	$1,580	$14,744	$181,991

TABLE 11-7 How to Accumulate Seven Times Your Pre-Retirement Income by Age 55

Age	Your Pay	Your Investment	Employer's Contribution	Total Return	Year-End Value
45	$54,778	$5,478	$1,643	$16,699	$205,811
46	$56,970	$5,697	$1,709	$18,856	$232,073
47	$59,248	$5,925	$1,777	$21,233	$261,008
48	$61,618	$6,162	$1,848	$23,851	$292,869
49	$64,083	$6,408	$1,922	$26,733	$327,932
50	$66,646	$9,997	$1,999	$26,714	$366,642
51	$69,312	$10,397	$2,079	$29,828	$408,946
52	$72,085	$10,813	$2,162	$33,235	$455,156
53	$74,968	$11,245	$2,249	$36,952	$505,602
54	$77,967	$11,695	$2,339	$41,571	$561,207

Opening up options at 60

Assume that your contribution rate remains at 15 percent, your employer's contribution rate remains at 3 percent of your salary, and your pay continues to increase by 4 percent per year. Your investment return remains at 8 percent. Table 11-8 gives you the numbers.

TABLE 11-8 How to Accumulate 10 Times Your Pre-Retirement Income by Age 60

Age	Your Pay	Your Investment	Employer's Contribution	Total Return	Year-End Value
55	$81,085	$12,163	$2,432	$45,480	$621,282
56	$84,329	$12,649	$2,529	$50,311	$686,711
57	$87,702	$13,155	$2,631	$55,573	$758,130
58	$91,210	$13,682	$2,736	$61,307	$835,855
59	$94,858	$14,229	$2,845	$67,551	$920,480
60	$98,652	$14,798	$2,960	$74,348	$1,012,586

At this point, you should be in a good position to consider various alternatives — including retirement, working fewer hours at your current job, or shifting to some other income-producing activity that interests you. You have successfully accumulated ten times the income you are earning when you retire. This is a good level to achieve if you are retiring at the age when you will qualify for full Social Security benefits. You will need more if you retire at an earlier age.

REMEMBER

These projections are based on assumptions that may differ considerably from your actual experience. Take all these figures as guidelines to help you understand the important features of investing for retirement.

WARNING

If you plan to retire before age 65, don't forget to factor in the cost of medical insurance. The availability and cost of medical care is a major issue if you plan to retire before you and your spouse are eligible for *Medicare*, the government-sponsored medical program for those age 65 and older.

Counting on compounding

The purpose of the sample plans in the preceding sections is to show you how a specific plan gives you a tangible way to measure your progress each year. It's helpful for you to know some assumptions in the previous savings goal examples:

>> Money is saved for retirement every year. You should even add to your retirement savings during periods that you're not eligible to contribute to a 401(k) using an IRA and other investments if necessary.

>> All the money is left in the plan until retirement. None of the money is withdrawn for other purposes.

>> The assumed return requires at least 60 to 70 percent in stock investments (mutual funds or a diversified mix of individual stocks) up to age 55. After age 55, the stock holdings drop to the 50 to 60 percent range. (I talk more about investment strategy in Chapter 13.)

Your retirement nest egg comes from your own contributions and your employer's contributions, and the investment return that's earned on these contributions. Table 11-9 shows this final breakdown among the three sources, using the example of savings progress at age 60 from the previous section.

TABLE 11-9

Account Breakdown by Source

Source	Amount
Your contributions	$226,173
Employer contributions	$57,812
Investment return	$728,601
TOTAL	$1,012,586

You've probably heard about the magic of *compounded growth* — a term used to explain how money can grow over time.

Figure 11-1 looks at the cost of waiting to save $1,000 a year. See how much more the person who starts at age 25 ends up with than the one who waits until age 35.

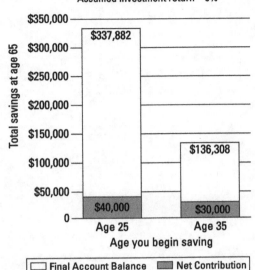

The Power of Compounding

$1,000 Annual Contribution
Assumed investment return – 9%

FIGURE 11-1:
A quick look at
the importance of
compounding.

The benefit of compounded growth is very real, but this magic is significant only over long periods of time — 20 to 30 years or longer. This is why starting to save at an early age and sticking with your program is so important. If you wait 10 years before you start, you'll substantially reduce your investment return. The difference can be made up only by a much larger savings rate or by working and saving longer.

Chapter **12**

Determining How Much to Save

S o you're retired. No more 9 to 5, no more boss to answer to, no more commute, no more meetings . . . and no more paycheck. Even though you no longer get a paycheck, you still have expenses, and that's why you started saving for retirement all those years ago — or yesterday. This chapter gives you the tools to use to fund your retirement.

Improving Your Chances of an Ideal Retirement

Investing in a retirement plan or an IRA can mean the difference between merely surviving retirement and actually living it up.

REMEMBER

Most financial planners suggest that you'll need at least 70 to 80 percent of your pre-retirement income to maintain your lifestyle in retirement. But many people may need closer to 100 percent, or more.

Some people think their Social Security benefits alone will be enough to cover their retirement needs. The unfortunate fact is you shouldn't rely on Social

Security to finance your retirement. Financial security during retirement requires income from a variety of sources. Social Security was never intended to be the sole source of retirement income for Americans.

When you retire, you'll have to manage your nest egg so that you don't run out of money before you die. Chapter 11 explains why and how to set up a savings plan for your 401(k) or IRA during your working years, and Chapter 17 looks at ways to make your money last after you retire.

Deciding How Much of Your Salary to Put Aside

How do you decide what percentage or dollar amount to put aside for your retirement? To begin with, you need to consider several factors:

>> Whether you can enroll in an employer-sponsored retirement plan

- If yes, the plan documents prompt you for decisions

- If no, you need to become the captain of your own retirement plan by starting an IRA. See the chapters in Part 3 for info on IRAs

>> The government's restrictions on contributions to IRAs and 401(k)s

>> Your own plan's restrictions

>> Your budget's limitations

>> The amount you need to get the full employer matching contribution

The next sections help with all these issues.

Making use of your salary deferral agreement

When you enroll in a 401(k) plan, you fill out a *salary deferral agreement*. Salary deferral refers to the pre-tax amount of your pay that you want your employer to put in the 401(k) plan rather than in your paycheck. It probably also gives you the option to make after-tax Roth contributions.

The form may require you to select a percentage of salary to contribute, or it may ask for a dollar amount. In fact, it may even give you a choice, such as the one shown in Figure 12-1. What's the difference? Take a look:

>> The percentage of salary is easy because it's the same no matter how many pay periods you have. If you want to contribute 10 percent of your pay, you simply list "10%" on the form.

>> For a dollar amount, you need to figure out the total amount you want to contribute for the year and then divide it by the number of pay periods. Say you get paid twice a month. If you earn $50,000 and you want to put $3,000 a year into your 401(k), you list "6%" on the form. This will result in a $125 per pay deduction ($3,000 divided by 24 equals $125).

SECTION I - Salary Deferral Election
Participant should complete A or B.
A. ☐ I **elect to contribute** the following pay to the Plan each pay period:
☐ _____ % **OR** ☐ $_____
B. ☐ I elect **NOT to contribute** to the Plan.
SECTION II - Salary Deferral Election of Bonuses and Commissions
I **elect** ☐ **to apply** ☐ **not to apply** the percentage or fixed dollar amount specified in Section I(A) above to any bonuses and/or commissions I may receive as compensation.

FIGURE 12-1:
Sample 401(k) salary deferral form.

If you work irregular hours or earn variable pay such as overtime, bonuses, or commissions, contributing a percentage of pay means a variable amount is deducted each pay period.

TIP

Some employers won't let you include overtime or other forms of non-base pay as compensation for the purposes of contributing to a 401(k). In this case, contributions may be based only on your base pay or something less than your total compensation.

REMEMBER

The most important thing is to start contributing as soon as you're eligible. Even if you only contribute 1 percent of your salary to begin with, it's a start. After you're in the habit of saving, it gets easier and easier. But if you put it off, it only gets harder.

Measuring your plan's maximums

Your 401(k) plan isn't allowed to let you contribute more than the federal limits discussed in the previous section, but it probably restricts you to less because there are other things that must be deducted from your pay including federal and state income taxes, local wage taxes, and Social Security. Your plan may also have a priority that will be followed due to other deductions for medical coverage, charitable donations, and so on. Your employer decides the pecking order for your 401(k) contributions.

Being highly paid means different rules

Under federal law, employers must test their 401(k) plans each year to ensure that no discrimination exists in favor of highly paid employees.

The key question is: How much do you have to earn to qualify as a highly compensated employee, or HCE? The rules are pretty tricky. If you earn less than $130,000 and you don't own more than 5 percent of your company (and you aren't related to, or married to, anyone who does), you aren't highly compensated. If that's the case for you, feel free to skip this section. Otherwise, keep reading — but do a few jumping jacks first to make sure that you're fully alert.

What makes you an HCE?

You're considered highly compensated in a given year if you own more than 5 percent of your company in that year or the previous year. You may also be considered highly compensated in a given year if you earned more than a specified salary in the previous year. Here's a concrete example: You're considered an HCE in 2021 if you owned more than 5 percent of your company in either 2020 or 2021. Also, you *may* be considered an HCE in 2021 if your salary in 2021 is more than $130,000. (I say "may" because a possible exception exists for the salary rule. See the "Being highly paid but not an HCE" sidebar in this chapter for details.)

The contribution percentages of HCEs are added up as one group, and the contribution percentages of lower-paid employees are added up as a second group. The average contribution percentage of the highly paid employees can't be more than 2 percentage points above those of the lower-paid group. For example, if lower-paid employees as a group contribute an average of 4 percent of salary to the 401(k), highly paid employees can only contribute 6 percent. (The formula is actually more complex, but this example gives you the basic idea.)

Safe harbor and Qualified Automatic Contribution Arrangement 401(k) plans, which I talk about in Chapter 18, are exempt from these requirements.

TECHNICAL STUFF

Highly compensated employees are often referred to as *HCEs*, while lower-paid workers are referred to as *non-HCEs*. I mention these terms so you'll be familiar with them if you come across them should you encounter them.

How do HCE contributions work?

If you're highly compensated, your contributions will likely be limited to bring your combined contributions down to an acceptable level (in other words, in line with lower-compensated employees).

BEING HIGHLY PAID BUT NOT AN HCE

If you earn more than the HCE salary limit, you still may not be considered an HCE even if your company has a lot of highly paid employees. A company is allowed to limit its designated HCEs to only the top 20 percent of employees. So, for example, if 40 percent of employees at your company earned more than the $130,000 dollar limit in 2021, your company can choose to designate only the top-paid 20 percent of non-excludable employees as HCEs who may have their contributions capped or receive refunds in 2021. This flexibility doesn't exist with the ownership rule, though. If you own more than 5 percent of the company in 2020 or 2021, you'll be considered an HCE for 2021.

Say you're highly compensated and you want to contribute 10 percent for a year in which HCE contributions have to be capped at 6 percent. If your plan is on the ball, you'll find out about the problem early and have your contributions capped at 6 percent.

By the way, there's another way your employer can resolve this problem. Your employer can give an extra contribution to some or all of the lower-paid employees to make up for the discrepancy. This contribution is called a *qualified matching contribution* (QMAC) or *qualified nonelective contribution* (QNEC). If you receive one of these contributions, it must be vested right away. This option is less popular among employers, because it costs them extra and it's complicated. (Go figure, right?)

CALCULATING AN HCE REFUND

If your plan fails the nondiscrimination test during any year, refunds will probably be made. The system for determining who gets a refund, and how much it is, is somewhat complicated. First the plan has to determine how far the highly compensated employees were over the limit. Say the lower-paid employees in the plan contributed 4 percent on average, and there are three highly compensated employees in the plan. One of the highly compensated employees contributed 8 percent, one contributed 7 percent, and one contributed 6 percent. Their average contribution is 7 percent, which is 1 percent too high. (Because the lower-paid employees contributed 4 percent, the highly compensated employees are limited to 6 percent.)

The HCE who contributed the largest dollar amount (rather than highest percentage of pay) is the first to get a refund. This rule can cause tension among highly compensated employees, because the person who caused the plan to fail by contributing 8 percent isn't the one who has to take a refund.

Another limit may come into play: In 2021 you're not allowed to make 401(k) contributions or receive employer contributions based on more than $290,000 in compensation. So, if you earn $320,000 and contribute 5 percent of your salary, your contributions have to stop at $14,000 (5 percent of $290,000) instead of $19,500 if you are under age 55. Any employer match applies to the $14,000, as well.

TECHNICAL STUFF

If your plan doesn't require whole percentages, you may have signed up to contribute 6.724 percent, which gets you to the $19,500 maximum contribution — and your employer can match it. Signing up for 7 percent if your plan requires a whole percentage lets you contribute the $19,500 maximum but matching contributions stop when you have contributed this amount because you will no longer be contributing. You will have earned $278,571 at that point ($278,571 times 7 percent); therefore, $11,429 of your income that is less than the $290,000 won't be matched ($290,000 minus $278,571). If your employer matches 6 percent of your compensation, $685.71 is the amount that won't be matched ($11,429 times 6 percent). The matching contributions you will miss depend on the employer matching rate. You will lose $342.86 if the matching rate is 50 percent ($685.71 × 0.50).

Estimating what your budget can afford

Talking about how much you're allowed to put into a retirement plan is fine, but what about how much you can afford to put in? If money is tight, you may be tempted to wait and start saving in a couple of years when you're earning more or have less debt. The problem with that strategy is that the longer you wait to start saving, the harder it gets psychologically. You get used to spending the money you have. Also, by waiting to participate, you lose a lot of potential earnings.

The following example (also illustrated in Figure 12-2) shows how you can cheat yourself big-time by waiting just a few years to start saving.

Ken, Rasheed, and Lisa all earn $50,000 a year. They all decide to contribute 5 percent of their salary, or $2,500, to their 401(k) plans, but over different periods of time. Assuming that each has an average annual return (how much the money increases in value when it's invested) of 8 percent, look at the surprising results:

>> Ken waits eight years to begin saving. In years 9 through 30, he contributes a total of $55,000 to the plan ($2,500 × 22 years), and his account balance grows to $143,654. (The extra comes from his 8 percent return, which is reinvested in the account each year without being taxed.)

>> Rasheed starts saving right away, but he stops after eight years. He contributes only $20,000 to the plan ($2,500 × 8 years), but because he started earlier, his money has more time to grow through the magic of compounding. He ends up with $149,794 — $6,000 more than Ken after 30 years.

>> Lisa saves for the entire 30 years. She contributes only $20,000 more than Ken, in total (over the eight years when Ken doesn't contribute), but her $75,000 contribution grows to $293,448 — twice that of Ken's, because her money benefited from compounding for a longer period of time.

Advantages of Starting to Save Early Through a 401(k) Plan

Year	A) KEN waits 8 years to start saving		B) RASHEED starts saving early, quits after 8 years		C) LISA starts saving early and keeps at it!		What you invest and what you earn
	Annual Investment	Year end value @ 8%	Annual Investment	Year end value @ 8%	Annual Investment	Year end value @ 8%	
1	$0	$0	$1,250	$1,295	$1,250	$1,295	A – started late
2	0	0	1,250	2,694	1,250	2,694	22 years @ $1,250
3	0	0	1,250	4,205	1,250	4,205	Total saved $71,827 Amount invested 27,500
4	0	0	1,250	5,836	1,250	5,836	Investment return 44,327
5	0	0	1,250	7,598	1,250	7,598	B – started early
6	0	0	1,250	9,501	1,250	9,501	8 years @ $1,250
7	0	0	1,250	11,557	1,250	11,557	Total saved $71,827
8	0	0	1,250	13,777	1,250	13,777	Amount invested 27,500 Investment return 44,327
9	1,250	1,295	0	14,879	1,250	16,174	
10	1,250	2,694	0	16,069	1,250	18,763	C – started early & continued
15	1,250	11,557	0	23,611	1,250	35,167	30 years @ $1,250
20	1,250	24,579	0	34,692	1,250	59,271	Total saved $71,827
25	1,250	43,713	0	50,973	1,250	94,687	Amount invested 27,500 Investment return 44,327
30	1,250	71,827	0	74,897	1,250	146,724	

FIGURE 12-2: Payoffs of saving early in a 401(k).

The figures indicated reflect employee contributions only. In this example, investment return is calculated at 8%. Your own 401(k) investment return may be higher or lower, depending on the performance of the funds offered and how you invested the money in your account.

You can see that it pays to start saving early and to keep saving. In this example, each person is saving a little more than $200 per month. If that seems like too much for you now, consider contributing a smaller amount. Sometimes that's the best way to get started. For example, consider saving $20 per week, or $1,040 a year.

If you're contributing to a 401(k), you can save $20 while only reducing your take-home pay by about $16 per week, because you save the $20 before paying taxes if you opt for pre-tax contributions, while you get your take-home pay after paying taxes. Just about anyone who's earning $50,000 can probably find a way to save $20 a week. If you keep a record of your nonessential spending for just one week, you may find that eliminating one or two things is easy. (In Chapter 11, I suggest ways to find money to save if you're on a tight budget.)

Remember that even a small amount of savings makes a big difference over time. That $20 per week invested for 35 years with an 8 percent return can eventually become $180,000! Any employer matching contribution increases this amount (see Chapter 4 for more on employer matching).

TIP

After you start saving, make it a goal to increase your savings rate each year. Perhaps the easiest way to do this is to save more each time you get a raise. If you start by contributing 1 percent of your pay, and you receive a 4 percent pay increase, use part of the raise to increase your contribution rate to 2 percent. Keep doing this each time you get a raise, until you reach a point where your savings plus any employer contribution is likely to provide an adequate level of retirement income. (Check the guidelines in Chapter 11.)

Building Your Nest (Egg)

You'll probably need at least 100 percent of your income in the year before you retire in order to maintain your standard of living. How much savings will it take to provide this level of income? The answer is a lot.

TIP

I recommend trying to save 10 times the income that you expect to earn in the year before you retire. This formula is a good starting point if you plan to retire at your Social Security normal retirement age. If you plan to retire earlier, you'll need to save more. If you have a company pension or other sources of income or if you retire later, you may be able to get away with saving a bit less.

If you're retiring in the near future

Assume that you're retiring at the end of this year, and your salary for this year is $50,000. According to my benchmark, you should save $500,000 to hit the 10-times goal.

Sound like a lot of money? It is, but it would provide approximately $30,000 a year of *inflation-adjusted income* (see the sidebar "What goes up — or inflation-adjusted income" in this chapter for more information) over 25 years, assuming

>> The rate of inflation is 3 percent.

>> Only a small cushion will remain at the end of 25 years.

>> You invest 50 percent of your nest egg in stocks and 50 percent in bonds during this period.

WHAT GOES UP — OR INFLATION-ADJUSTED INCOME

What is inflation-adjusted income? *Inflation* is the rate at which prices increase over time. When you plan for the future, you have to plan for prices to go up; otherwise, you'll run out of money too soon. Inflation-adjusted income essentially refers to the *purchasing power* of your money — what your bucks can buy. It means that if over the next 25 years you want to be able to buy what will cost $30,000 today, you'll need significantly more than $30,000.

You can't know for sure what the inflation rate will be. You need to make an assumption. I use 3 percent, which is on the low side from a historical perspective but realistic for long-range planning, I believe.

The following table shows how much income is needed to keep the buying power of $10,000 over the years. (Using $10,000 makes it easy to adjust to whatever income you think will be right for your situation.) For example, you can calculate that you'll need $60,984 in the 25th year of your retirement to buy what $30,000 will buy in the first year ($20,328 × 3).

A yearly income of $30,000 may not sound like much, but remember that your taxes will be lower when you retire, and you won't need to save for retirement anymore. Your expenses will likely be less than when you were working. Your income should also be supplemented by your taxable savings and Social Security, giving you an adequate level of retirement income.

Number of Years After You Retire	Annual Income Needed
1	$10,000
2	$10,300
3	$10,609
4	$10,927
5	$11,255
6	$11,593
7	$11,941
8	$12,299
9	$12,668
10	$13,048

Number of Years After You Retire	Annual Income Needed
11	$13,439
12	$13,842
13	$14,258
14	$14,685
15	$15,126
16	$15,580
17	$16,047
18	$16,528
19	$17,024
20	$17,535
21	$18,061
22	$18,603
23	$19,161
24	$19,736
25	$20,328

If your retirement is farther off

I can hear you calling, "Hey, a little help over here. . . I'm not retiring tomorrow, so how do I know how much I'll be earning the year before I retire?" Not to worry. Table 12-1, Ted's Inflation Adjustment Table, is here to help.

Assume that you're 41, and you want to retire when you're 62. You need to project your current income to what you think you'll be earning 20 years from now (at age 61, the year before you retire). Decide on an average rate that you expect your income to increase — say 3 percent. Go down the Number of Years column in Table 12-1) to 20, and over to the 3% column, where you see the factor of 1.80. Multiply your current income, say $50,000, by 1.8, and you'll see that your expected income at retirement is $90,000. Using the 10-times rule, your desired nest egg becomes $900,000 (10 × $90,000). This is an easy way to get a rough idea of how big a retirement account to build — regardless of your current age or income.

TABLE 12-1

Inflation Adjustment Table

Number of Years	Assumed Annual Rate of Change				
	3%	3.5%	4%	4.5%	5%
1	1.03	1.035	1.04	1.045	1.05
2	1.06	1.07	1.08	1.09	1.10
3	1.09	1.11	1.12	1.14	1.16
4	1.12	1.15	1.17	1.19	1.22
5	1.16	1.19	1.22	1.25	1.28
6	1.19	1.23	1.27	1.30	1.34
7	1.23	1.27	1.32	1.36	1.41
8	1.27	1.32	1.37	1.42	1.48
9	1.31	1.36	1.42	1.49	1.55
10	1.34	1.41	1.48	1.55	1.63
11	1.38	1.46	1.54	1.62	1.71
12	1.42	1.51	1.60	1.70	1.80
13	1.46	1.56	1.67	1.77	1.89
14	1.51	1.62	1.73	1.85	1.98
15	1.56	1.68	1.80	1.93	2.08
16	1.60	1.74	1.87	2.02	2.18
17	1.65	1.80	1.95	2.11	2.29
18	1.70	1.86	2.02	2.21	2.41
19	1.75	1.93	2.10	2.31	2.53
20	1.80	1.99	2.19	2.41	2.65
21	1.86	2.06	2.28	2.52	2.79
22	1.91	2.13	2.37	2.63	2.93
23	1.97	2.21	2.46	2.75	3.08
24	2.03	2.29	2.56	2.87	3.23
25	2.09	2.37	2.66	3.00	3.39
26	2.15	2.45	2.77	3.14	3.56

(continued)

TABLE 12-1 *(continued)*

Number of Years	Assumed Annual Rate of Change				
	3%	3.5%	4%	4.5%	5%
27	2.22	2.53	2.88	3.28	3.74
28	2.28	2.62	3.00	3.43	3.92
29	2.35	2.72	3.12	3.58	4.12
30	2.42	2.81	3.24	3.74	4.33

Using a retirement calculator

Another way to develop a workable retirement plan is by using one of the many retirement calculators and other tools available on the internet or through the financial organization that handles your money. Remember that each calculator uses different methods and makes different assumptions; so different calculators can produce widely varying results. Check the assumptions each calculator uses to see if they make sense for you and your situation.

TIP

The major benefit of using a retirement calculator is that it gives you an investment reality check. Will the amount you're saving and the investment mix enable you to accumulate what you need? A good retirement calculator will answer this question and also help you decide how to close any savings gaps. Generally, you can close a gap by increasing your contributions, adjusting your investments to achieve a higher long-term return, or a combination of the two.

As of September 18, 2021, employers are required to inform each 401(k) participant of the value of the life annuity income that can be provided beginning at age 67 using the current account balance. Hopefully, participants will start receiving this information during 2022.

It would be even more helpful if the service providers would include other income projections such as how much monthly income you can expect assuming you continue to contribute your current contributions until age 67 or an even broader range of income projections. This type of assistance to help 401(k) participants plan for retirement is long overdue.

If your retirement plan is an IRA, you can use retirement income calculators available through many financial organizations and AARP.

Chapter **13**

Selecting Your Investments

W hen you drive somewhere, what kind of ride do you like? A bumpy one that rises and dips like a rollercoaster, leaving you with a stomachache by the time you reach your destination? Or a smooth one that lets you arrive feeling rested and relaxed? Unless you truly enjoy discomfort, you probably prefer the smooth ride.

Investing for retirement is a lot like car rides. And I have news for you — *diversifying* your investments (choosing a range of different ones) puts you on a smoother investing path than not diversifying. How so? Different types of investments, such as stocks and bonds, tend to move up and down in value at different times. If you choose several investments, one may go down in value as another begins to go up, giving you a relatively even ride.

"Why not just put everything in the one investment that performs better than the others?" you ask. Great idea, in theory. But in practice, you can't possibly know which investment will perform better than others. As all mutual fund companies will tell you, *past performance does not guarantee future results.* (They don't tell you this just to be nice, either. They're required, by law, to inform you of this.) Just because a fund performed well over the last year, or even several years, doesn't mean that it will continue to do so if you invest all your money in it. (According to Murphy's Law, as soon as you put all your money into it, it will do terribly.)

Your 401(k) plan probably lets you choose from many different investments, probably more than a dozen. How can you choose? You can close your eyes and point or throw darts, but that's not advisable. What you need is a strategy.

This chapter outlines the main categories of investments likely offered by your 401(k) plan, how to compare and combine them so that they're likely to keep increasing in value, and where to go for more help.

IRA investments are different because you have the sole responsibility for picking your investments, including where you set up your account. How and where you can invest is unlimited; however, the basic information about investing covered in this chapter also applies to IRAs.

Looking Over the Investment Menu

When your employer set up your 401(k) plan, it chose a selection of investments to offer. If you're new to investing, the list may appear baffling — like trying to order dinner from a menu written in a foreign language. Although making a mistake while ordering a meal may set your stomach back for a day or two (pan-fried calves' brains? Oops, I meant to order risotto!), choosing the wrong 401(k) investments can set back your retirement plans considerably.

Most investments offered by your 401(k) plan are likely mutual funds. *Mutual funds* pool together money from many investors and use that money to buy a variety of investments. Different types of mutual funds exist, such as stock funds, bonds, or other fixed-income (non-stock) funds, and money market funds, which are generally named after the type of investment they favor. Within those broad categories are more specialized mutual funds, as I describe in the following sections. Mutual funds give you an advantage as an individual investor because they let you invest in many more investments than you probably can on your own.

Your plan may also offer non-mutual fund investments, such as company stock or a brokerage window, which I describe later in this chapter.

TIP

Being broadly diversified may be the first and most important investment strategy. This means owning many different types of investments. Some investments do well even during times when many investments melt down.

However, broadly diversifying your investments isn't likely to avoid significant losses when a major crash occurs like the one in 2008. Hopefully your losses will be less than what they would have been without a good diversification strategy.

Most 401(k)s also offer funds that enable you to be broadly diversified even though you are investing all your money in one fund. The most common of these funds is Target Maturity or Target Date Funds (TDFs). Each fund is designated by a year indicating our proposed retirement date, such as 2020, 2025, 2030, 2035, 2040, 2045, and 2050. TDFs are readily available for IRA investors.

As you look at your investment choices, you may wonder whether to invest a little bit in each fund or just choose the one that performed best during the past year. The answer is likely somewhere in between. Your job is to decide what combination makes sense for *you*.

How do you do that? First you need to understand the degree of risk and potential return of the investments. (I discuss these concepts in detail in Chapter 14.) Here, laid out roughly from lowest risk to highest (based on past performance), are broad categories of investments:

» Money market funds

» Stable value funds (not available to IRA investors)

» Bond funds (short, intermediate, long term, or some of each)

» Balanced funds including TDFs

» Stock funds

» Company stock (only available in 401(k) plans)

Looking at past performance of any investment option is of limited value because there's no way of knowing how specific investments will perform in the future.

Money market funds: Show me the money

Money market funds are considered the least risky investments. They invest in very short-term debt instruments (called *cash equivalents*) issued by banks, large U.S. companies, and the U.S. government. A fund earns interest on the instruments it holds, but the instruments themselves do not increase or decrease in value. Your money isn't expected to lose value in money market funds, and it will probably gain a bit.

These funds generally have low returns, and they shouldn't be used for long-term investing because they probably won't beat inflation over the long run. However, they can be a good place to park your money temporarily while you try to figure out what to do with it. Also, you may want to invest in one as part of a diversified portfolio if your plan doesn't give you another fixed income (non-stock) option, or if you desire added stability, especially as you approach retirement.

THE DUBIOUS VALUE OF AN ANNUITY IN YOUR 401(K)

Insurance companies have been pressuring the government to make it easier for them to sell annuities to 401(k) participants. For many reasons, mostly based on my own experience, I don't think you should invest in an annuity in your 401(k). *Note:* I strongly suggest considering buying a guaranteed life income annuity when you retire; just don't buy one for your 401(k).

My first job was in the pension department of an insurance company. I was responsible for determining the amount of monthly annuity that can be purchased each year for each participant with an amount that was contributed into what was known as a money-purchase pension plan. The annual annuity unit that was purchased each year guaranteed a monthly lifetime income beginning at age 65. For example, the insurance company was guaranteeing a monthly benefit payable 35 years later for a 30-year-old participant. The annuity rates were loaded in favor of the insurance company. Insurance company actuaries who determine these rates don't take risks because doing so puts their jobs at risk.

I was trained to use guaranteed annuities rates as a major reason to buy an insurance product with future guaranteed annuity rates when I transferred from an administrative to a sales position. I bought into what I was taught until I learned the future rates that were being guaranteed were considerably higher than the current annuity rates. As a result, the future rate guarantees weren't likely to be of any value.

Participants didn't get any benefits when they died prior to age 65 with the annuities I administered. The same may or may not be true for annuities inside a 401(k). At best the annuity insurer may offer to pay a beneficiary the amount used to buy the annuity without any investment gain. If they offer payment to a beneficiary, this will result in a smaller annuity unit being purchased each year because the insurance company won't be able to keep the money.

Locking money into guaranteed life income annuity payments means giving up much higher potential investment returns and the flexibility to withdraw funds for other reasons such as buying a first home, or the birth or adoption of a child. It is also highly probable that you will be able to buy a much larger monthly annuity by investing in mutual funds until you retire and then buying the annuity.

Too many major life events can occur during your active employment years for it to make sense to lock up your retirement savings in an inflexible annuity product.

Keeping things reined in with stable value funds

Stable value funds are fixed-income investments commonly backed by insurance companies or other financial institutions. Many 401(k) plans include these as conservative investments, but they aren't widespread outside retirement plans. Their values don't fluctuate the way bond funds sometimes do (see the next section).

You can consider these an alternative to bonds for the fixed-income portion of your investments. But remember that even though the word "stable" may appear in the name, they aren't fully guaranteed. If an insurance company (or other financial institution) backing the investment fails, or if another asset held in the portfolio is in default, you may lose money. Also, your return can decline in a period of rising interest rates and increasing inflation. The long-term return of stable value funds has generally been below that of bond funds but higher than money markets.

Bonding your funds: Single portfolio seeks stable relationship

Bond funds invest in U.S. government bonds and/or corporate bonds (bonds issued by companies). The risk level and potential return of the fund depends in part on whether it holds more long-term bonds (that mature in 20 to 30 years), medium-term bonds (5 to 10 years) or short-term bonds (1 to 3 years). In general, funds holding mostly short-term bonds have lower risk and lower return than funds holding intermediate- and long-term bonds. Another factor that affects your investment results is the quality of the bonds the fund owns. *Junk bonds* have a potentially higher return but also potentially greater losses.

WARNING

A fund company isn't going to call its fund that invests in junk bonds a "junk bond fund." It will more likely be called a "high-yield fund." Read the prospectus or other material carefully before actually investing your money in any fund.

In a 401(k), you generally invest in a bond fund to add stability to your portfolio. Sticking to less-volatile short-term and intermediate-term bonds makes sense. The name of the fund may indicate what kinds of bonds it holds; otherwise, you can look at the list of bonds in the fund. (Short-term bond funds sometimes have "low duration" in their name.) Like stock funds, bond funds can be *index funds* or *actively managed funds*. I explain these terms in the section "Stock funds: A feather in your cap" later in this chapter.

Changes in interest rates can affect the return of a bond fund. (The relationship isn't what you may think, though — when interest rates rise, bond values may decline, and vice versa.) In addition, a company that issues a bond (a corporate bond) may go kaput. If you invested in a fund holding those bonds, it can affect your return.

Some municipal bonds are tax-free investments — the interest earned isn't taxed. Although these may be good investments *outside* of a 401(k) don't buy them *in* your 401(k); you'll be wasting the tax advantage. Money in a 401(k) grows tax-deferred, but you must pay income tax when you take money out, whether it was invested in a tax-free bond fund or not.

Deciding one and done: Balanced and TDF funds

Balanced funds and TDFs are mutual funds that invest in a set mixture of stocks and bonds and are generally designed for one-stop shopping. Investment professionals choose the balance of stocks and bonds for balanced funds. (The mix for balanced funds is usually around 60 percent stocks and 40 percent bonds, but the combination may vary.)

TDFs are a type of balanced fund aimed at a particular age group, based on the number of years until retirement. These funds are designed to be most effective if you choose one that's right for you and invest only in that fund rather than mix it with other investments. For example, the investment mix in a 2040 TDF is what is thought to be an appropriate mix for someone who is expected to start withdrawing money from that fund in 2040. If you want an easy answer, pick the TDF that aligns with the year you think you may start withdrawing money. These funds are designed to make it easy for those who don't know much about investing.

Stock funds: A feather in your cap

Stock funds, also called *equity funds*, invest mostly or entirely in the stock of U.S. and/or foreign companies.

Many factors influence individual stock prices, such as

>> Political events in the United States and around the world

>> Unpredictable events, such as the 9/11 attacks, natural disasters such as an earthquake, and a pandemic like COVID-19

>> The company's revenue and profits

>> A change in company management

- >> New products recently introduced by the company (or a competitor)
- >> The company's prominence within its industry
- >> The industry climate
- >> General market trends
- >> The opinion of large institutional investors, such as mutual fund managers
- >> The opinion of key analysts

Because so many things can impact the price of a stock, you may wonder why in the world you should invest your retirement savings in something so uncertain. The answer is that, historically, stocks have provided the highest average investment return over the long term. Also, by investing in a mutual fund rather than a single stock, you can reduce your risk level.

Active versus passive management

Some stock funds are *index funds* that invest in companies that make up a stock index. Many stock indexes exist; one of the best known is the *Standard & Poor's 500* (S&P 500), which is comprised of 500 large U.S. companies considered leaders in their fields (or economic sectors). Contrary to popular belief, the companies that make up the S&P 500 are not necessarily the 500 largest U.S. companies. The S&P 500 is often used as a broad measure of the U.S. economy.

REMEMBER

Fees for index funds are generally lower than for managed funds, because index fund managers don't spend a lot of time making decisions about what stock to buy and what to sell. Index funds are sometimes referred to as *passively managed funds.* (I give more examples of indexes in the section "Mistake #2: Comparing different types of funds" later in this chapter.)

An *actively managed* stock fund is a different cup of tea. This type of fund is run by a fund manager who tries to get better returns than the index that applies to the fund. (For example, the S&P 500 is an index for measuring the performance of *large-cap* stocks; I explain large-cap stocks in the following section.) The manager of an actively managed large-cap stock fund wants to earn a better return than the S&P 500, but they don't? worry about doing better than a bond index, for example, because that's a different type of investment. To beat the index, the manager needs to pick stocks that they expect? will do especially well. Because of additional operating costs in managed funds, the manager must beat the index by 0.05 to 1.0 percent in order for your return to be the same as if you had invested in an index fund. The fees for some actively managed funds are in excess of 2.0 percent. That's a big hurdle. Studies show that most actively managed funds don't beat the indexes over time: However, debates still rage in the investment world as to which is better — active or passive management.

TIP

You may decide to choose an actively managed fund, even if it doesn't achieve as high a return as its benchmark, if the stocks selected by the manager have lower risk than those in the benchmark. The fund prospectus and third-party sources such as Morningstar or Value Line tell you how much risk the manager takes.

TIP

I prefer funds that have good historical returns but smaller up and down swings. The average annual returns commonly shown for each mutual fund won't give you this information. You need to dig deeper by going into the fund prospectus or the website of the fund manager to get the actual return for each year the fund has been in existence.

Table 13-1 compares the latest returns of two actual funds over a ten-year span ending December 31, 2020. It can help you understand why just looking at average annual returns isn't enough.

TABLE 13-1

Annual Returns Comparison

	Year 1	Year 5	Year 10
Fund A	11.65%	8.19%	6.69%
Fund B	9.04%	7.74%	7.42%

Fund A is an indexed 2015 TDF. Fund B is an actively managed fund. The one-year and five-year average returns may cause an investor to select Fund A, but taking the long view shows Fund B is the more profitable option. I also explain in Tables 13-2 and 13-3 that average annual returns aren't the best way to evaluate funds.

TIP

Take a look at how different funds perform during sustained market downturns. The last one occurred in 2008, more than ten years ago. It's easy to get the average annual returns for recent years, but you may have to do some digging on the fund company's website to get historical yearly returns. It can be worth the effort to know how a fund rebounds — or doesn't — after market stress.

Capitalizing on a company's assets

Stock funds often concentrate on companies of a certain size or *capitalization*. (Capitalization, or *market cap*, refers to the number of shares on the marketplace multiplied by the price per share. If a company has issued 10 million shares of its stock and the stock is valued at $10 per share, the company's market cap is $100 million.)

Generally, *large-cap* refers to companies with capitalization of more than $10 billion, such as Microsoft or Walmart. *Small-cap* companies have capitalization under about $2 billion, such as Twitter and Chipotle Mexican Grill. (Yes, I realize that $2 billion is hardly small change, but these definitions are relative. Kind of like the coffeehouse whose smallest size drink is labeled "tall.") These definitions are somewhat fluid (different experts may use different cutoffs). What you need to know is that large-cap companies as a whole are considered less volatile investments than small-cap companies, which tend to be newer, less proven companies. However, small-cap companies are generally seen as having greater potential for growth (as well as for failure).

There's also a *mid-cap* category for companies that are bigger than small-caps but not big enough for the big leagues. This category is very fluid. It may not be included in an asset allocation recommendation you get from an advisor, because a mix of large and small-cap companies may give you a similar investment result.

If you want to go whole hog, you can further divide stock funds into *growth* and *value funds*. (A mutual fund that mixes growth and value stocks is often referred to as a *blend*.) Here's the skinny on growth and value funds:

>> **Growth funds** invest in companies that are expected to earn a lot of money over a sustained period, such as some technology companies (Apple) or social media companies like Facebook. They generally plow their earnings back into the company rather than pay dividends to shareholders. The price of these stocks tend to be high compared to the companies' earnings, but the expected revenue and profit growth attracts investors.

>> **Value funds** invest in companies that are seen as bargains — their stock prices are low compared to their assets, revenues, and earnings per share. The stock price may be low because the company is in a *sector* (part of the economy) that is going through a slump but is expected to recover, such as energy companies or some telecommunications and technology companies in 2002 (ExxonMobil or Comcast, for instance). Another reason for a low stock price may be that the company or industry has fallen out of favor with investors for a reason unconnected to its performance — similar to a fickle public's treatment of some rock stars and professional athletes.

Put all those categories together, and you end up with funds called "Company X Small-Cap Growth" or "Company Y Value Equity." The first would likely invest in small-growth companies, and the second in value stocks — potentially from a company of any size.

TIP

There's obviously a lot more to a mutual fund than its name. In fact, the name may be misleading. You should look at the fund's *prospectus* (a description of the fund that you can get from your employer, plan provider, or the fund company) to see where the fund is invested. Small-cap growth funds may also have investments in bonds and cash. Why does that matter? Say you've figured out that 15 percent of your money should be in bonds, and you've already invested that much in a bond fund. If the stock fund you invest in also holds bonds, you'll end up with more bonds than you want, which probably means a lower return over the long run.

You should also check how an independent third party such as Morningstar or Value Line identifies the fund. (I explain more about these and other services in the "Seeking Help from the Pros (and I Don't Mean Martha Stewart)" section at the end of this chapter.)

International investing

Your 401(k) plan may offer a mutual fund (or funds) that invests in companies outside the United States. Foreign investments may move up and down at different times from the U.S. stock market, meaning that international investments can help diversify your portfolio. An "International" fund generally invests only in non–U.S. companies, while a "Global" or "World" fund may also include U.S. investments.

International funds may be named after the specific region they invest in: Europe, the Pacific Rim, Latin America, or Emerging Markets (developing economies), for example. Be sure to research any fund (before you invest in it) to find out exactly what it holds. Also, read up on the politics and economics of the countries the fund invests in — instability increases the risk to your investment. For example, Emerging Markets investments generally are riskier than investments in developed economies such as Europe.

Investing where you work: Company stock

Your 401(k) plan may let you invest your contributions in your employer's stock. Although doing this can seem like a good idea, especially if your company is the greatest, think twice before you decide whether to do it. Company stock isn't a diversified investment such as a mutual fund. Although your company's stock may do really well, it can also do really badly at some point and wipe out your entire nest egg if you invested it all in company stock. Remember your parents' admonition about not playing with matches? It's the same with company stock. Hold it too long, and eventually you'll get burned.

I don't recommend investing any of your own 401(k) money in company stock. Having a large portion of your savings in company stock is a disaster if the company goes out of business. You can lose your job and much of your retirement savings at the same time. If your company offers a stock purchase plan — a plan that permits employees to buy company stock at a discount — go ahead and buy some stock for your personal portfolio; just don't put it in your 401(k).

TIP

If you have a lot invested in your company's stock, it may pull your entire account down, even if you also have money invested in mutual funds. Many financial planners advise holding no more than 10 percent of your retirement investments in company stock (including the portion your employer may give you as a contribution), and some encourage investors to sell all their company stock and buy mutual funds instead (if their plan's rules allow them to follow this advice).

Brokerage window: Don't fence me in

Like cowboys living out on the range, some 401(k) investors don't like to be fenced in. They want to invest in more than just the options chosen by their employer. To make these employees happy, some companies offer a *brokerage window* (sometimes called a *self-directed option*). This isn't really a class of investment, but I include it here because it's a way of investing in a 401(k) plan that is becoming more common. The "window" may let 401(k) participants invest in any stock, bond, mutual fund, or exchange-traded fund they like, not just the ones offered by their plan.

For more info, check out "What Is an ETF? A Beginner's Complete Guide" by Kevin Voight at NerdWallet, www.nerdwallet.com/article/investing/what-is-an-etf.

WARNING

Using a brokerage window or nontraditional investments puts more responsibility on you to research your investments to make sure that they're right for you. I recommend getting help from a reputable advisor if you choose to go this route.

Broadening 401(k)s

If your plan offers a brokerage window, you probably have to pay extra for it. Also, some companies don't give you complete freedom, because they don't want you to use a brokerage account to *day-trade* (buy and sell investments frequently, trying — and usually failing — to make a quick buck) or to invest all your 401(k) money in a single stock. I advise employers who offer a brokerage window to limit investments to professionally managed mutual funds.

Your employer may set up a 401(k) where each participant has their own broker-age account. An independent recordkeeper is needed to do that. (Chapter 18 contains information about independent recordkeepers.) With an independent recordkeeper, employers may also allow participants to invest in non-traditional investments such as real estate. I am not encouraging doing that, but it's legally possible.

Feeling free with IRAs

IRA investors can open their accounts where they have access to a brokerage account without having to get anyone's approval. You have complete freedom to open the account wherever you want, including the opportunity to invest in non-traditional investments. Traditional investments are those that are liquid and are traded on any of the many market exchanges such as the New York Stock Exchange, Nasdaq, London Stock Exchange, and the Japan Stock Exchange.

IRAs with access to a brokerage account may be opened at stock brokerage firms like Charles Schwab, E*Trade, TD Ameritrade, and so on. They also may be opened at some of the large mutual fund companies like Vanguard and Fidelity.

WARNING

The only prohibited investments for IRA investors are life insurance, collectibles, and real estate you live in. Permitted investments for 401(k) participants are a bit more restrictive because these plans are subject to ERISA's fiduciary rules. These rules require that all investments must be selected by the employer considering what is in the best interest of the participants. Any self-dealing is also a prohib-ited transaction.

Nontraditional investments include things that are not traded on stock or other exchanges. For example, you're permitted to buy real estate provided you don't live in the property you purchase for your IRA account. You can buy gold and other precious metals, cryptocurrency, and so on. Having your IRA own an LLC is another possibility, but this one is more of a stretch with possible serious ramifi-cations. I am not suggesting these investments, but I would be remiss if I didn't let you know that they are possible.

Making such investments provides an opportunity for broader diversification but should be considered for only a portion of your retirement funds after you build a rather large nest egg.

If you want to do nontraditional investing with an IRA, you need to set up an IRA account using a custodian that enables you to make such investments. It is imper-ative to select a custodian that has lots of these types of IRA accounts and that has been in business for many years. The Retirement Industry Trust Association (www.rita.org) provides services to this type of custodian, and they also have some standards that members must follow.

I also found The Entrust Group's website to be helpful when I was looking for information about this type of custodian. Their fees and a lot of other useful information is on their site at www.theentrustgroup.com.

Forging Your Own Investment Trail

Different types of funds serve different investment *objectives*. Broadly speaking, objectives can include growth (capital appreciation), income, and capital preservation (which I explain in just a second).

Long-term investors (those with at least ten years before they may need the money) usually invest primarily for *growth*. When you invest long term, you don't want an immediate return such as interest or dividends. Instead, you want your investments to increase in value, so that when you're ready to sell them, they'll be worth a lot more than you paid for them. You're willing to take on a certain amount of risk for the possibility of a higher return. The most common investment for this type of strategy is stocks — of all kinds.

Within five to ten years of retirement, you can cut back your level of stocks by shifting into less volatile investments, such as bonds and stable value funds, to reduce your risk. You may also shift the remaining stock portion of your portfolio from more risky stocks (generally growth-oriented companies) to less volatile ones (generally value-oriented companies). This is a *capital preservation* strategy. You want your money to grow at a rate that will at least beat inflation, but you want to reduce your risk of losing money. The long-term return of this portfolio will probably be lower, but at this point, you're more concerned with preserving your capital.

Some retirees who are very concerned about preserving capital during their retirement years typically invest to generate an income through interest and dividends. A problem with this strategy is that you have little or no *hedge* (protection) against inflation. In addition, you can't count on companies that pay high dividends to always do so. Dividends are one of the first things to be cut when profits shrink. You need income during your retirement years, but you can collect it in other ways. I recommend using an automatic withdrawal plan from mutual funds or an annuity rather than trying to find investments that will generate enough income through interest and dividends. In any case, you should probably still keep at least 25 percent of your money in stocks, because retirement can last for 20 years or more, and your money needs to keep growing.

Baking Your Asset Allocation Pie

Figuring out the right investments for you is an important part of 401(k) and IRA investing. It requires some time at the outset, but when you're done, you shouldn't have to spend too much time on managing your account, except for periodic maintenance.

The first step is to figure out what percentage of your investments should go into the different asset classes. The five asset classes that are generally used are large-cap stocks, small-cap stocks, international stocks, fixed income (bonds and stable value funds), and "cash" (money market funds). Pie charts are the financial planners' preferred method for illustrating *asset allocation,* or how to divide your money among different investments. Figure 13-1 shows a sample allocation for someone 25 years from retirement who is a moderate investor (not too conservative, not too aggressive).

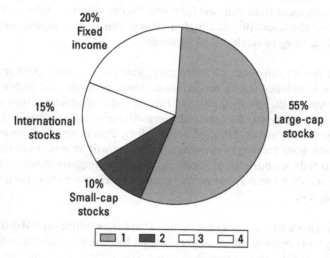

FIGURE 13-1: Pie chart with 55 percent large cap, 20 percent bonds, 10 percent small cap, and 15 percent international.

WARNING

Everyone's situation is unique, and the sample allocation shown here may not necessarily represent the right strategy for your situation. You may need or want something more aggressive (riskier) or less risky. These are guidelines to put you in the ballpark — whether you end up sitting behind home plate, in the bleachers, or somewhere in between is up to you.

REMEMBER

The right asset allocation for your situation depends on a number of factors, including your time horizon, retirement goals, and comfort level with investment risk. It also depends on whether you expect your 401(k) or IRA to be your principal source of retirement income, or whether you have other substantial resources to rely on, as well. (If you have other resources, you may be able to take less risk with your 401(k) or IRA and still meet your retirement goals.) You and your next-door-neighbor may both be 25 years away from retirement, but she may require a more conservative portfolio, while your situation may warrant one that's more aggressive.

For example, someone with a 25-year time horizon who doesn't mind investment risk may decide on a 401(k) allocation that's 100 percent stocks, as shown in Figure 13-2.

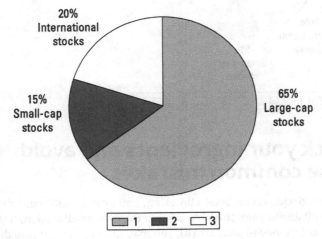

FIGURE 13-2: Pie chart showing 65 percent large cap, 15 percent small cap, and 20 percent international.

Someone else with the same time horizon who is risk-averse may move more into bonds and even a money market (cash) investment, as shown in Figure 13-3.

After you determine an appropriate asset allocation for you, the next step is to determine which funds in your 401(k) plan and those available with your IRA match up with the *asset classes* you want to invest in, and decide which funds to invest in. The following section, "Check your ingredients and avoid these common mistakes," gives some tips for choosing investments.

How you go about completing these steps depends on whether you prefer to do things yourself or seek professional advice, as well as on what resources are available to you at work. In the "Seeking Help from the Pros (and I Don't Mean Martha Stewart)" section at the end of this chapter, I give suggestions for where you can go for help.

Another option is to put all your money into the Target Date Fund that aligns with the year you expect to start withdrawing money — the 2035 TDF, for example.

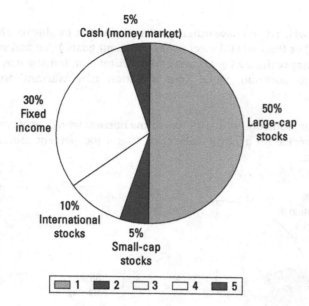

5%
Cash (money market)

50%
Large-cap
stocks

30%
Fixed
income

10%
International
stocks

5%
Small-cap
stocks

FIGURE 13-3:
Pie chart with 50
percent large
cap, 5 percent
small cap,
10 percent
international,
30 percent
bonds, and
5 percent cash.

| ▭ 1 | ▬ 2 | ▭ 3 | ▭ 4 | ▬ 5 |

Check your ingredients and avoid these common mistakes

When you decide on an asset allocation, you need to split your money among the funds available in your 401(k) to achieve the desired allocation. If you have already contributed money to your 401(k), you may need to move it into different funds to achieve the mix that you want. You should also make your new contributions in these proportions.

TIP

With a 401(k), you can move money among investments without paying fees. Most plans let you move money when you want to by using your service provider's website. You can also change your IRA investments by accessing your IRA account online using the website of the financial organization that holds your account.

When choosing specific funds, be sure to focus on the right information. Following are some common mistakes 401(k) and IRA investors make.

Mistake #1: Basing investment choices on the past performance of the investments

Good results are often fleeting. Many of the funds that appear on "Top 10" lists aren't repeat stars.

Many technology funds were top performers prior to 2000. They then dropped into the worst-performing category in 2000 and early 2001. One mutual fund that invested in small Japanese technology companies gained 100 percent during the first six months of 1999 and 114 percent in the second half of 1999. If you were shopping around for a fund back then, boy, would that have looked like a winner. But (there's always a "but," right?) when technology companies took a dive in 2000, the fund dropped by 71.8 percent. If you'd been paying attention to analyst predictions about the tech sector and had looked at the companies held by the fund, you would've been forewarned. You probably would have chosen another fund and ended up better off. That said, I ran across an internet message board with entries from three investors who were in the fund in April 2000, when the fund was nosediving. Two of the three said that they were hanging on to the fund because they thought it would go back up. (The fund no longer exists, by the way.)

The potential exists today for some major downturns. For example, growth stock index funds were up 64 percent during the past year and an average of 25 percent for the last five years. Bitcoin increased in value from $1,290 on March 2, 2017, to $54,806 on March 17, 2021. It is highly unlikely that similar levels of growth can be sustained; therefore, investing new money into these types of investments today chasing their recent returns may be a bad idea.

Mistake #2: Comparing different types of funds

You can't compare apples with oranges, and you can't compare stocks with bonds. You must compare a fund's performance to that of others in its *peer group* (similar types of funds).

Identifying a fund's type can be difficult. The name won't always help you. Looking at a prospectus for the fund should help you figure out a fund's type, but it still may not be totally clear. An independent source, such as Morningstar or Value Line, can be your best bet for finding out what the fund invests in.

TIP

To measure your mutual fund's performance against a standard, use an *index*. Indexes are made up of a large number of companies that fall into the category being measured, so they provide a good indication of how the category is doing.

You need to make sure that you measure the mutual fund's performance against the appropriate index. In general, you can measure

>> Large-cap stock funds against the S&P 500 or Wilshire 5000

>> Small-cap stock funds against the Russell 2000

>> International funds against the MSCI-EAFE (Morgan Stanley Capital International Europe, Australasia, Far East Index)

>> Bond funds against the Lehman Brothers Aggregate Bond Index

The financial institutions listed also have a number of more specialized indexes for measuring performance of specialized funds such as large-cap growth, small-cap value, and so on.

Mistake #3: Failing to look at both short- and long-term performance

Compare the fund's most recent returns, and also longer-term (three- to-five-year) performance, with that of other funds from the same category. Looking at long-term results helps you tell whether the fund is relying on one good year for its overall good performance.

Mistake #4: Assuming that the fund with the highest average return will give you the most money

This is not necessarily the case, believe it or not. For proof, look at the year-by-year comparison of two different funds in Table 13-2.

TABLE 13-2   Net Annual Return Comparison (In Percent)

Fund	Year 1	Year 2	Year 3	Year 4	Year 5	3-Year Avg.	5-Year Avg.
A	35.3	22.4	(–8.7)	18.5	(–7.6)	16.33	11.98
B	21.1	17.3	(–0.5)	13.2	2.7	12.63	10.76

The natural assumption from looking at the numbers listed in Table 13-2 is that Fund A is better because its five-year average return is 11.98 percent, which is higher than Fund B's return of 10.76 percent. However, you arrive at a different conclusion when you look at Table 13-3, which shows the dollar amounts you'd accumulate in both funds if you invested $10,000 in each at the beginning of each year.

TABLE 13-3   Amount Accumulated With $10,000 Annual Investment (In Dollars)

Fund	Year 1 (end)	Year 2 (end)	Year 3 (end)	Year 4 (end)	Year 5 (end)
A	$13,530	$28,801	$35,425	$53,829	$58,978
B	$12,110	$25,935	$35,755	$51,795	$63,463

Looking only at percentage returns (Table 13-2), Fund A would have appeared in the winner's circle after the first three years, with a 16.33 percent average annual return, while Fund B's 12.63 percent average three-year return probably would have attracted little or no attention. But Fund B accumulated a slightly larger amount than Fund A after three years (Table 13-3). The difference is even more dramatic after five years.

After five years, Fund A achieved an 11.98 percent average return compared to 10.76 percent for Fund B, but the dollar amount accumulated in Fund B is 7.6 percent more than Fund A!

The essential things to keep in mind about watching performance over time are

REMEMBER

>> A fund that has less dramatic ups and downs can perform better than a more volatile fund.

>> Average performance results are of limited value.

>> Don't consider "Top 10" listings the final word. Find the funds that can sustain top performance.

>> It can take a long time to get back to where you were after a bad year.

The last point of the list is especially important. Assume, for instance, that you have $100,000 invested in a fund that drops 20 percent to a value of $80,000. A 20 percent gain the next year brings your value up to $96,000. But you're still 4 percent behind. If you're counting on an 8 percent annual return to get you to your retirement goal, you have a lot of ground to make up. Your $100,000 at the beginning of this two-year period would have to be worth $116,640 to be on track, but it's worth only $96,000 after the recovery. You need a 31 percent gain the third year to get on track, which is highly unlikely.

The combination of setting unrealistic return expectations and picking funds that don't do well during down markets may eventually result in a serious gap between what you need to save and what you actually have in your account. Somewhere along the way, you need to make up for the investment gains that didn't occur. This is another reason why it makes sense to pick funds with less dramatic ups and downs.

In the final analysis, the funds you choose must meet your personal objectives. You're not always going to follow conventional wisdom — you need to make informed investment decisions that are right for you.

Open the oven door once in a while to check your progress

After you develop your asset allocation pie, leave it alone but don't ignore it completely. Check it at least once a year to see whether you need to *rebalance*, or bring your investments back in line.

To take a simple example, say you have 75 percent in stocks and 25 percent in bonds. Say stocks take off and do really well. The stock portion of your account increases in value at a much faster rate than the bond portion, to, say, 85 percent of your total account. The bond portion is now worth only 15 percent of your total account. You're in a position to lose a lot of money if the stock market drops — more than if you had 75 percent in stocks. You need to sell some stocks and use the money to buy bonds to move your account back to a 75/25 split, if that's the right asset allocation for you. You may not want to do this, because your stocks have been doing so well, but it's the right thing to do.

Studies show that many participants never rebalance their 401(k) or IRA accounts. Many workers over age 55 entered the market slump that began in 2008 with a higher percentage invested in stocks than ever in their careers. They lost a lot of money from their accounts because they didn't rebalance. In fact, at their stage in life, they should have actually gone one step further and *reallocated,* or changed, their fundamental asset allocation. They should've reduced their stock investments to a lower level than when they joined their plans. For example, a 50/50 split of stocks and bonds would be more appropriate for a 60-year-old than a 75/25 split. If the participant had 85 percent in stocks, the unfortunate result would be greater losses than they should have had.

TIP

Another advantage of TDFs is that they automatically rebalance your investment mix so you don't have to do it. They will also reduce your stock exposure as you get older. Check your TDF to see when they do both these things.

REMEMBER

After you determine an appropriate asset allocation, you probably shouldn't change your allocation pie unless a major life-changing event occurs, such as inheriting a million dollars, winning the lottery, or approaching retirement age.

Make sure that your pie complements the rest of the meal

One of the cardinal rules of planning a menu is that, if you serve a main dish with a crust (such as Beef Wellington or quiche), you shouldn't serve pie for dessert. Otherwise, you have too much crust for one meal. Likewise, make sure that your

401(k) and IRA investments go well with other investments you have. They should balance as a whole.

For example, say your company matches your 401(k) contribution in company stock, and you've built up quite a lot of it — 50 percent of your 401(k) balance. Assume that you can't change this distribution, because your employer requires you to hold the stock until you turn 55, and you're only 40. You also buy additional shares through a stock purchase plan. What can you do? You should count the company stock as a high-risk stock investment when you decide how to invest your own contributions to your 401(k) and try to use your own contributions to adjust your overall risk to a more comfortable level.

You should also take into account how you're investing in your IRA or outside savings account. If you're married, you can look at your 401(k) and your spouse's as one investment and compensate for the aggressive company stock investment in yours with more conservative investments in your spouse's account.

You should also take into account any guaranteed retirement benefit payment that you expect from your employer with either a defined-benefit or cash balance pension. With a defined-benefit plan, you may receive a regular defined payment when you retire. Having either of these plans gives you room to invest your 401(k) money somewhat more aggressively, but only if you've been, or expect to be, with your employer for enough years to qualify for a significant pension payment. (That may be quite a few years.)

Of course, things can change very quickly. Your company may change or terminate the plan, the company may be sold or go out of business, and so on. Your investments should be reevaluated if changes such as these occur.

Seeking Help from the Pros

A common mistake 401(k) participants make is to randomly pick their investments without any idea of what they're investing in or why. Becoming informed about investing doesn't necessarily require a major time commitment.

Finding books and publications

You can buy, or borrow from the library, a number of books that cover the basics of investing, starting with the latest editions of *Investing For Dummies* and *Mutual Funds For Dummies,* both by Eric Tyson (Wiley Publishing). Many public libraries also carry investing resources, such as mutual fund reports from Morningstar and

Value Line, which are packed with information, including various funds' holdings, risk levels, and past returns. You may also want to talk to friends who seem to be successful investors and ask them what resources they find helpful.

Consulting a real live person

Investing is like any other life experience — the result usually depends on the effort you're willing to put into it. If you're like me and most other retirement savers, you don't have a lot of time to manage your investments. (That's why you're reading this book and not a 500-page tome on the theory of investing, right?) Consider getting professional investment advice. Your plan may offer advice, or you can get advice independently from outside your plan.

An advisor can analyze the funds offered by your 401(k) plan and match up a specific investment recommendation with your risk tolerance and goals. The advisor will recommend exactly how much you should invest in each option and also whether you need to move around what's already in your account.

With an IRA you will probably be charged a *wrap fee,* which pays for the financial advisor. An advisor who is part of a large financial organization, investment firm, or bank usually puts your money into a canned investment package. *Canned* means they are tightly controlled by their employers and are typically able to offer a limited number of pre-packed alternatives. These alternatives are similar to the asset allocation mixes of TDFs, but the total fees are usually in the 1.5 to 2.0 percent range for the same type of investments you can get on your own for less than 0.10 percent. The fee for Charles Schwab's index TDFs is only 0.08 percent. You can easily access them by entering "Charles Schwab target date funds" in your browser. Vanguard is another good choice with TDF fees in the 0.13 to 0.15 percent range. One sure way to improve your investment return is to reduce the fees you pay. In my opinion, paying an additional 1 to 1.5 percent or more fee for an advisor isn't worth the added cost.

Vanguard and Charles Schwab both also offer investment advisor services. Vanguard's fees are currently 0.30 percent up to $5 million and 0.20 percent over $5 million and under $10 million. Charles Schwab's fees currently vary depending on the type of services you receive.

You can also select an investment advisor who lives in your area. I recommend one who operates independently rather than being limited to canned solutions dictated by the firm the advisor works for. By "canned," I mean the typical eight to twelve portfolios that are offered to all investors. Each investor is placed into one of these portfolios.

TDFs are canned portfolios that have roughly the same investment mix as those offered by non-independent investment advisors, without the additional fees. The fees for canned portfolios offered by non-independent advisors range from 1 to 1.75 percent compared to 0.08 percent for Charles Schwab's TDFs.

Another real-person option is to find an independent advisor who is able to provide customized services to fit your situation. Clear View Advisors is an example in my area.

Determine whether the advisor makes money by advising you to invest in a particular fund or funds. Some are independent, or fee-based, while others earn a commission on what they sell. Possible sources for finding a good advisor include the following:

>> Word of mouth — but make sure that you ask people who seem to be doing well, not your colleague who's always asking to borrow five bucks.

>> Professional associations or companies, such as

- The National Association of Personal Financial Advisors (www.napfa.org)

- The Financial Planners' Association (www.fpanet.org for the FPA Planner Search)

- Dalbar, Inc. (www.dalbar.com) for company information

Going online for info

Many resources for retirement investors are available online including robo advisors, which I cover in the next section. For asset allocation and fund allocation advice, you can look at independent online advice providers.

Each online advice provider has a different presentation, fee, and technology, but they all gather information about you and make a specific recommendation for how to invest your money. You can either take the recommendation as is, or compare it with one you've come up with on your own.

You can also find mutual fund reports by Morningstar and Value Line on their websites — www.morningstar.com and www.valueline.com, respectively. Value Line charges a subscription fee, and Morningstar asks you to register with its site. (Morningstar also charges for certain services.) Both companies rate mutual funds, but keep in mind that the ratings are based on past performance, which is no guarantee of how the funds will perform in the future. Another resource for mutual fund information is Charles Schwab, a large online broker. Go to www. schwab.com and click on "What We Offer" then "Mutual Funds" to see how Schwab classifies various funds.

Going online for advice

Robo advisors are a class of financial advisors that provide financial advice online with moderate to minimal human intervention. A robo advisor uses computer algorithms and advanced software to build and manage your investment portfolio. Wealthfront, Vanguard, Fidelity, Charles Schwab, Stash, and Betterment offer this type of advice, as do many of the other large investment firms.

A $3,000 minimum balance is required for Vanguard Digital Advisor service, and their current fees are about 0.15 percent annually. Charles Schwab requires a $5,000 minimum balance for its Schwab Intelligent Portfolios, and there currently isn't any fee. A $25,000 minimum balance is required for Schwab's Premium service. Charges entail a $300 initial planning fee plus $30 per month for unlimited guidance.

Whatever you do, remember that investing is not an exact science. The important thing is to do *something*, and make sure that what you do is reasoned. Even when you use an advisor, you should know enough about investing to determine whether the advice you're getting makes sense.

IN THIS CHAPTER

» **Getting a handle on investing basics**

» **Taking the plunge during a downturn**

» **Recognizing risk**

» **Realizing that risk and reward go hand in hand**

» **Finding your risk tolerance**

Chapter **14**

Taking Reasonable Investment Risks

The whole reason you invest your money is so it can earn more money. Otherwise, you may as well just lock your savings up in a safe. (Of course, inflation would eat away at the value of your money while it sits in the safe. So investing your money is really your best bet.)

The bad news is that investing money involves a certain amount of risk. The good news is that you can use this risk to your advantage and score a higher return on your money.

Like many things, investment risk isn't that scary after you understand it. This chapter explains the different types of risk involved with your 401(k) and IRA investments. The goal is not to frighten you away from investing but to make you comfortable by familiarizing you with the unfamiliar. After all, the key to successful long-term investing is building a good plan and sticking to it. Finding the level of investment risk that's right for you will help you stick to your plan.

Defining Some Investment Basics

In general terms, investment risk refers to the fact that the value of your investment goes up and down over time. Another term often used to refer to the movement in an investment's value is *volatility*. Essentially, the more volatile an investment is, the higher its risk.

In order to fully understand these concepts, you need to grasp some investment basics. If you're already familiar with debt, equity, and the concept of diversification, feel free to skip down to the next section, which defines different types of investment risk.

Playing debt instruments and making equity investments

Debt and *equity* instruments are the two types of investments you use to make money with your money.

When you invest in a *debt instrument,* such as a bank certificate of deposit (CD), you essentially loan money to an entity for an agreed-upon period of time. In return, you receive interest payments, and you get your principal (initial investment) back at the end of the term (maturity).

Debt instruments also include bonds and money market securities. They're often referred to as fixed-income investments because the amount you earn is fixed and predetermined. The two main investment risks that you face with debt instruments are as follows:

>> **Whoever you loan your money to can *default* on the loan — in other words, miss interest payments and/or not pay back your principal.** In this case, you lose money. Bonds run the spectrum from what are considered the safest (short-term U.S. government bonds) to the most risky (high-yield or junk bonds, issued by corporations with low credit ratings). The interest paid on a short-term government bond is less than that promised on a junk bond because the government bond is less risky. But the likelihood that you'll see your principal again is much higher with a government bond than with a junk bond. Agencies such as Standard & Poor's and Moody's give credit ratings for bonds issued by companies (corporate bonds).

>> **You may not get the full price back if you try to sell bonds before the maturity date.** The essential thing to remember is that longer-term bonds are more volatile than shorter-term bonds if you try to sell them before they mature.

Equity refers to the stock market. When you put your money in equity investments, you're buying a piece of a company. The amount you gain or lose depends on how well or poorly the company does.

REMEMBER

Unlike debt investments, equity provides *no* specified interest or payment.

With equity investments, the main risk is that the company you invest in will do poorly or even go bankrupt. In the first case, the value of your investment goes down; in the second, you may lose all your money. On the other hand, if the company does phenomenally well, so does your investment. That's why equities are generally considered more risky than fixed-income investments. However, the potential rewards (investment gains) of equities can be bigger than with fixed-income investments.

If a stock investment loses value, it's often referred to as a *negative return* rather than a loss. Technically speaking, it's not really a loss unless you sell the stock. If you hold onto the stock, its value may go back up over time, and you will have lost nothing. However, holding on to a stock and waiting for this to happen may be a bad idea, depending on the stock.

Taking a dip in the mutual fund pool

Mutual funds are a common investment option in retirement plans. When you invest in a mutual fund, your money is pooled together with that of many other people and invested under the direction of a professional money manager or in line with an index.

Mutual fund investments in your 401(k) may include the following broad categories:

>> Money market funds

>> Bond funds

>> Stock funds (U.S. and international)

Your 401(k) may also offer a stable value fund, which is a different type of fixed-income investment similar to a bond mutual fund.

I explain these types of investments (and more) in Chapter 13. For this chapter, what you need to know is that the different categories of funds carry different levels of investment risk and expected return. In general, money market funds are the least risky and historically have had the lowest return, while stock funds are the most risky and historically have had the highest return over long periods of time, such as 10 to 20 years. (Investing is all about trade-offs!)

Because of the large pool of investor money, mutual funds can invest in a number of different investment vehicles, which is known as *diversification*. Diversification benefits you by lowering your overall risk. (Read more in the "Diversifying for fun and safety" section later in this chapter.)

Watching the return of the mummy . . . er . . . money

Participants often ask what return to expect on their 401(k) or IRA. That's a great question, and I wish I could answer it definitively — but I can't. Why? Because the return on your investments depends on a number of factors. I can provide guidelines based on past results of different investment types and generally accepted figures. These are long-term averages based on past performance; you can't assume that your investments will turn in exactly the same return or that they'll have the same return year in and year out, because they won't. The return will fluctuate. For example, it's reasonable to expect stocks to return an average of 9 percent over a period of about 20 years or more, but it's not reasonable to assume that this will occur over shorter periods such as five years. Historically, stocks have periodically produced a much higher or much lower return during shorter time spans.

Investment returns over the long term, meaning 20 years or more, depend on the type of investment:

>> **Money market funds** depend on how high or low current interest rates are. These rates have been historically low over the last ten years, so returns in these funds have ranged between 0.05 and 1.0 percent during this period.

>> **Bond funds** vary depending on the duration you select — short-term, intermediate, or long-term — ranging from 1.5 to 6 percent.

>> **Stock funds** can be expected to return around 9 percent but will vary substantially depending on market activity, such as the major downturn in 2008.

Because you'll probably hold a combination of investments, the highest overall return for your account as a whole likely won't exceed 7 percent — and it may be that high only if you're holding at least 75 percent in stock investments. If your investment strategy is more conservative, you can reduce your expected return to 5 to 6 percent (even lower if you're really conservative).

WARNING

The robust stock market performance since 2008 has been great, but that has probably created unrealistic expectations. Stock returns have been in the 10 to 15 percent range during the last ten years but aren't likely to do as well during the next ten years. Returns in this range should never be built into your retirement planning. (Note: The impact of the COVID-19 pandemic was too brief to have a lasting effect on the market due to the huge influx of money by the Fed.)

Diversifying for fun and safety

The best way to reduce your risk of loss, whether you invest in bonds, stocks, or other investments, is to *diversify* your investments — in other words, spread your money around. That way if one investment does badly, the others may do well and make up for the loss. Also, if one investment does extremely well, you'll benefit.

Here's an example of how it can pay off to put your money in a combination of different investments:

Manuel and Sophia both have $5,000 in their 401(k)s. Manuel chooses to invest his entire balance in a "safe," stable value fund with an average return of 2.5 percent a year. Sophia decides to diversify her 401(k) money by investing $1,000 in each of five different categories. Her first investment choice fails, and she loses the entire $1,000 — a scenario that isn't likely, but I use it to prove a point regarding the benefit of diversifying. Sophia's second option doesn't do well, and although she doesn't lose any money, she doesn't make any either. Her third, fourth, and fifth investment choices have average to above-average returns.

After 25 years, Manuel has $9,270 ($5,000 at 2.5 percent return for 25 years). Sophia, however, has $22,070. How did she do it? Table 14-1 shows the comparative returns.

TABLE 14-1

The Advantage of Diversifying Your Investments

Investing $5,000 as follows . . .	Results in . . .
$1,000 and loses it all	$0
$1,000 at 0% return	$1,000
$1,000 at 5%	$3,386
$1,000 at 8%	$6,849
$1,000 at 10%	$10,835
Total	**$22,070**

If Sophia had invested her entire account in the first option, she would've lost everything. By spreading her money over different investments, she overcame that loss and even ended up making more money than Manuel did.

WHAT GOES UP . . .

Most people have heard of the great stock market crash of 1929 that heralded the beginning of the Great Depression. That drop was 86 percent from the high point to the low point. The following table looks at the biggest market drops since the Great Depression, as measured by the S&P 500 index of 500 of the most influential companies in the United States.

Event	Decline in S&P 500 Index Before Recovery
Nixon Shock/OPEC Oil Embargo 1973–1974	48%
Black Monday 1987	29%
Burst of the Dot-Com Bubble, 2000	49%
Global Financial Crisis, 2008	57%
COVID-19 Crash 2020	34%

These percentages reflect the *average change* for the 500 companies in the S&P 500 index from a high point to a low point, usually over several months. Some stocks fare better than the general market decline, and some fare worse. Because some stocks fare worse, the stocks of some S&P companies actually dropped by a lot more than 35 percent during the decline that began in 2000, when the dot-com bubble burst. The big problem with owning a single stock is that your company may be the one that drops by 80 percent (or more) during such a period. This decline can be a big problem if it happens a year or two before you need your money.

The dot-com bubble burst cost investors $5 trillion. Venture capitalists and other investors poured money into funding tech and internet start-ups, resulting in highly inflated stock prices. Low interest rates also made capital easily accessible.

The 2008 Financial Crisis was caused by high-risk trading practices of Wall Street banks, and it nearly resulted in the collapse of the U.S. economy. No one knows when the next market collapse will happen, but you can know that there will be one.

The most efficient way for most 401(k) participants and IRA investors to diversify is through collective investment funds such as mutual funds and exchange-traded funds, or ETFs. Mutual funds and ETFs invest in a number of different companies or other investments. Some are run by professional money managers who decide what investments to hold. Some mutual funds and ETFs are *index funds*, meaning that they hold most or all the same stocks in an index such as the S&P 500 (which contains 500 of the largest companies in the United States). The manager doesn't pick stocks for index funds. The other types of mutual funds and ETFs are *actively managed* funds in which the fund manager buys and sells stocks in order to try to get a better return than with an index.

It can be useful to own a mutual fund or ETF. Say you buy shares in a mutual fund that owns only stocks. The value of that fund can conceivably *increase* on a day that a single stock drops by 30 percent if the fund doesn't own that stock. Even if your fund does own this particular stock, your account value may drop by only a few percentage points for the day — compared to 30 percent for a person who owns only this one stock.

It's usually not enough to own just one mutual fund unless it is a TDF or similar fund that includes a broadly diversified range of stocks and bonds. I explain how to put together a good combination in Chapter 13.

The smartest people in the investment business incur major losses when the market collapses even when they hold widely diversified investments. I know this is scary, but the only way to avoid investment risks is to not invest any money — not a good option. Keep in mind that major market downturns generally aren't a big problem for younger investors who have many years to continue investing.

Staying In It to Win It

It's tempting to want to jump ship when stock prices take a downturn, but that is precisely what not to do. You also want to limit the times that you're buying when prices are high. This section covers downturn opportunities and averaging buying low and high.

Seizing the opportunity of a downturn

I remember telling the younger members of a group of 401(k) participants during the 2008 crisis that they should be celebrating because their chances for getting a 50 percent positive return during the next five years had become much better as they can buy many more fund shares at reduced prices. I encouraged them to keep investing as much as they can afford into the plan, which is what younger investors should do when there's a major market downturn.

As one example of how investing during a downturn can pay off, Table 14-2 shows the result of an annual $1,000 investment on January 1 of each year in Vanguard's 2040 target-date fund (TDF).

TABLE 14-2   ## Vanguard 2040 Target

Year	Annual Return Percentage	Annual Investment	End-of-Year Value
2008	–35.11	$1,000	$649
2009	28.67	$1,000	$2,122
2010	15.33	$1,000	$3,601
2011	–2.11	$1,000	$4,504
2012	15.58	$1,000	$6,362
2013	24.79	$1,000	$9,187
2014	7.61	$1,000	$10,962
2015	–1.25	$1,000	$11,812
2016	8.98	$1,000	$13,963
2017	20.86	$1,000	$18,084
2018	–7.23	$1,000	$17,697
2019	24.19	$1,000	$23,220
2020	16.31	$1,000	$28,170

In 2008, the fund lost more than 35 percent of its value, but the table shows that continuing to invest pays. If you still have years to invest, there's no need to panic when big market drops occur.

TIP

One of the benefits of Target Date Funds is that they keep your stock allocation balanced by periodically rebalancing and also by reducing the percentage of stocks in your account as you get older.

Buying more when prices are low

When you invest a specified amount at regular intervals, as you do with automatic 401(k) contributions or automatic IRA deposits from your paycheck, you use an investment strategy called *dollar cost averaging*. (You didn't know you were that smart, did you?) This investment strategy may lower the average price that you pay for your investments. How? Because you're spending the same amount each time you invest, you end up buying more shares of your investments when prices are low and fewer shares when prices are high. By averaging high and low prices, you reduce the risk that you will buy more shares when prices are high.

Of course, if stock prices only go up for the entire time you invest, this strategy won't work. But if you contribute to a retirement account over a long period of time, there will likely be periods when prices go down.

Continuing to invest new contributions when stock values drop also helps because you accrue new shares at a reduced price. Everyone likes buying things at a discount, which is what you can do when stock prices drop a lot.

Classifying Different Types of Risk

Several types of risk come into play when you're investing. The following sections explain what those types are, but keep in mind that this isn't an exhaustive list of *all* kinds of risk.

Losing more than you can stand

No one wants to lose any money, but folks are especially fearful of losing more than they can afford. You probably won't lose everything in your 401(k) account, but losing to the point of severe pain is a very real possibility (especially if you don't diversify your investments).

REMEMBER

The amount of risk you can take depends to a large extent on how soon you'll need your money — your *time horizon*. If you won't need the money for 20 or 30 years, it doesn't matter if the stock market goes into a slump for a few years. Historically, the market has always recovered, so if you hold on to your investments, they'll probably rebound (provided that you had a good reason to buy them in the first place).

If you'll need your money in five years or less, however, you may not have time to recover from a drop in the stock market. This is when you need to move some of your money out of high-risk investments and into more stable investments that safeguard your principal, such as money market funds, stable value funds in a 401(k), and shorter-term bonds.

Older participants are in a much different position than younger ones during a strong market downturn. If you're 60 years old and have a $250,000 account balance, having it drop to $125,000 is horrible because you don't have that many years to continue investing. You won't be buying a lot of shares at a discounted price. Such losses have occurred in the past because older 401(k) and IRA investors have benefited by having the stock portion of their accounts achieve great returns. As a result, participants approaching retirement age often have larger portions of their accounts invested in stocks than at any other time they have been 401(k) or IRA investors. Excess exposure to stocks has resulted in 50 percent losses in retirement holdings.

A common mistake 401(k) investors made during the late 1990s was putting too much into certain stocks that were doing extremely well such as computer and software producers instead of diversifying their investments. (They may have thought that they were diversifying by buying a high-tech mutual fund instead of stock in a single company, but that didn't help when the entire industry bubble burst.) When those companies' performance began to suffer, many portfolios lost a lot of value. After the dot-com bubble burst in 2000, younger investors picked themselves up, dusted themselves off, and started all over again with diversified portfolios. But investors within a few years of retiring had a completely different outlook. Many had to delay retirement.

Even if you put together a portfolio that contains good, solid performers, you're at the mercy of general economic conditions. This type of risk is known as *systematic risk*, or *market risk*. It's the risk that your investments will decline in value simply because current economic conditions are making most investments decline in value. These general declines have happened periodically over history and will happen again. You need to look carefully at your investments. If you decide that your investments are the right ones for you, hang on and ride it out. Historically, the stock market has always recovered, although sometimes it can take a few years. If you're an investor nearing retirement, be sure to have enough of your investments in less risky securities that'll keep your principal intact in case you need to tap it.

Losing your entire investment

The stock market slump that began in 2000, combined with the Wall Street collapse in 2008, caused many people to worry about losing all their retirement savings. Some workers want to know if they should pull their 401(k) money out of stocks and invest in something safer during such times.

Before you do something rash (such as pull all your 401(k) money out of stocks), you need to understand that there's no such thing as a completely risk-free investment. Even if you bury your money or hide it in your mattress, your dog can still dig it up and eat it for lunch, or the money can be stolen. Even the investments most people consider completely safe — FDIC-insured bank savings accounts and certificates of deposit (CDs) — are only guaranteed to a certain point. They still carry some risk of loss.

TECHNICAL STUFF

The *FDIC* (Federal Deposit Insurance Corporation) is federal government insurance that protects your money up to a certain amount ($250,000 per person as of 2021) should the bank where you parked your money in a savings account go bankrupt. Not all financial institutions are FDIC-insured. Mutual funds are never covered by the FDIC. What's more, the FDIC doesn't have enough resources to back its guarantees in a total economic collapse.

REMEMBER

The important fact is that you'll probably never lose all your money, even if it's all invested in stocks. One important exception is if you have too much invested in your own company's stock or any other single stock. This type of investment can be a ticket to either riches or rags, as I explain in the next section.

Owning too much company stock

A number of 401(k) investors face the very real risk of holding too much stock in their employer's company. *Company stock* may be available in a number of ways:

>> Your employer can use it to make matching contributions to your account.

>> Your employer can give it to you as an additional contribution.

>> Your 401(k) may offer it as an investment option for your own contributions.

>> Your employer may give you the opportunity to buy stock via a stock purchase plan.

WARNING

Employers who contribute company stock to a 401(k) as a matching contribution or other contribution may place restrictions on when you can sell that stock — you may only be able to sell it when you turn 55, for example. This restriction puts you in a difficult situation because you won't be able to diversify that part of your account even if you want to. In this situation, remember two things:

>> Your other investments need to balance out the fact that you have so much invested in your company's stock.

>> Don't increase your holdings by investing your own contributions in company stock.

The second point is very important. The fact that many companies prospered throughout the 1990s, and their stock values consistently increased, led a number of employees to invest some or all of their own contributions in company stock. Just how bad an idea this is became apparent in 2000, when the stock market began to decline and many investors lost big chunks of their retirement accounts. The old adage about not putting all your eggs in one basket can't be more true.

Yes, it can be hard not to invest a lot in your own company. After all, you work there, and you want to support the company, as well as feel that you have an ownership stake in how well it does. What's more, you may have gotten a big sales pitch from senior management on the benefits of owning company stock. Many senior managers want employees to own as much company stock as possible. Interesting psychology is at work here. According to at least one study, 401(k) plan participants who receive a matching contribution in company stock are more likely to also invest their own contributions in company stock if such an option is available in their plan. So, if your company matches your contribution in stock, you're more likely to direct your own contributions into company stock, when really, the rules of diversification dictate that you should put your own contributions somewhere else.

Not to be ignored is the possibility that your buddies at work may laugh at you for investing your money in mutual funds when they're making a ton of money investing in company stock. The pressure to not miss out on this "once-in-a-lifetime opportunity" can be great. One solution: Ignore your buddies.

If your employer gives you company stock, you certainly shouldn't look a gift horse in the mouth. Take it! But think twice before you invest your own money in company stock. The risk of a major loss is simply too high. Many large, well-known companies watched their stock prices drop by more than 50 percent during the market downturn that began in 2000.

REMEMBER

Every stock's value goes down at some point — it seems to be only a question of when and by how much. It's virtually impossible for a stock to only go up for 20 years or more.

Unfortunately, many 401(k) investors with a lot of company stock learned this lesson the hard way, at the worst time — in their 50s and nearing retirement. For years they saw the value of their accounts grow as they rode the company stock rocket. Then, seemingly overnight, they watched much of what they had gained flame out and disappear.

A single stock has much more potential to move up and down than a diversified collection of investments. Keep your ownership of company stock at the lowest level permitted by your plan in order to avoid unnecessary risk. This type of risk is called *company risk* or *unsystematic risk*, and the only way to reduce or eliminate it is to diversify your investments.

Not having enough money to live on during your retirement

Considering the risks outlined in the previous sections, you may wonder why investing your money in anything other than a relatively safe bank savings account is even necessary. The answer is that you need to beat *inflation*, the gradual rise in prices over time. You may be able to avoid many investment disasters, but inflation isn't one of them.

If prices rise by an average of 3 percent a year, your money will lose more than 60 percent of its value over 30 years. This means that the $100,000 you have today will be worth only $40,000 when you need it at retirement 30 years from now. This loss is just as real as waking up tomorrow morning to find that your account value has dropped by 60 percent. Ouch!

REMEMBER

You have to invest your retirement funds — it's the only way to beat inflation.

Understanding the Risk-Reward Relationship

When you think about it, retirement investing is a 40- to 60-year event that includes both your working and retirement years. You can't afford to accept a safe return over this time period, because it may not keep up with inflation.

"Simple," you may be saying. "All I have to do is invest in something risky, and that will bring up my average return." Unfortunately, it's not that easy. Although you generally have to take on more risk to get a higher return, or reward, that doesn't mean that every high-risk investment will give you a high return. Some may fail miserably.

REMEMBER

You need to choose reasonable investments that are right for your goals as well as for your personal risk tolerance. Investments with the same level of risk can produce very different returns. Your goal is to find the investments that will give you the best returns for your risk level.

I explain general guidelines in Chapter 13. You can also hire a financial planner to do an analysis for you or use financial planning software and services available over the internet. A financial planner (or software) will run a number of different scenarios through the computer and come up with a combination of investments that should give the greatest potential return for a given level of risk. This would be nearly impossible to do on your own.

As an example of why it's so important to try to get the best return possible at your desired risk level, Figure 14-1 shows the impact of an additional 3 percent return on your ending balance.

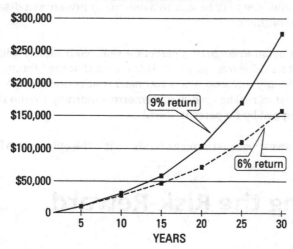

FIGURE 14-1: How returns affect investment growth.

As the table shows, a 9 percent return results in an end balance of $273,000 after 30 years versus $158,000 at a 6 percent rate of return. The 3-percent-higher return generates a 73-percent-higher 401(k) nest egg and a 73-percent-higher retirement income. To achieve the same result over 30 years at the lower rate of return, you'd need to make an annual contribution of $3,460 instead of $2,000.

Deciding How Much Risk You Can Stand

The key to managing risk is knowing how much you can tolerate. When you know how much risk you can handle, you can find investments that you can live with over the long term. If you panic and sell your investments following a price plummet, all you'll do is lose money. If you can stick it out and not sell the investments when they're low, you'll be in better shape.

REMEMBER

Let me clear up a common misconception: The amount of investment risk that's right for you has nothing to do with whether you like to go bungee jumping on weekends or drive race cars as a hobby. When it comes to investments, the amount and type of risk you can tolerate has more to do with your time horizon than with your personality (although personality does factor in to a degree). Your time horizon is the length of time between now and when you'll need your money. The longer your time horizon, the more time your investments have to increase in value, even if they have a bad year or two. That generally means that you can take on more investment risk, as part of a carefully thought-out investment strategy, if you have 20 or 30 years until retirement than if you have, say, 5 years until you'll need your money.

Can you handle drops of 20 percent, 30 percent, 40 percent, 50 percent, or even more in the value of your account? Answering questions like this helps you determine whether to invest in risky stocks or safer bonds. Imagine yourself with a retirement account of $100,000 that drops to $50,000 in value. Would you be able to hang on, or would you, like so many others, be tempted to sell those investments and put the money in lower-risk investments? If you sell, you'll have to dramatically increase your contributions to make up both the loss *and* the lower investment return you'll get in the future. Many investors are comfortable owning stocks when things are going well but tend to sell when stocks are down. This is generally the wrong thing to do.

Stocks have averaged an 8 to 10 percent return since 1926. Bonds have averaged a 4 to 6 percent return. These average returns are indicative of the broad stock and bond markets. Your average annual returns should have been in these ranges if you owned a broad range of stocks and bonds during this entire period and didn't panic and sell out during bad years.

Being highly diversified means you own large-, mid-, and small-cap growth and value stocks. One way to do this is to invest in a TDF. A TDF, or Target Date Fund, is a mutual fund containing a diversified group of investments. It automatically adjusts the stock/bond ratio to become more conservative as you get closer to your retirement age. Table 14-3 illustrates the risk-reward trade-off. The numbers in the table are based on the assumption that stocks produce an average of 8 percent return and bonds an average 4 percent return over the long term of 20 years or more. Average returns over shorter periods will be much different, and the average returns also vary substantially depending on what stocks and bonds you own. Actual historical returns vary depending on the time period selected and the mix of stocks and bonds included in the averages.

The results vary substantially depending on the beginning and ending dates. A change of only one year can result in quite different average returns, particularly if the time period selected is only ten years. The same is true depending on what mix of stocks and bonds are included in the results. This is why I am using 8 and 4 percent average returns because they are indicative of what can be expected over longer periods of time — 20 years or more.

In Table 14-3, the first column indicates the stock/bond ratio. The second column is the expected average annual return over a period of 20 years or longer. The worst and best years are based on historical results during the past 20 years. No one has any idea when the worst and best years will occur over the next 20 years, which is one of the things that makes investing so difficult.

TABLE 14-3

Sample Historical Average Investment Returns

Bond/Stock Ratio	Average Return	Worst Year	Best Year
100%/0%	4.0%	–8.1%	32.6%
70%/30%	5.2%	–14.2%	28.4%
50%/50%	6.0%	–22.5%	32.3%
0%/100%	8.0%	–43.1%	54.2%

Some investors focus only on the average annual return when deciding how to invest. Others may focus on what's currently hot — the fund that had the highest return during the past year. Those who focus on the highest average annual return may be tempted to invest 100 percent in stocks because they have the highest average annual return. They are very content when things are going well; however, they may panic and cash out when their accounts drop by 30 or 40 percent. That is why you must consider how well you will handle a major drop in value.

Those who chase what is currently hot run the risk of getting hammered when that market segment drops out of favor and becomes very cold. This is what happened with tech and internet stocks during the 2000 dot-com bubble. The same potential exists today for tech stocks and cryptocurrencies.

The stock market is at an all-time high as I write this. It is highly unlikely from a historical perspective that 2022 will be the year that produces the highest return during the next 20 years. The same is true for bonds because bond prices decline when interest rates rise. At the same time, inflationary pressures are increasing. Interest rates historically increase during inflationary times. As a result, 2022 also isn't likely to be the year that produces the highest return on bonds during the next 20 years.

REMEMBER

The whole point of finding a comfortable risk level is that it helps you stick to your investment plan. Investing more aggressively (taking more risk) gives you a chance of getting a higher return, but it may also mean more ups and downs than you want. It's a trade-off. The bottom line is that you have to feel comfortable with the investments you choose.

Long-term investing gives you a lot of time to recover from market slumps. The important thing is to choose good, solid investments and reduce your stock holdings as you approach retirement, when you'll have to start generating an income from your investments. (Within your stock investments, you can also shift from growth stocks toward value stocks, which tend to be less volatile.)

5
Money In,
Money Out

IN THIS PART . . .

Putting money into your retirement account can be as easy as choosing a percentage on the enrollment form you fill out when you join. It can be more challenging if you're the one deciding how much and when to make your contribution.

Taking money out of your retirement account before you retire isn't generally a good idea. Withdrawing money from your account early is almost always accompanied by tax penalties and fees. One exception is when you use money you've saved to buy your first home — you may pay a modest fee, but you can avoid heavy taxes by doing the withdrawal at the right time.

Staying on top of your retirement money becomes even more important after you retire. Paying attention to tax planning and investment issues are ever-present concerns.

Chapter 15

Making Contributions

The people in power — from legislators to employers to you — know that investing in a retirement plan is smart. However, those same legislators and employers set some limits on how much you can put into a retirement savings account. On the plus side, the employer, at least, may make deposits into your account while you work for them, and eventually, those employer contributions become yours.

This chapter goes through the limits on how much you and your employer can put into your account and talks about when an employer's contributions can become yours.

Checking Out How Much You Can Contribute

"How much can I contribute to my retirement plan?" seems like a fairly simple question. However, the answer isn't as straightforward as you may think. The federal government sets limits on contributions, but your 401(k) plan is allowed to be more restrictive. Also, high-income earners may have their contribution levels capped due to special restrictions required by law. (I explain rules for highly compensated employees in more detail in Chapter 12.)

Gauging the limits of the law

The federal dollar limit for pre-tax salary deferrals is probably the best-known 401(k) limit (not to mention a mouthful to say!). Despite its scary title, this limit is easy to understand. It's the cap on how much income you can have your employer put into the 401(k) rather than into your paycheck. In 2021 the limit is $19,500, plus an additional $6,500 catch-up contribution if you're age 50 or older. The limits rise in $500 increments due to inflation and occur as often as inflation warrants.

The 2021 IRA limits are $6,000 if you're under age 50. If you're 50 or older, you can put in an additional $1,000 catch-up contribution.

REMEMBER

Another federal limit to be aware of is the *percentage-of-pay limit.* This limit applies to all contributions made to your 401(k) by you and your employer, as well as to all contributions to other defined contribution plans, such as profit-sharing plans or 403(b) plans. These contributions can't total more than 100 percent of your pay, or $58,000 for 2021, whichever is less. The $58,000 limit is expected to rise periodically with inflation.

REMEMBER

The 100-percent-of-pay limit includes catch-up contributions, but the $58,000 dollar limit does not.

Seeing what Uncle Sam allows (he's extra generous if you're 50 or older)

Your contribution limit to a 401(k) plan in 2021 is $19,500. This maximum increases in $500 increments for inflation periodically. These may be all pre-tax or Roth contributions or a combination of the two. (*Pre-tax contribution* refers to money taken out of your paycheck before you pay federal income taxes — it reduces your taxable income so that you pay less federal income tax for the year.) Roth contributions can also be taken out of your paycheck, but you pay tax on the amount, so your taxes aren't reduced.

The $19,500 contribution limit applies only to your contributions and doesn't include contributions from your employer. The 2021 combined employee/employer contribution limit is $64,500.

In the year that you hit the big 5-0 and every year thereafter, you can make an additional pre-tax or Roth contribution, known as a *catch-up contribution,* which raises your total possible contribution by $6,500 in 2021. The catch-up limit increases in $500 multiples for inflation periodically. Why the special tax break? You can speculate that it's because Uncle Sam is well over 50 himself (look at his white hair, after all). In reality, Congress approved this extra tax break to help workers who may not have contributed much to their own retirement savings early on, particularly workers, typically women, who stepped out of the work force to raise children or care for ailing relatives.

A small number of 401(k) plans allow you to make after-tax contributions. You can't deduct these contributions from your income tax, but you can benefit from them in another way — the gain on your investment isn't taxed every year. It grows *tax deferred,* and you pay income tax only on the investment gains when you withdraw them. Please note that after-tax contributions are not the same as Roth 401(k) contributions. However, you may be able to achieve a better result by making Roth contributions because the investment gains are never taxed if you follow the applicable rules.

TECHNICAL STUFF

Some small businesses offer what's known as a SIMPLE (Savings Incentive Match Plan for Employees) IRA plan. These plans have fewer administrative requirements for the employer, but the trade-off is lower contribution limits ($13,500 under age 50 plus an additional $3,000 age 50 and over in 2021) than for 401(k)s. Safe Harbor 401 and Qualified Automatic Contribution Arrangement (QACA) 401(k) plans also have fewer administrative requirements for the employer but allow the higher 401(k) contribution limits presented here. I explain Safe Harbor, QACA 401(k)s, and SIMPLE IRAs in Chapter 18.

Paying attention to the percent-of-pay limit

Believe it or not, you can contribute all your wages to your retirement plan if you don't earn more than about $60,000. The combined employee/employer limit is 100 percent of your pay with a $64,500 maximum. (This includes the $6,500 catch-up contribution.) However, your employer may set a lower percentage in its plan.

In reality, you can't contribute a full 100 percent of your salary, even if your employer doesn't make a contribution, because you must pay Social Security taxes, and possibly state and local taxes, on your income before making your 401(k) contributions. You may also have other pre-401(k) pay deductions for medical coverage or contributions to a Section 125 flexible benefits plan.

But, if you can afford to do so, you may be able to contribute quite a chunk of your pay as long as you remain under the limit. If you're a lower-income saver, or if you start a second career after earning a military, police, or other pension, being able to contribute a higher percentage can be a real plus for you. For example, if you retired from the military with a pension that covers most or all of your everyday expenses, but you became bored and decided to go back to work part-time earning $14,000, you can contribute the entire amount after other deductions.

Heeding limits on your personal IRA

The only limit on IRA contributions is the $6,000 you're allowed to contribute annually for 2021. When you're 50 or older, you get to make an extra catch-up contribution of $1,000.

WARNING

Your earned income must be at least as much as your IRA contribution. If you contributed more than you earned, you need to withdraw the excess contributions by your tax deadline to avoid a penalty.

The amount you're eligible to contribute may be reduced or eliminated if your taxable income is too high or if your spouse is covered by a 401(k). Check Chapter 2 for more info.

IRA-based employer-sponsored retirement plans such as a SEP-IRA and a SIMPLE-IRA have different contribution limits. See Chapter 18 for information on those small business plans.

Maxing Out Matching Contributions

Many employers match the funds you put into your 401(k) up to a certain percentage or amount. The amount of money you receive from your employer depends on how much you contribute, so it makes sense to contribute enough to get the most possible.

Your employer sets the matching rate as well as the limit of how much it will match and the vesting schedule for the employer contributions. The match rate may be as little as 10 cents (or less) for each dollar you contribute up to a percentage of your salary.

The most common matching rates are 25 cents or 50 cents for each dollar you contribute, usually up to 6 percent of your salary. Some employers match dollar-for-dollar, and a few have even higher matches.

TIP

If you can't afford to contribute the full amount matched by your employer now, start with a lower percentage and increase your contribution rate as soon as possible to reach the full amount. The easiest time to do this is when you get a raise. Increase your contribution rate by 1 percent every time you get a raise. You don't have to stop there, either. It always makes sense to contribute as much as you possibly can.

If you're married, you and your spouse can each contribute the maximum amount to get the full match in your plans. If you can't afford to do that, consider the following options:

>> See which plan has the higher match and best vesting schedule and put what you can into that plan.

>> Decide who's likely to stay long enough to qualify for the vested employer contributions and consider pooling your contributions to that plan to get the full match.

>> Consider which plan has better investment options, and, if you expect to tap your 401(k) plan resources in the future, which one permits in-service withdrawals or loans. You can then contribute more to the plan that offers the best options.

TIP

There's no delicate way to put this, so I'm just going to say it: If you think there's a chance that you won't stay married, you may be better off continuing to fund your own 401(k) to the extent possible rather than putting some of your money toward your spouse's 401(k) plan. Divvying up retirement accounts after a divorce can be tricky.

Timing Is Everything

When you put money into your retirement account isn't quite as important as how much you put in, but timing can make a difference. The next sections talk about timing issues for 401(k)s and IRAs.

Spreading out your 401(k) contributions

How you time your contributions is important. Some people like to contribute more to their 401(k) early in the year to ensure that they reach the maximum before, say, having to think about buying holiday gifts at the end of the year. This is sometimes referred to as *front-loading* the 401(k). The potential problem with this strategy is that it can cause you to lose some of your employer matching contributions. Before you decide to go with this strategy, ask your employer about its timing for depositing matching contributions. Many employers only make these deposits during the pay periods when you contribute to the plan because it's easier for them. If this is how your plan works, you'll lose out by front-loading.

For example, say your employer matches 50 cents on the dollar, up to 6 percent of your salary. If you earn $150,000 and you contribute at least $9,000 (6 percent of your salary), you should receive an employer match of $4,500. Now, say you want to contribute the full $19,500 permitted in 2021, and you want to do it early in the year. You fill out your form indicating that you want to contribute 20 percent of your pay every pay period. You're not allowed to contribute $30,000 to a 401(k), so you'll be forced to stop contributing partway through the year when you reach the $19,500 limit, unless you are at least age 55 and eligible to make a catch-up contribution. (You'll get there after you've earned $97,500, because 20 percent of $97,500 is $19,500.) Say your employer stops making matching contributions then, because you're no longer making contributions at that time. You will have received only 3 percent of $97,500 in matching contributions, or $2,925, which is lower than the $4,500 you would've received if you had spread out your contributions evenly over the year. By using this strategy, you lose $1,575 of employer contributions.

In this case, it makes more sense to reduce your contribution rate so that you contribute for the entire year and still hit the $19,500 limit. In this instance, 13 percent would be the percentage to use (13 percent of $150,000 equals $19,500).

Spreading out your IRA contributions — or not

The deadline for making IRA contributions is the date you file your tax return for that year. So, you can put money into your IRA for the previous year up until April 15.

The fact that you *can* doesn't mean you necessarily *should*. Participants in 401(k) plans have contributions deducted from their pay each pay period. Following this pattern with your IRA contributions makes sense. Saving each pay period is much easier than making one lump-sum contribution for most workers.

You can't make payroll deduction IRA contributions unless your employer sets up a payroll deduction IRA plan; however, you can have money transferred from your bank account into your IRA each pay period. You can set a more flexible schedule if it makes more sense to transfer funds once a month or once a quarter, so long as you make the contributions.

TIP

Making periodic deposits is a good idea if you are serious about contributing to an IRA for your retirement and/or some other purpose such as buying your first home. Periodic contributions can also reduce your investment risk because you are buying shares throughout the year when shares are both higher and lower. April 15 may or may not be a good time to invest a lump-sum contribution.

Chapter **16**

Withdrawing Money Before You Retire

L ife is so unpredictable. Just when you think you have everything under control . . . wham! An unexpected expense jumps out of a dark alley, bops you on the head, and runs off with your wallet. At times like that, it's nice to know that you may be able to tap your retirement funds to tide you over.

Uncle Sam permits two ways for getting money out of your 401(k) while you're still working — hardship withdrawals and loans. However, your employer isn't *required* to allow you to do either one. Before you go any further with this chapter, check your summary plan description (summary of your plan's rules) to see what your plan allows. It may permit both loans and hardship withdrawals, only one or the other, or neither. Many plans don't permit loans because administering them can be a hassle. You're probably wondering why you can't get your money any time you want. After all, it's your money, right? Yes, it is, but remember that Uncle Sam gives you big tax breaks to help you save in a 401(k). He really wants you to use this money when you retire, so he makes it difficult to take it out earlier.

If you *are* allowed to take a loan or make a hardship withdrawal, you'll be much better off if you understand the rules and how much you may have to pay in taxes and penalties, before doing so. You may decide that it's better for your long-term future to look for another source of emergency funds first.

IRAs don't restrict when you take money out so you can do that at any time without having to ask for approval; however, a tax penalty may be imposed.

TIP

The rules I discuss in this chapter apply if you're still working for the employer that sponsors your 401(k) plan. The rules are different for taking money out after you leave your employer. I discuss those details in Chapter 17. That chapter also covers withdrawals from your IRA to provide retirement income.

Taking Money from Your IRA

You can withdraw money out of a traditional IRA without a tax penalty if you're over age 59½. You also pay no tax penalty for a number of other purposes or in specific situations:

>> To purchase a first home (you're limited to $10,000 over your lifetime)

>> To pay qualified higher education expenses for you, your spouse, or relatives such as the children or grandchildren of you or your spouse

>> You experience total and permanent disability

>> To pay an IRS levy

>> To pay health insurance premiums while you're unemployed

>> Certain distributions to qualified military reservists called to active duty

>> To pay expenses related to the birth or adoption of a child

These exceptions enable you to utilize your IRA for reasons other than retirement, making an IRA account even more valuable. Easier access to the money in your IRA than in a 401(k) is a big reason to consider transferring your 401(k) into an IRA when you change jobs.

At your death, your beneficiaries can withdraw the money without penalties, but it's too nice a day to think of that, right?

This is a more extensive list than what you can do with money in a 401(k) plan.

Accessing Your 401(k) Plan Money While Working

It can be difficult, if not downright impossible, to make a withdrawal from your 401(k) while you're working for the company that sponsors the plan.

The tax breaks you get with a 401(k) plan come with a price. It can be very costly to take your money out of the plan before you retire — if you can even do it at all. Many employers permit you to borrow money from your 401(k), but not necessarily for any old reason. Most plans permit *hardship withdrawals,* which are withdrawals from your account to pay expenses when you're in financial difficulty. Your employer may permit withdrawals only for reasons approved by the IRS.

People often think that they're automatically allowed to withdraw money from a 401(k) for higher education expenses or for buying a home, and that they won't owe an early withdrawal penalty on the amount. This is false. Your plan *may* allow you to make a withdrawal for these reasons, but it doesn't *have* to.

When you leave your employer, either to retire or to change jobs, you generally have a window of opportunity to get your money. In most cases, you can receive payment of your account or transfer the money into an IRA or another employer's retirement plan (see Chapter 10). I highly recommend transferring the money to another plan or IRA, or leaving the money in the plan to avoid a high tax bill.

TIP

Don't wait for an emergency to check on the rules for accessing your money. You may find that you can't make a withdrawal or that you will lose about half the value in taxes and penalties if you do make a withdrawal.

Federal law allows three ways to get money out of your 401(k) while you're working for the employer sponsoring the plan. But keep in mind that your employer isn't *required* to allow these features, so they may not be available in your plan. The three ways to obtain money from your 401(k) are as follows:

>> **Unrestricted access to plan assets after you reach age 59½:** The amount withdrawn becomes part of your taxable income for that year.

>> **Withdrawals for financial hardships as defined by law and IRS regulations:** *Hardship withdrawals,* as they're known, are fully taxable and are usually also subject to an additional 10 percent federal early withdrawal penalty (and possibly additional state and local taxes, as well).

>> **Plan loans:** These are subject to numerous restrictions. You may get a plan loan to pay for excessive medical expenses, but you won't get one to buy a yacht.

The first two options listed are known as *in-service withdrawals*, because you make them while you're "in the service of" your employer.

Strangely enough, federal law makes it theoretically easier to withdraw your employer's contributions than your own pre-tax deferrals while you're working. Your employer may allow you to take the employer contributions out for any reason. But most employers place restrictions on withdrawals of their contributions because they want you to use the money for retirement, so you won't be able to use those to buy your yacht.

TIP

Loans and in-service withdrawals are a mixed blessing because, while they give you some flexibility with your money, they'll likely reduce the ultimate value of your retirement nest egg. But being able to withdraw these savings can be an important plan feature if you think that you may need your money before reaching age 59½. This is particularly true for younger employees who have a long way to go until retirement.

Facing Hardship with Your 401(k) at Your Side

Most 401(k) plans allow hardship withdrawals, but not all of them do. Why *wouldn't* a plan let you withdraw money to pay for an emergency? Your employer may want you to use the money only for retirement — period. In the following sections I assume that your 401(k) plan offers a hardship withdrawal possibility.

Defining a hardship

You can't take a hardship withdrawal if your yacht breaks down and you need to buy another one before the spring thaw. Hardship withdrawals are limited to specific situations and are permitted only if you have an *immediate and heavy financial need* that can't be satisfied from other resources.

Certain expenses are deemed to be immediate and heavy, including

» Costs related to the purchase of your primary residence

» Tuition and related educational expenses for the next 12 months for you, your spouse, a dependent, or a nondependent beneficiary

» Medical expenses for you, your spouse, dependents, or a primary beneficiary not covered by insurance

- » Payments necessary to prevent either eviction from your principal residence or foreclosure on the mortgage for your residence

- » Burial and funeral expenses for you, your spouse, dependents, or a primary beneficiary

- » Certain expenses for the repair of damage to your primary residence such as fire, flood, hurricane, or earthquake that qualify for the casualty deduction under IRC Section 165

WARNING

A distribution isn't considered necessary to satisfy an immediate and heavy financial need if you have other resources available to meet the need, including your spouse's and minor children's assets. You must also have obtained all other currently available distributions from the 401(k) plan and all other employer plans maintained by your employer.

Your employer has the option to require you to take a plan loan rather than a hardship withdrawal.

You can also withdraw Roth contributions to a 401(k). Any investment gains withdrawn are taxable, and the 10 percent penalty tax applies if you haven't made contributions for at least five years, and you haven't reached 59½. The penalty tax doesn't apply for distributions due to death or total and permanent disability. Any Roth contribution withdrawal must include a pro-rata portion of any investment gains.

All withdrawals of non-Roth contributions prior to age 59½ are taxable including the 10 percent early distribution penalty except in the following circumstances:

- » You're a highly compensated employee required to take a distribution to make the plan comply with a nondiscrimination test.

- » Your death.

- » To pay a qualified domestic relations order (QDRO), issued as part of a divorce decree.

- » To pay an IRS levy of your account.

- » A series of substantially equal periodic payments (SEPP), which I explain in Chapter 17.

- » To pay medical expenses in excess of 10 percent of your adjusted gross income.

- » You withdraw money within 30 to 90 days of your first automatic enrollment contribution deduction. You forfeit any matching employer contributions if you do this.

>> To add a child to the family. The Secure Act passed by Congress in December 2019 permits each parent who has an IRA or 401(k) account to withdraw $5,000 for the birth or adoption of a child.

>> To make certain payments to a reservist called to active duty.

>> You are totally and permanently disabled.

The IRS definition of total and permanent disability requires you to be "unable to perform substantial gainful activity" because of an identifiable physical or mental impairment that is expected to be of "long-continued and indefinite duration." Your doctor needs to confirm that you are unable to work due to a physical or mental disability and that you will continue to be unable to work permanently or at least for a very long period of time. You must submit IRS Form 5329 when you submit your tax return to claim the exemption. Enter Code 03 for disability where it asks for the code for the exemption. Also look at Box 7 of the 1099-R you received for the distribution to be sure that the distribution code used is 03. If not, contact your former employer or service provider to get a corrected form.

Participants who are unhappy with their 401(k) investments frequently ask whether they can take their money out of the plan as a hardship withdrawal, while they're working, and roll it into an IRA. The answer is no. You can only transfer your money to an IRA under the conditions explained in Chapter 10.

If you manage to withdraw your money using a hardship withdrawal before you turn 59½, you'll be heavily taxed. Not only will you owe federal and perhaps state and local income tax on the amount withdrawn, but you'll also owe a 10 percent federal early withdrawal penalty on the entire amount unless the withdrawal is for one of the reasons that qualify for an exemption. If you take a hardship distribution, the money you withdraw is no longer eligible for a rollover.

Taking out a loan lets you avoid these penalties; however, other costs are involved. I explain these costs in "Both a Borrower and a Lender Be" later in this chapter.

Determining the amount

You can withdraw only the amount you need to meet your hardship expense. Because you have to pay tax on a hardship withdrawal, you can include the taxes you'll owe. The next section, "Calculating the tax you owe," provides an example.

The money you're allowed to withdraw for a hardship may be limited to the money you've contributed (excluding investment gains), or it may include vested employer contributions and money you have rolled into the plan from an IRA or another retirement plan. Your employer decides the rules. Many employers don't permit their contributions to be withdrawn for a hardship because they want this money to stay in the plan and be used to provide retirement benefits.

If your plan lets you borrow money from your 401(k), you may be required to take a loan before taking a hardship withdrawal. It depends on your plan's rules. In this case, you take the maximum loan allowed to you, and then if you still need money, you take the rest of what you need as a hardship withdrawal. I discuss loans in more detail in the section "Both a Borrower and a Lender Be" later in this chapter.

Calculating the tax you owe

You need to pay federal income tax, and state income tax if applicable, on the amount of your hardship withdrawal. (You didn't think you'd be able to avoid taxes, now, did you?) Additionally, if you're under 59½ years old, you have to pay a 10 percent early withdrawal penalty on the amount you take out unless it is for one of the reasons mentioned in the preceding "Defining a hardship" section. Some states also impose an early withdrawal penalty of a few percentage points. In total, you'll probably have to pay 25 to 40 percent of the amount withdrawn, and you may have to pay even more.

For example, say you need $10,000 for a down payment on a house, your federal tax rate is 22 percent, and you're under 59½. Because of your age, you'll owe a 10 percent early withdrawal penalty along with taxes, for a total of 32 percent. Without taking into account state and local taxes, you'll need to withdraw $14,706 in order to have $10,000 for your down payment and $4,706 to pay 32 percent in taxes. (To get this amount I subtracted 32 percent from 100 percent leaving 68 percent, which is 0.68. I then divided $10,000 by 0.68, which equals $14,706.)

Don't spend all the money you withdraw without first determining how much you owe in taxes! Your employer normally withholds 20 percent of the hardship withdrawal. However, this mandatory tax withholding has no relationship to the amount of federal and state tax you'll owe — it's simply a deposit to the IRS. You'll determine the actual taxes owed when you figure your taxes for the year you receive the distribution, and you'll have to pay the difference. Determine how much tax you'll have to pay — and pay it — before you do anything else. Many participants fail to do this and end up with an unexpected, whopping tax bill.

Participants often ask me whether withdrawing money to buy a home or to pay for college expenses exempts them from the 10 percent early withdrawal penalty. The answer is no. The confusion arises because you *can* avoid this penalty if you withdraw money from an IRA to buy a home or pay for higher education expenses. I discuss rules for IRAs in Chapter 8.

REMEMBER

Another consequence of hardship withdrawals is that you disrupt your retirement savings. Say you withdraw $14,706 in order to end up with $10,000 after paying taxes (as in the earlier example). You don't just lose the $14,706 from your 401(k); you lose what this money would've been worth by the time you retire. If that money had stayed invested for 30 years with a 9 percent return, it would be worth $195,115. You'll have to substantially increase your contributions to make up this loss by the time you retire.

Dipping into Your 401(k) Money to Buy Your First Home

The tax bite and disruption to your retirement account are two good reasons to avoid a hardship withdrawal, unless, of course, the withdrawal is absolutely necessary. But withdrawing money to buy your first home may be a smart financial decision.

Investing in a home can bring you a good return. Assume that you take a hardship withdrawal of $25,000 at age 35 to buy a $250,000 home with a 30-year mortgage. Assume that the value of your home appreciates at a rate of 3 percent per year. After 30 years, your house would be worth $604,000. Of that, $354,000 is capital appreciation ($604,000 – $250,000).

If the $25,000 had stayed in your 401(k) plan and earned a 9 percent return until you turned 65, it would've grown to $331,667, which is less than the capital appreciation on your house. This is a simplified example to show you the potential value of home ownership.

TIP

If you're using some of your 401(k) money to purchase your first home, take a smart approach that either eliminates or substantially reduces your tax bite: Essentially, you need to buy your home as close to the beginning of the year as possible.

Assume the following:

>> Your first home costs $250,000.

>> You have to withdraw $25,000 to help cover the initial costs.

>> The property taxes are $3,500 per year.

>> The mortgage will be $225,000 at a 3.5 percent interest rate.

>> The settlement date is January 15.

In the year you buy the home, the property taxes you pay will be $3,353, and the mortgage interest will be $7,575, because you will have owned the home for only 11½ months. You start to receive the tax benefits of first-time home ownership by deducting the interest and taxes — $10,928 of deductions that will offset some of the impact of having to add the $25,000 withdrawal from your 401(k) to your total income.

But this strategy only works if you withdraw the $25,000 during the same year that you buy the home. You get less of a benefit the later in the year that you buy the home, because you have to include the full withdrawal in your income. But you can deduct interest and tax payments only for the period that you own the home. The worst case is to buy your home in December because you get the tax break related to home ownership only for part of one month. In this case, you'd have a $25,000 taxable distribution minus a $910 tax break, meaning that $24,090 is taxable income.

TIP

You may have to borrow the money, rather than withdraw it, if your plan gives you both options. Again, this is one of those crazy government things.

Both a Borrower and a Lender Be

Most 401(k) plans allow loans, but your plan may limit your ability to borrow from your 401(k). Your employer may not want you to squander your retirement money on something that's not really a necessity.

The following sections lay out general rules for loans. Keep in mind that the rules for your specific plan may differ.

Giving one good reason . . .

You can take out a loan only if your 401(k) plan document allows you to borrow for the specific reason that you have in mind. Some plans permit borrowing for any reason, but another common approach is to permit loans only for the reasons included on the hardship withdrawal list earlier in this chapter in the section, "Defining a hardship." You can get specific details about account loans from your summary plan description or from your benefits office or 401(k) plan provider.

Figuring out how much you can borrow

The government sets the limits on how much you can borrow. Generally, you're allowed to borrow no more than 50 percent of your account value up to $50,000 maximum. The other half stays in the account as collateral. However (there always seems to be a "however"), government rules permit borrowing 100 percent of an account up to $10,000. For example, if your account value is $15,000, you may be able to borrow $10,000, even though 50 percent of $15,000 is only $7,500. Some plans don't allow this, though — they limit all loans to 50 percent of the account value for the sake of simplicity. Some plans also impose a minimum loan amount because it's not worth the hassle for them to administer a loan for only a few bucks.

Determining how much interest you pay

The interest that you pay on your 401(k) loan is determined by your employer and must be at a level that meets IRS requirements. It's usually the *prime rate* (the interest rate that banks charge the most creditworthy companies) plus 1 or 2 percentage points. In most plans, the interest that you pay goes back into your account, so you're in the interesting position of being both the borrower and the lender (what would Shakespeare have said about *that?*).

Paying the piper: Repayment rules

You normally have to repay the loan within five years, but you can repay it faster if your plan permits. Also, your employer may permit a longer repayment period if the money is used for a home purchase.

Employers usually require you to repay a loan through deductions from your paycheck. The loan repayments are taken out of your paycheck after taxes, not pretax like your original contributions. Then, when you eventually withdraw this money in retirement, you pay tax on it again. I repeat: *You pay tax twice on money used to repay a 401(k) loan.*

WARNING

The fact that most employers require you to pay back the loan with payroll deductions means that if you're laid off or you quit your job, it becomes impossible to keep repaying the loan. What happens then? You have two choices: Either repay the entire outstanding loan balance right away or take the amount as a taxable *distribution* (payment from the account).

If you don't have the money to repay the loan, you must declare the entire unpaid loan balance as income on your tax return. Adding insult to injury, if you're younger than 55 when you leave your job, you'll probably have to pay an early withdrawal penalty of 10 percent. As I explain in the earlier section, "Calculating the tax you owe," this withdrawal penalty hurts. Also check out Chapter 17 for information on an exception to the rule known as 72(t) withdrawals.

If you take a loan, you should be pretty sure that you're going to stay with your employer long enough to repay it. At the very least, try to have a Plan B in the works (other than robbing the nearest bank) to help you scrape together enough money to repay it in full if you're laid off.

To Loan or Not to Loan (To Yourself, That Is)

Although the ability to take a loan is nice in an emergency, don't use the privilege lightly. Taking a loan from your 401(k) rather than from another source has definite disadvantages.

The most attractive feature of a loan is that it isn't taxable when you receive the money.

However, you eventually have to pay tax on the loan. You have to repay the loan and interest with after-tax deductions from your paycheck, so you simply pay tax on the loan every pay period rather than all at once. And when you withdraw money at retirement (including those repayments that were already taxed), you pay income tax again. You're taxed twice on the amount of a loan.

If you can't afford to continue making pre-tax contributions to the 401(k) at the same time that you're repaying the loan, your eventual account balance will be lower than if you hadn't taken the loan. It will be worth much less if you can't afford to pay the loan and to contribute the amount needed to get the maximum employer matching contribution.

Say you're contributing $1,800 a year pre-tax to your 401(k), and you receive an employer matching contribution of $900. If you stop contributing for five years, you lose out on $9,000 of your own contributions ($1,800 × 5) and also on $4,500 in employer matching contributions ($900 × 5). If those amounts are invested in the 401(k) plan over 30 years, with an average return of 9 percent, they will grow to $139,340.

If you take a loan, try to continue making pre-tax contributions to your 401(k) while you're repaying the loan. Doing so will help build up your 401(k) balance over the long run.

Weighing a Hardship Withdrawal versus a Loan

You may come up against a situation where you're required to tap into your 401(k), either by using a hardship withdrawal or a loan, because you have no alternative.

Table 16-1 compares the end result of a loan and a hardship withdrawal on the balance of a hypothetical account after five years. In this case, the person repaying the loan isn't making new contributions to the account. The interest rate for the loan is 4 percent.

TABLE 16-1 **Impact of Loan versus Hardship Withdrawal on Account Balance**

	Loan	Hardship Withdrawal
Beginning account balance	$20,000	$20,000
Amount borrowed or withdrawn	$10,000 (borrowed)	$14,706 (withdrawn to have $10,000 left after tax)
Monthly repayment (loan) or contribution (hardship withdrawal)	$202.76 monthly loan repayment for 60 months	$259.95* monthly contributions for 60 months
Annual investment return	9 percent	9 percent
Balance after five years without employer contribution	$28,545	$24,406
Balance after five years with employer contribution of 50 cents on the dollar	$28,545	$32,780

*Calculating $259.95 times 22 percent (your tax rate) equals $57.19 of tax savings ($259.95 minus $57.19 equals $202.76) — the same amount as the monthly loan repayment.

You can see that the decision regarding whether to take a loan or hardship withdrawal isn't cut-and-dried. If your employer makes a matching contribution, the hardship withdrawal may work out better for you in the long run, if you can't afford to pay the loan and continue making new contributions. However, if you can afford to keep making pre-tax contributions to your account while paying back a loan, the loan may be a better long-term solution. A loan may also work out better if your employer doesn't make matching contributions.

TECHNICAL STUFF

You can withdraw up to 100 percent of your vested account balance for a hardship withdrawal but no more than the amount necessary to meet the financial need. You can borrow 100 percent of the first $10,000 or 50 percent of your vested account balance when it exceeds $20,000. If your account balance is between $10,000 and $20,000, you may borrow $10,000. You can borrow $15,000 if your account balance is $30,000. The maximum amount you may borrow is $50,000. Remember that your plan doesn't have to allow you to make hardship withdrawals and loans and that you'll owe taxes on hardship withdrawals.

Saying No to Yourself

The bottom line is that both loans and hardship withdrawals are much less attractive than they first appear for most purposes. As a result, you should use them only when absolutely necessary rather than as a convenience.

By taking a loan or hardship withdrawal, you're most likely reducing the eventual balance of your retirement account. It may make sense to take money out of your 401(k) to buy a first home because a home generally gives you a good return on your investment. Likewise, borrowing from your 401(k) to start a business may be a smart move if the business does well — but not if it flops.

People also often ask whether to take money out of a 401(k) to pay off credit card debts charging high interest rates. The thinking is that it's better to pay 4 percent interest to yourself (with a 401(k) loan) than 22 percent interest to a credit card company. This may be true, but the danger is that you'll simply rack up more debt, and you'll have no 401(k) to bail you out. If you use 401(k) money to pay off credit card debt, make sure that you cut up your credit cards or that you always pay the full balance each month so that you don't dig yourself back into the same hole.

Chapter **17**

Managing Your Plans after Retirement

L iving out your retirement years is supposed to be easy, but it isn't. It takes careful planning even with good professional help. It occurred to me as I was writing this book that for me it has been similar to running a business. Running a successful business requires having a budget each year. A good business plan includes expected expenses and income for each month of the year. You track both during the year and make adjustments as needed to keep things on track. I do that with my personal planning. I keep monthly tabs to confirm that things are on track. My planning includes the likely sources of income during my 70s and soon-to-be 80s. My gene pool and current health are good; therefore, I may have to keep at this beyond my 80s.

This chapter helps you decide what to do with the money in your retirement accounts when you retire from your job, and how to manage it to give you comfort and peace of mind (and maybe even have a little something left over for your heirs).

Looking Forward to Retirement

Did you ever stop to think how much money you'll need in retirement to keep up your current lifestyle? You need to have realistic goals and prepare to be flexible.

The trick is to try to estimate how big a retirement account you'll need and develop a savings plan to try to accumulate that amount. When you retire, you'll have to manage your nest egg so that you don't run out of money before you die. Chapter 11 explains why and how to set up a savings plan to accumulate ten times the amount you're earning when you retire.

When you retire, your investment job isn't over. In some ways, the job's just beginning. You have to convert your account balance (your *nest egg*) into a healthy income stream that will last the rest of your life. This means that you not only have to decide how to invest your money, but you also have to decide how and when to spend it. Making a bad investment decision or two when you're young is pretty normal and doesn't have to be a tragedy. Chapter 14 shows how losing all your money in one investment and earning nothing on another investment isn't a serious problem if you also have investments that perform well — proving the benefits of diversification.

It's great if you can invest the money in a way that would let you live off the investment income without touching the *principal* (the amount in your nest egg before withdrawing any money), but for most people this isn't possible. You have to spend the principal, as well. Spending your account's principal is often referred to as *drawing down* your account. The trick is spending just enough to make things comfortable but not using everything up before you go to the great beyond.

Note: All the recommendations I provide in this chapter are directed toward individuals, not couples. That's because both you and your spouse need to do your own retirement planning — unless you operate on a combined income. If you and your spouse have joint accounts and a "what's yours is mine" attitude, a combined plan is fine. But remember that, unless you have other resources, both incomes need to be replaced to maintain your lifestyle.

Decisions, Decisions: What to Do with Your 401(k) Money

One of your first decisions as a retiree is what to do with the money in your 401(k). You essentially have two choices with your 401(k):

>> Leave it in the plan.

>> Take it out of the plan.

Well, okay, the choices are a bit more complicated than that. On the first point, you can leave it in the plan if your vested balance is more than $5,000 and you haven't reached the plan's normal retirement age, usually 65. Leaving your money in your former employer's plan is probably fine if you like the 401(k) plan investments and if you're not going to need the money soon. However, remember that the employer can change the plan investments at any time, and you have to go along with it. Also, most plans won't let you take installment payments, so if you need to withdraw some money from the plan, it'll probably be all or nothing.

That brings me to the second option — taking it out of the plan. When you take money out of a 401(k), you have to act carefully to keep taxes and penalties in check. The untaxed amount you take out has to be added on top of your other taxable income for that year.

TIP

The only portion of your account withdrawals that won't be taxable are any Roth contributions you made and the investment income on those contributions. You must have made Roth contributions for at least five years and be over age 59½ to get this tax break. Other withdrawals are taxable, and this additional untaxed income can push you into a higher tax bracket if you have a healthy account balance that you withdraw all at once.

If your plan lets you take installment payments, you can arrange to take out what you need and pay income tax only on that amount each year. (This works until you hit age 72, when you must start taking a *required minimum distribution* each year.) I explain these distributions (RMDs) in the section "Paying Uncle Sam His Due: Required Withdrawals" later in the chapter.

However, most 401(k) plans have an all-or-nothing policy — either leave it in the plan or withdraw a *lump sum* (the entire amount). With all-or-nothing plans, the best solution is generally to transfer the money into an IRA to preserve the tax advantage and withdraw money periodically from the IRA as you need it. Again, you pay income tax only on the amounts that you withdraw, which works out to be less than paying tax on the entire amount all at once.

You may also transfer Roth contributions and the earnings on them into a Roth IRA so this portion of your account will continue to grow without being taxed. You can also convert some or all of your untaxed 401(k) account into a Roth IRA. See Chapter 10 for more details about such a conversion.

TIP

What you decide to do, and when you decide to do it, should depend largely on two factors:

>> Your age when you leave your employer
>> When you plan to start using the money

The next sections explore both points.

Being older can save you money

Your age when you leave your employer is important because it determines whether you have to pay a 10 percent early withdrawal penalty on money you withdraw from the 401(k), in addition to taxes.

If you're at least 55 years old when you leave your employer, you don't have to pay the penalty on money withdrawn from that employer's plan. You still have to pay income tax on the untaxed portion of your account withdrawal, though.

REMEMBER

The exemption from the 10 percent early withdrawal penalty doesn't apply to any untaxed 401(k) money you still have with employers you once worked for but left before turning 55.

If you're under 55 years old when you retire, you will owe a 10 percent early withdrawal penalty on any 401(k) money you withdraw, in addition to taxes. (There are a few exceptions called 72(t) withdrawals, which I explain in the following section.) When you reach age 59½, though, you can withdraw your 401(k) money without a penalty, even if you retired from your employer before age 55.

WARNING

Just to complicate matters, your plan can refuse to let you withdraw money until you are the plan's "normal retirement age," which is often 65. This is unusual but make sure to find out the rules for your plan before you do anything drastic, like retire.

No matter how old you are, you can avoid the early withdrawal penalty tax by rolling over your untaxed 401(k) money into an IRA. Remember, though, that after it's in the IRA, you'll generally owe a 10 percent early withdrawal penalty on any money you withdraw before you turn 59½. (The mysterious 72(t) withdrawal exception, which I explain in the following section, applies here, too.)

Foiling the dreaded early withdrawal penalty

But what if you need your money before age 55 or age 59½? Here's where the 72(t) withdrawals (distributions) come into play — you can use them to avoid the early withdrawal penalty. It's called a Section 72(t) distribution because it comes under that section of the Internal Revenue Code. These distributions are a list of exceptions to the penalty, such as being disabled or having medical expenses exceeding 10 percent of your income (see Chapter 16 for the complete list). However, one of the exceptions, called a SEPP, can be used by anyone. (SEPP stands for substantially equal periodic payments.)

When you use SEPP withdrawals, you set up a schedule of periodic payments that continue for five years or until you're 59½, whichever is longer. Monthly, quarterly, semi-annual, annual, or some other form of equal payments work provided you withdraw the same amount each year. (You determine the amount using an IRS formula based on your life expectancy. Several approved methods exist. The simplest is the same one used to determine required minimum distributions, described in the section "Paying Uncle Sam His Due: Required Withdrawals.") You can set up SEPP payments with your 401(k) if your plan allows these periodic payments. If it doesn't allow them, you can roll your 401(k) balance into an IRA and take the SEPP payments from the IRA.

The three methods for SEPP withdrawals are

» **The amortization method:** Your annual payment is determined by amortizing your balance over a single or joint (you and your spouse) life expectancy. This method produces the largest and most reasonable amount you can remove. The amount is fixed annually.

» **The minimum distribution (or life expectancy method):** This method uses a dividing factor from the IRS's single and joint life expectancy table. This factor is divided into your annual account balance. The annual withdrawals are likely to vary each year but not substantially. The lowest possible amounts can be withdrawn with this method.

» **The annuitization method:** This option requires using an IRS annuity factor to determine a fixed annual payout that typically falls between the other two methods.

TIP

Use a SEPP to avoid the 10 percent penalty tax if you retire before age 55 and start withdrawals from your 401(k) before age 59½, or if you need to make withdrawals from your IRA before age 59½.

WARNING

If you move your 401(k) money into an IRA, remember to have it transferred directly. Don't accept a check made out to you personally. If the 401(k) service provider makes the 401(k) check out to you, 20 percent of the amount must be withheld for taxes. You must make up this difference when depositing the money in the IRA; otherwise, the 20 percent withheld will count as taxable income.

Here's an example of a situation requiring SEPP withdrawals. Say you stop working at age 56 and leave your money in your 401(k). Everything's fine for two years, and then you decide you need to withdraw some money. You don't have to worry about the 10 percent early withdrawal penalty because you were at least 55 years old when you left your employer. However, you still have to think about income tax. If you withdraw the entire 401(k) balance, you'll have a big tax hit. Your employer may allow you to take installment payments from your 401(k) in the amount of your choosing, which would solve your problem. However, if your employer requires you to take a lump-sum withdrawal, what do you do? (If you've read the earlier chapters, I expect you to belt out this refrain like a Broadway chorus by now.) That's right, roll over the 401(k) into an IRA to preserve the tax advantage.

There's one complication, though. (There's always something.) If you take a distribution from an IRA before you're 59½, you have to pay the 10 percent penalty tax. It doesn't matter that you were over 55 when you left your employer. To get the money out of the IRA without the penalty tax, you need to take a Section 72(t) distribution that must continue for at least five years — until you're 63, in this example.

An alternative is to take a partial distribution from your 401(k) for just the amount you need right away, and roll over the rest of the money into an IRA. For example, assume that you have $200,000 in your account, and you need to use $35,000 before you turn 59½. You can take $35,000 (plus enough money to cover the tax) from your 401(k) plan and transfer the rest of the money directly to the IRA.

TIP

I recommend having the bulk of your savings in an IRA after you retire because IRAs give you greater withdrawal flexibility after age 59½ and more investment flexibility than a 401(k).

Leaving money with your former employer

If you don't need to use any of your 401(k) money for retirement income and your account exceeds $5,000, you can leave the money in your 401(k). Your employer can't force you to take the money out prior to your plan's normal retirement age. Participants who are comfortable with the investments they have in their 401(k) and/or who don't like making decisions are more likely to leave their money in the plan. Those who aren't thrilled with their 401(k) investments usually can't wait to get their money out of the plan and into other investments they think are better.

There is no right or wrong decision. Either arrangement is fine if your 401(k) investments are satisfactory. One thing to remember is that money in a 401(k) may have somewhat greater protection from creditors than money in an IRA, depending on your state of residence, should you declare bankruptcy. (IRA protection depends on state law where you live, whereas 401(k) protection is afforded by federal law.)

On the other hand, an IRA offers much greater investment flexibility. An IRA also gives you greater flexibility in naming a beneficiary: You don't have to get your spouse's approval before you can name someone else as beneficiary, as you have to with a 401(k).

TIP

As you decide whether to leave your 401(k) money with your former employer, also consider the fact that the corporate landscape changes constantly. In a continuous merger-and-acquisition climate, I usually advise participants to get their money out of the 401(k) plan as soon as they can. Not only can former employers be elusive, but they can also change your plan investments at any time. Your money can be moved from one set of investments to another without your approval.

Making Withdrawals from Your IRA

You may hold some or all your retirement savings in a traditional and/or Roth IRA. You can withdraw money from either type at any time; however, there are tax penalties if you don't follow the rules that exempt you from a penalty tax. The same rules apply to a traditional IRA as to withdrawing untaxed money from a 401(k), so check "Foiling the Dreaded Early Withdrawal Penalty" earlier in this chapter. *Note:* My comments in this section are limited to IRA withdrawals to provide retirement income. You can make IRA withdrawals for other reasons without tax penalty.

Withdrawals from a Roth IRA aren't taxable if your account is at least five years old. Otherwise, withdrawing any of the investment income means you pay a 10 percent penalty tax on the investment income. Amounts you contributed to a Roth IRA are never taxable because you already paid tax on this money.

You can also take Section 72(t) distributions known as substantially equal periodic payments (SEPP) from your IRA accounts without tax penalty. This is a way to access the money in these accounts prior to age 59½ to generate retirement income without paying a penalty tax. You must follow an IRS-approved specific schedule. There are three different methods, which I cover in the section "Foiling the dreaded early withdrawal penalty." You must stick with the schedule you select for five years or until you reach age 59½, whichever comes later (unless you are disabled or die). A tax penalty will be applied to all payments you have received up to that point if you vary from the schedule.

REMEMBER

A key issue when you have different types of retirement savings accounts is how to manage them. They're much easier to manage when you combine them into one account or at least into one investment organization. You need to put thought into how to generate the amount of retirement income you currently need and to keep doing so.

Never having to pay tax on the investment gains with a Roth IRA is an important issue because you aren't required to take money out of your Roth IRA during your lifetime. As a result, delaying withdrawals from a Roth IRA is usually a great idea; however, withdrawing some nontaxable money from the Roth IRA and taxable money from a traditional IRA or 401(k) gives you less taxable income.

Careful planning will also be necessary if your total income will be coming from your retirement savings during the early years of retirement because you either aren't eligible for Social Security (SS) or because you decide to delay taking your SS benefit. Getting help from a good accountant is advisable.

Paying Uncle Sam His Due: Required Withdrawals

You must begin taking your money out of the 401(k) plan and a traditional IRA by the time you're 72. If you're still working for the employer that maintains the 401(k) plan, you don't have to start withdrawing money until you leave that job. (However, if you own more than 5 percent of the company, the age-72 rule applies, even if you're still working.) The government wants to collect tax on your money at some point, which is why you can't leave it in a 401(k) or traditional IRA forever.

Withdrawals from a Roth IRA aren't required during your lifetime.

REMEMBER

The amount that you're required to withdraw each year from your 401(k) or traditional IRA is called your *required minimum distribution,* or RMD. Again, 72 is the magic age when it comes to your first RMD. The requirement kicks in during the year you turn 72, but you have until April 1 of the following year to take the installment. You then have to take required distributions by December 31 of each year.

WARNING

You have a few extra months to take your first required distribution (until April 1), but because that distribution is for the previous year, you still have to take a second required distribution for the current year before December 31 of that same year. Be aware that the withdrawals increase your taxable income for that year. You may not want to put off taking your first withdrawal.

For example, if you turn 72 in 2023, you have to take your first RMD by April 1, 2024. But you can take it in 2023 if you like. Why would you take it in 2023? Because you'll also have to take a distribution by December 31, 2024, for the year 2024. If you put off your 2023 distribution until 2024, you'll have a higher taxable income that year, all else being equal. You may also have to pay tax on a larger portion of your Social Security benefit if you have more taxable income. See Chapter 2 for more details on taxing your Social Security benefits.

Calculating your RMD isn't terribly difficult if you have the right information. Be prepared to have the following items at hand:

>> **The balance of your retirement account as of December 31 of the year before the one that you're taking the distribution for.** In other words, if you're calculating your 2023 distribution, you need to know your account balance as of December 31, 2022.

>> **The IRS life expectancy tables that apply to you and the correct number for your age.** You can find these tables in a supplement to Publication 590-B (2020), Distributions from Individual Retirement Accounts (IRAs), which is available at www.irs.gov/pub/irs-pdf/p590b.pdf. Use Table III if your spouse is less than ten years younger than you, if you're single, or if you're married but your spouse isn't your named beneficiary. Use Table II if your spouse is more than ten years younger than you and is your sole beneficiary. Don't worry about Table I — it's for beneficiaries who inherit an IRA.

For example, if you reach age 72 during 2021 and are married, and your spouse is 65, use Table III, provided in Table 17-1. On that table, the distribution period for a 72-year-old is 25.6. You divide your account balance by that number, and the result is your required minimum distribution. Say your account balance on December 31, 2021, is $250,000. Your required minimum distribution is $9,765.63 ($250,000 divided by 25.6). That's how much you have to take out the first year. For the following year, you do a new calculation with your updated account balance and the next distribution period number on the table.

TABLE 17-1

IRS Life Expectancy Table III

Age	Distribution Period	Age	Distribution Period
70	27.4	93	9.6
71	26.5	94	9.1
72	25.6	95	8.6
73	24.7	96	8.1
74	23.8	97	7.6
75	22.9	98	7.1
76	22.0	99	6.7
77	21.2	100	6.3
78	20.3	101	5.9
79	19.5	102	5.5
80	18.7	103	5.2
81	17.9	104	4.9
82	17.1	105	4.5
83	16.3	106	4.2
84	15.5	107	3.9
85	14.8	108	3.7
86	14.1	109	3.4
87	13.4	110	3.1
88	12.7	111	2.9
89	12.0	112	2.6
90	11.4	113	2.4
91	10.8	114	2.1
92	10.2	115 and over	1.9

Source: www.irs.gov

REMEMBER

The trustee, custodian, or issuer that held the 401(k) or IRA at the end of the pre-ceding year must either report the amount of the RMD to you or offer to calculate it for you. This entity must include the date the RMD must be distributed. The report is due by January 31 of the year the distribution is required.

By the way, the rules for calculating required minimum distributions are the same whether your money is in a 401(k) or a traditional IRA. And you can always take out more than the required minimum with no penalty. However, if you take out less, the IRS will fine you 50 percent of the required amount that you didn't withdraw.

Developing a Strategy to Deal with the Tax Man

It would be nice if taxes disappeared when you retired, but unfortunately, they don't. The earlier sections of this chapter talk about minimizing taxes when you first move your money out of your retirement fund, but you need to look at a few other situations, too, which I put forth in the following sections.

Which comes first: Plucking the chicken or emptying the nest egg?

You most likely have some money saved in *taxable* (nontax-advantaged) accounts like Roth 401(k) contributions or a Roth IRA as well as in your 401(k) or traditional IRA. How do you decide which money to spend first?

Historically, many professional advisors recommended keeping as much money as possible in a tax-deferred account, even during retirement. The rationale was that you would continue to benefit from the fact that no interest, dividends, or gains were taxable while the money was in the account.

But the game changed in 1984 when Congress revised the tax rules regarding Social Security benefits. Although this tax-deferred advantage is still true, you also have to factor in taxation of your Social Security benefits. When you start receiving Social Security, your benefits are taxed if your income is over certain limits. Non-Roth distributions from a 401(k) or traditional IRA are taxable retirement benefits included in the income you must count to determine what portion, if any, of your Social Security benefits are taxable. So, if you take money out of your 401(k) or traditional IRA when you start receiving Social Security benefits, you may have to pay tax on your Social Security benefits.

TIP

Do some basic planning before deciding on your retirement withdrawals, bearing in mind that receiving income over a certain level means you pay tax on your Social Security benefits. Chapter 2 explains when your Social Security benefits are taxable, and you can check the Social Security Administration website at www.ssa.gov for updates.

If you retire a few years before taking Social Security benefits, you may want to use up your tax-deferred accounts first, rather than your other savings, per the following example that assumes you

>> Retire at age 60

>> Plan to start receiving Social Security benefits when you reach age 62, before you reach your full retirement age

>> Have $150,000 of personal savings

>> Have $350,000 in your retirement account

>> Will need $45,000 of income (after taxes) each of your first two years of retirement (before Social Security kicks in)

You can either use your personal savings or withdraw approximately $50,000 from your retirement account during each of these two years. (I am assuming that a $50,000 withdrawal will leave you about $45,000 after paying taxes. If you have other taxable income, your tax rate may be higher.) Withdrawing the money from your 401(k) right away will reduce the size of the taxable distributions you'll receive after you become eligible for Social Security. It reduces your taxable income after you start to collect Social Security benefits, so perhaps you won't have to pay as much, or any, tax on your benefits. This may be a better tax deal than the tax break you receive by keeping more money in your retirement account. And you'll still have your personal savings available, which you've already paid taxes on.

TIP

You need to do some fairly complex calculations to see what's better in your situation, so I strongly encourage you to consult an experienced accountant or other qualified advisor who does this type of planning.

Dealing with that darned company stock

You need to consider taxes when you decide what to do with the company stock you may have accumulated in your 401(k) account or other employer-sponsored plan, such as an employee stock ownership plan (ESOP). As I discuss in Chapter 13, you get a special tax break when you receive company stock as a distribution. You pay tax only on the value of the stock when it was credited to your plan account, not on its current value. You pay a capital gains tax on the difference whenever you eventually sell the stock. These capital gains taxes are lower than the income taxes you would otherwise pay. Finally, if you pass the stock to your heirs when you die, they won't pay tax on any gains that occurred before it was given to them.

This type of estate planning is feasible only if you don't expect to use the stock during your retirement, and you're willing to take the risk of having a chunk of money tied to one stock for many years.

REMEMBER

Holding stock in an individual company is much riskier than investing in a number of different investments. If you're not sure why, check out Chapter 14.

If you roll your company stock into an IRA, you can sell it and diversify into other investments. You have to pay income tax on your eventual withdrawals. If you take your distribution of stock, you must pay tax on the value of the stock when you received it in the plan. You can then sell the company stock, paying only capital gains tax on the gain, and use the money to invest in more diversified mutual funds or a portfolio of stocks. However, returns on these "taxable" investments will be subject to income tax every year. Still, the benefits of diversification probably make either one of these strategies more palatable than holding on to the company stock, unless you really aren't going to need the money during your lifetime.

REMEMBER

Don't let the tax tail wag the dog. Passing company stock on to your heirs is an instance when tax planning for them may get in the way of good investment planning for you.

Managing Your Investments in Retirement

Investing to build up an adequate retirement nest egg takes most people an entire working career. But, believe it or not, managing your investments is even more critical *during* your retirement years, because what took many years to build can go "poof" in an instant, like one of those big soap bubbles kids blow. When you're younger, you can do some really dumb things and still have time to recover. If your investments lose 20 percent or more when you're 30, it's a non-event. When you're 70, it can be a disaster.

REMEMBER

As a retiree, you really have to pay attention to your investments, so that you can convert your retirement account and other resources into an income stream that will last for the rest of your life.

As you decide how to manage your nest egg during your retirement years, I can't emphasize enough the importance of consulting a professional. This is probably the best investment you can make for your retirement. Ask co-workers, friends, or family members for recommendations on financial professionals in your area. A good resource is www.napfa.org, the website of the National Association of Personal Financial Advisors. Chapter 13 includes more detailed information about advisor services.

Live long and prosper

Maintaining an income stream that will last for the rest of your life is more difficult now than it used to be. A generation or two ago, retirees commonly converted all their available funds into income-producing investments. For most retirees, this meant converting their funds into bank certificates of deposit (CDs). Those who owned stocks typically stuck to the ones that were popular for widows and orphans — in other words, stocks such as utilities that paid high dividends and had a history of steady income with low price fluctuation and modest long-term growth.

Keeping up with inflation wasn't a big deal when the average retiree lived for only 10 to 12 years after retiring. A 3 percent inflation rate reduced the amount of income a retiree can spend by only 23 percent after 10 years.

Today, if you retire during your 50s or early 60s, you need to plan for at least 30 years of retirement income. Your buying power will be reduced by 58 percent after 30 years of inflation at 3 percent. You've probably read that you have to keep some money invested in stocks during your retirement years to help offset the impact of inflation. This advice makes sense because stocks have produced a higher level of return on average than other investments over 20- to 30-year time periods. But you also need to know how much stock, and which types of stock, to own.

Stay practical

WARNING

When you do your retirement planning, don't expect an annual return of 10 percent or higher. Too many 401(k) and IRA investors have come to expect just that during the high-performance 2010s and early 2020s. The stock returns that investors experienced during these years can't continue indefinitely — you can expect a typical market crash. It appeared the crash would happen in 2021 due to the COVID-19 pandemic, and it most likely would have if the Federal Reserve hadn't printed a lot of money. I don't know when the next prolonged, major downturn will occur.

Retirees who were following traditional investment advice during 2008 incurred losses in the 30 percent range. Such a loss shortly after you retire is a horrible way to start your retirement years. More aggressive retiree investors incurred even larger losses.

A $100,000 account that drops to $70,000 due to a 30 percent loss must increase by 43 percent to get back to $100,000. Assume you need to withdraw $4,000 per year from your retirement accounts — the 4 percent generally recommended by investment professionals. You assumed your $100,000 would grow by 6 percent each year. If both happened during the first year of your retirement, you would have roughly $102,000 in your account at the end of the first year. If, instead of a 6 percent gain, you experience a 30 percent loss, your account becomes worth approximately $66,000 after the first year rather than $102,000 — a 55 percent gap from which you most likely will never recover.

It's important to have a plan in place and reserves at the ready in case there is a drop in the market. Read on to find out how to manage your investments when things don't go quite according to plan.

Managing Risk

After all the years you worked hard to reach your retirement goal, you probably want, and deserve, a break that's free of investment stress. I wish I could tell you how this sort of break is possible, but I can't, because it's not. At this point, you need to withdraw money from your account to live. The combination of a low or negative return for a couple of years and regular withdrawals can really disrupt your carefully laid plans.

Balancing investments

One way to avoid having to sell stocks when they're down is to invest about 20 percent of your nest egg in low-risk, fixed-income investments, such as a money market fund or short-term bond fund. Hold these investments in your regular IRA or in a separate IRA. Use this money as a special cash reserve fund during down periods. You can tap this fund rather than be forced to sell stocks and bonds when their value is down.

Imagine you have a retirement nest egg worth $250,000. You withdraw 4 percent, or $10,000, for living expenses the first year. The next year you withdraw $10,300 to keep up with 3 percent inflation. Now say the value of your investments drops 10 percent the first year and another 4 percent the second year. Finally, assume that you based your plan on a 6 percent return during your retirement years.

REMEMBER

If you're particularly thrifty, you may think that you don't need to adjust for inflation. Don't fool yourself. You're not living on the same income now that you had 20 or 30 years ago, and you won't want to live on today's income 30 years from now. Some argue that, despite inflation, expenses decrease during retirement years. That's true for some expenses, but medical expenses usually increase, and you may ultimately need to cover the cost of an assisted-living facility. Keeping some of your investments in stock should help you make up the gap that inflation causes.

A 6 percent return may have looked like a sure thing when you retired, but instead the market drops by 14.6 percent during the first year and gains 10.8 percent the second year as it did in 2008 and 2009. Table 17-2 shows returns for a mutual fund with a 47/53 stock/bond mix that was considered appropriate for a retiree early in the 21st century. Table 17-2 shows the fluctuations in value of a $250,000 nest egg in these circumstances, compared to your original investment plan, which assumes 6 percent gains per year.

TABLE 17-2   ## How Actual Results Can Differ From Your Plan

	Beginning Amount $250,000 Your Plan	Beginning Amount $250,000 Actual Results
Withdrawal Year 1	$10,000	$10,000
Withdrawal Year 2	$10,300	$10,300
Investment gain (or loss) Year 1	$14,700	($35,770)
Investment gain (or loss) Year 2	$14,973	$26,507
Ending balance Year 1	$254,700	$204,230
Ending balance Year 2	$259,373	$215,431

The actual results were a 14.6 percent loss during 2008 and a 10.8 percent gain during 2009. If your plan is based on a 6 percent average annual return, this example shows how badly your plan can be disrupted if the year you retire is when the market crashes.

Although no one can predict when the market will go up and down, you do need a predictable stream of income during your retirement years. But withdrawing money when the value of your investments is declining can be gut-wrenching.

Buying an annuity

Buying a fixed-income annuity is an option to consider if you have less than a few million in assets to provide the retirement income you need.

WARNING

There are many types of annuities on the market. The only one I recommend is a fixed-income annuity that provides a guaranteed monthly income for the rest of your life. A joint life annuity will provide a guaranteed income to both you and a spouse.

The amount you pay to buy a fixed-income annuity depends on your current age, the age when you want the monthly income to begin, and the monthly annuity amount. It costs a lot to buy $1,000 of monthly annuity income when you are age 67 with immediate monthly payments because the insurance company must pay you for the rest of your life — potentially 20 to 30 years.

You can choose from many annuity options:

>> Buy one that starts payments when you retire.

>> Buy one that doesn't start paying you until you reach an older age such as 75 or 80. Doing so will assure you a guaranteed monthly income at that age, reducing the risk that your nest egg will run dry while you are still living.

>> Buy two annuities — one that starts paying when you retire and another one that starts payments during your later years.

A life-income annuity is the reverse of life insurance. With life insurance, you pay premiums each year for a benefit paid to your beneficiaries when you die. This benefit is meant to help replace your lost income. With an annuity you receive monthly benefits for as long as you live. The annuity protects you from living too long. The monthly payments end when you die unless you select one that guarantees an income to a spouse or someone else after you die. You receive the largest monthly benefit if payments end when you die.

REMEMBER

The biggest risk with a life annuity is incurred if you die shortly after buying it, making the insurance company that sold you the annuity the big winner.

Your health and gene pool are factors to consider before buying a fixed income annuity. You need to judge how likely you are to live into your 80s or 90s based on your health and genes.

A lot more needs to be considered about this type of annuity than I can cover in this book. I think "Stan the Annuity Man" has the best information available. Go to www.stantheannuityman.com and order his free books to get access to a lot of good information even if you never buy an annuity from Stan.

The amount of annuity income you get varies a bit by state due to state taxes. Annuity rates also change frequently for a variety of reasons, with changes in interest rates the biggest factor. You can buy a larger annuity income when interest rates are higher because insurance companies factor their expected return into their pricing. Interest rates are low today making it less attractive to buy an annuity. Delaying your annuity purchase is an option to consider if you expect interest rates to go up in the near future.

READ THE CONTRACT BEFORE YOU BUY

I will briefly caution readers about other types of annuities that are marketed to those who are concerned about investment risk. One example is an annuity that enables you to stay invested in stocks and bonds with seemingly little or no downside risk. The sales material for these products is usually difficult to understand, but it makes attractive promises. The investment advisor of a friend recently encouraged him to invest $250,000 of his retirement funds into one of these annuities. I told my friend to get a sample contract from the insurance company before parting with his money. I have had many experiences over the years where insurance companies used what I call weasel language to get off the hook when financial conditions made it tough for them to fulfill their promises.

In this instance, the contract my friend was considering contained a provision permitting the company president, vice president, or secretary to amend the contract at any time without restriction. Language appearing after this sentence makes it look like this contract modification provision is limited to IRS-required changes, but that clearly isn't the case. The company can in fact use this provision to amend the contract at any time however they want.

Insist on getting a sample policy before you ever buy any annuity product. Carefully check the right to amend or modify the contract. Avoid any contracts that enable the company to amend the contract without your approval. Ignore comments such as "Don't worry; they have never done that and/or aren't likely to do it." My response to such a comment is, "Okay, then have the company president give me a letter stating that the company waives all rights to modify or amend my contract."

Take a look at some examples of how annuities work in different situations:

>> **Example #1:** The first example is how much monthly annuity income can be provided for a 65-year-old male with payments starting immediately. The answer on April 19, 2021, was $1,202.87 using $250,000 from an IRA. The $1,202.87 amount will be paid for as long as the buyer lives, and it will end when the buyer dies. A buyer who lives until age 100 would be a big winner.

>> **Example #2:** This example is the same as Example #1 except the monthly payment is reduced to $969.83 so payments continue to the buyer's spouse for the rest of the spouse's lifetime if the spouse outlives the buyer. This is known as a *100 percent joint and survivor annuity*. Monthly payments end when the buyer dies if the spouse pre-deceases the buyer. The buyer isn't permitted to name another joint survivor if the spouse dies prior to the buyer.

> **» Example #3:** This example is the same as Example #1 except the monthly payments are $1,079.51 to the buyer for life, with 50 percent of this amount continuing to the spouse after the buyer's death. This is known as a *50 percent joint and survivor annuity.*

The monthly payment for the above annuity payment options drops to $831.51, $637.26, and $747.79 when a feature is included that will increase the payments by 3 percent each year to help offset the impact of inflation.

Note: In all these examples, I assume the annuity purchase is made using a traditional IRA; therefore, the full annuity payment is taxable.

Consolidating Your Accounts

Many 401(k) and IRA savers have multiple accounts, often including one or more in former employer 401(k) plans. If this is you, you probably won't be able to tell me how these accounts are invested. At best, you may be able to name the investment organization where the money is invested.

Having multiple retirement accounts makes it much more difficult to manage your investments and to plan for retirement. You must decide how to structure your withdrawals when you retire to provide the income you need and to satisfy the minimum withdrawal requirements. Having multiple accounts with different financial organizations makes this much more difficult.

The larger and better financial organizations provide investment and other help when you have an account with them. They usually help you transfer money from a 401(k) or IRA without any additional fee, or you can pay an additional fee to get more extensive help. Such assistance is more effective when you have all or most of your retirement account assets with one organization.

I personally had to deal with this during my early 60s. I was avoiding combining my retirement accounts because I knew it would be a time-consuming and frustrating process. One day I decided to endure the necessary pain to make it happen. It was about as painful as I expected, but it was worth the effort. Having all my retirement accounts at one financial organization made it much easier to make investment decisions and to plan withdrawals.

TIP

When your money is invested with a major financial organization, you can easily transfer money from your account or accounts into your checking account via electronic transfers as needed. You can have a set amount transferred each month without having to do anything once the process is established. Or you can go online or call in to have money transferred as needed.

You can also hire an independent firm to take total control of the transfer process. Retirement Clearinghouse is one I prefer because I know their management team. Their fee to manage the transfer of a single account is $79.00. The fee drops to $49 for the next transaction and is free after that. Retirement Clearing House works directly with the financial institution, making the transfer as stress-free and pleasant as possible. They also don't get paid until the transfer has been completed. Their website is www.rch1.com, and the phone number is 888-600-7655.

Tending to Your Nest Egg

Some people think that they'll never run out of money if the amount they withdraw from their retirement account each year never exceeds their investment return. But how can you do this in years when your return is low or negative? Would you be able to live on 1 percent of your account? (Even with an account of $500,000, that's $5,000 for the entire year.)

Achieving an investment return such as 6 percent is not a given every year. Stock returns can be almost nonexistent even during extended periods. Living through one of these longer-term market funks when you're building your nest egg isn't easy — but it's much more painful when you're retired and watching your account shrink. In addition to good planning, a favorable economy during most of your retirement years will certainly help — but of course, you can't control that.

The recent pandemic is a reminder that we have limited control. The fact that the stock market has performed well after the significant COVID-19–triggered 2020 drop isn't a source of comfort to me because it has been driven by federal fiscal policies that aren't sustainable. As a result, I am not comfortable suggesting that readers approaching retirement or already retired follow traditional investment advice to invest 40 percent in stocks and 60 percent in bonds. Such a mix will leave you exposed to a 20 to 30 percent drop in your account value when the next market drop hits.

I hate to give specific recommendations because they can really be wrong in the short run; however, I recommend considering moving 50 percent of your holdings into cash because a major meltdown can occur soon based on historical records. You won't earn anything currently, but you shouldn't lose anything on the cash portion unless there is a total economic collapse. If that happens, who knows what will be safe? Such a move should cut your losses in half when the next major and prolonged downturn occurs. You will have the opportunity to invest all or a portion of this money in stocks and bonds after the market drops substantially.

Investors at or after retirement age need to be more concerned about protecting the retirement savings they have rather than pursuing higher investment returns.

Buying a fixed income annuity and/or holding a larger than normal portion of your invested assets in cash will provide a greater level of protection. The return on cash investments is crappy currently, but the reduced investment risk may be worth it.

Row, Row, Row Your Boat, Gently Down the Income Stream

Model plans for retirees generally recommend withdrawing only 4 percent per year from their accounts, increasing the withdrawal by 3 percent annually for inflation, and assuming a 6 percent investment return. I agree with such a model except I recommend reducing your expected investment return from 6 percent to 4 percent. Doing so will enable you to invest more conservatively and reduce the likelihood of a 20 to 30 percent drop.

Table 17-3 shows how this strategy would have worked for someone who retired during 2008, the year of the last market crash. At the end of 2021, $209,345 of the original $250,000 is left. The account will run dry during 2036 when the payout will have increased to $22,865 and the owner is 94, assuming the owner was 65 in 2008.

TABLE 17-3   **Planned Withdrawal Strategy**

Year	Beginning Balance	Annual Payout	Investment Return	Year-End Balance
2008	$250,000	$10,000	$9,800	$249,800
2009	$249,800	$10,300	$9,786	$249,286
2010	$249,286	$10,690	$9,758	$248,354
2011	$248,354	$10,927	$9,716	$247,143
2012	$247,143	$11,255	$9,661	$245,549
2013	$245,549	$11,593	$9,590	$243,546
2014	$243,546	$11,941	$9,503	$241,108
2015	$241,108	$12,299	$9,398	$238,207
2016	$238,207	$12,668	$9,275	$234,814
2017	$234,814	$13,048	$9,132	$230,898
2018	$230,898	$13,439	$8,967	$226,426
2019	$226,426	$13,842	$8,780	$221,364
2020	$221,364	$14,248	$8,570	$215,686

REMEMBER

Planning for a 4 percent rather than a 6 percent return frees you to pick investments that have less volatility. To do so, you must be willing to accept less upside potential because protecting rather than growing your investments is more important at this stage of your life. You can do this by investing in one or more mutual funds that have smaller up and down swings.

Table 17-4 shows the actual results rather than a model assuming you retired at the end of 2007 and invested all your retirement savings into a 2010 target date fund. This would have given you the asset mix considered appropriate for a retiree.

TABLE 17-4   **Actual Results for a Target Date Fund**

Year	Beginning Balance	Annual Payout	Return Percentage	Gain or Loss	Ending Balance
2008	$250,000	$10,000	–14.6	–$35,770	$204,230
2009	$204,230	$10,300	10.8	$21,501	$215,431
2010	$215,431	$10,927	5.8	$12,178	$216,682
2011	$216,682	$11,255	2	$4,221	$209,648
2012	$209,648	$11,593	5.3	$10,804	$208,859
2013	$208,859	$11,941	2	$4,058	$200,976
2014	$200,976	$12,299	3.5	$6,819	$195,496
2015	$195,496	$12,668	–3.7	–$6,999	$175,802
2016	$175,802	$13,048	3.2	$6,524	$169,278
2017	$169,278	$13,439	5.6	$9,103	$164,942
2018	$164,942	$13,842	–6.1	–$9,650	$141,450
2019	$141,450	$14,258	10.2	$13,701	$140,893
2020	$140,893	$14,686	5.8	$7,746	$133,953

If I were searching for a fund to invest in today, this fund would be attractive if I looked only at the average investment returns posted for this fund because the one-year return is 17.02, the five-year average return is 6.38, and the ten-year average return is 5.66 percent. Investing in this fund appears to be a great option if I want to achieve a 4 percent average annual return. But the results show I would have had only $133,953 left at the end of 2020. I needed $215,686 at the end of 2020 to be on track with my 4 percent average annual investment return plan. Very scary and much worse for someone who is attempting to get a 6 percent or higher average annual return. These average annual return results show why they aren't helpful when you're deciding how to manage your investments. You need to dig deeper by checking how the funds you are considering performed during the 2008 market crash.

Treating Your Home Like the Asset It Is

When you consider financial resources to fund your retirement, you may also wonder whether to convert your home into an income-producing asset. In some cases, this makes sense, but many people are emotionally attached to their family home and don't want to sell it. You may have to try to take a less emotional look, however, because you may need the equity from your home to achieve a comfortable level of retirement income.

Adding up the expenses

It may be smart to sell your home and use the proceeds to generate income, and then find a place to rent. Why rent if you own a home without a mortgage? Consider that a home is indeed an asset, but it doesn't produce money — it eats it up. It costs a lot of money to live in your home even if you don't have a mortgage. If you own a $300,000 home, your annual costs to maintain it are likely to be pricey:

>> Real estate taxes are probably in the $5,000 range.

>> Homeowner's insurance may be $1,000, more or less.

>> Routine annual maintenance and utilities, such as water, sewer, insurance, and lawn care are probably in the $6,000 range. (Check all your expenditures for a year if these estimates seem high.)

>> Periodic repairs, such as a new roof and indoor and outdoor painting or upkeep.

All told, you probably spend at least $12,000 per year for the privilege of owning your $300,000 home — even with the mortgage fully paid. This additional expense is okay if you have adequate retirement income but is less than okay if your retirement resources are limited. The situation is much worse if you still have mortgage payments.

You can probably find a nice place to rent for $1,500 per month in the same area as your $300,000 home. The rental will cost you $18,000 per year compared to the $12,000 it may cost to live in your present home. You're paying a bit more for the rental, but you don't have the hassle of home ownership. Most importantly, you can reinvest the money from the sale of your home and make up the difference. Investing $300,000 at a 4 percent return gives you an additional $12,000 annually, and you have the $300,000 available as needed.

Making use of your equity

A reverse mortgage or home equity loan are other ways to tap into your home's value if you really want to stay where you are and in the house you own. *Equity* is the difference between what your home is valued at and the amount you owe on it.

Up-front costs for a reverse mortgage are in the $10,000 to $15,000 range. All you get for those fees are the right to draw against your home equity as needed and no repayment schedule. No repayments are due during your lifetime, and you and your spouse can live in the house for the rest of your lives regardless of how long you live. You must keep up with taxes and maintain the home.

I recommend delaying applying for a reverse mortgage until you need to tap into your home equity; however, apply a year or more before you reach this point because the process takes a while.

WARNING

A reverse mortgage may not be in the best interest of your heirs. They may not have much time to pay off the balance after your death. The mortgage holder's primary interest is to get their money out of the property as soon as possible. Getting a price high enough so your heirs get some money usually isn't a concern.

Obtaining a home equity line of credit is another option to consider rather than selling your home. Do this while you're still working because a bank must approve your request based on your ability to repay the loan. Your income while still working should enable you to get the loan approved.

TIP

Save using your home equity loan until the later stage of your life for repayment reasons. Assume you obtain a $100,000 home equity loan when you're age 65 but don't need to use it until you reach age 80. Assume you start drawing $1,000 per month. My bank requires paying back 2 percent of the loan balance plus interest every month. There's usually no fee or only a small one with this type of loan, but monthly repayments are required, and they will grow if you make $1,000 monthly withdrawals. Eventually you will probably need to sell the home because you won't be able to make the monthly payments.

6

Helping Small Employers

Determine your best course for retirement saving if you're a sole entrepreneur or have just a few employees.

Weigh the merits of starting a 401(k) for your business against the flexibility of one of the IRA plans available to you.

Choose the type of 401(k) that suits you best, if you go that way, and make decisions and follow regulations about making employer contributions.

Chapter **18**

Plans from a Small Employer's Perspective

You're the proud, and probably very busy, owner of a small business looking to set up a retirement plan. Not only do you want to save for your own retirement, but you also know that your top-notch employees may move to another company with better benefits if you don't set up something.

This chapter is for owners of small businesses (from one to about 25 employees). It can help you determine which retirement plan will most benefit you and your employees.

Putting in the Effort

For a small employer, the cost and effort involved in establishing a retirement plan can be daunting. The typical small-business owner wears many hats in the start-up stages — which often include human resources manager and chief financial officer — and is usually the one responsible for developing a retirement plan.

As a small-business owner, you need to be extremely well informed before you set up a retirement plan. *You* will be responsible for complying with the law, not the person who sells you the plan or the organization that manages it. If you take time to find out about your retirement plan options — paying special attention to basic legal requirements — you should be able to avoid costly mistakes.

WARNING

Running a retirement plan, particularly a 401(k), can require a lot of your precious time. Don't trust salespeople who tell you otherwise. Beware especially of some internet-based providers who offer to design and get your plan up and running in five minutes — any plan that's hatched in five minutes isn't likely to meet your specific needs and is likely to be fraught with compliance problems. Remember, you're dealing with a bunch of IRS rules, so it can't be that easy!

Should you listen to the person trying to sell you a 401(k) plan? Not necessarily. Starting a retirement plan is a bit more complex than buying your favorite brew at the local gourmet coffee shop. You may be surprised to find out that the 401(k) is not your only retirement plan option — nor is it necessarily your best option. Other types of plans are easier to operate and make more sense for many small companies.

In case you're wondering why you should offer an employer-sponsored retirement plan, consider these points:

>> The most important benefit employees get from a 401(k) is that it can turn spenders into savers by making saving a top priority.

>> It can help you attract and retain good employees. Notice that most employment ads mention offering a 401(k).

Meeting Regular 401(k) Requirements Is a Pain in the Pocketbook

Regular 401(k) plans used by larger companies can be a real pain for a small employer. As an employer, you have to select a plan, decide how to administer it, find a company to provide the investments, comply with paperwork and other regulations, possibly contribute money to your employees' accounts, and so on. This may shock you since I'm known as the "father of 401(k)," but I believe that 401(k) isn't the best type of plan for many small employers, including solo entrepreneurs, family businesses, and other types of small employers.

The compliance requirements for tax-qualified retirement plans such as 401(k)s are very complex. A *tax-qualified plan* is one that gives the employer and employee special tax benefits. In return for these advantages, the employer has to follow (or comply with — hence the term *compliance*) certain rules about how the plan should be operated.

Compliance issues are the dark clouds that hang over any retirement plan. Your tolerance for fulfilling various requirements plays a large part in determining which plan you choose. The first compliance issue relates to employer contributions. This is a big issue for small-business owners, particularly for start-ups. When you have more expenses than revenue, you may not want to make contributions to your employees' retirement plan. But, depending on what plan you choose, you may be required to do so. Check "Finding Alternatives to a 401(k) Plan" later in this chapter for information on IRA-based plans that are simpler than 401(k) plans.

Getting to know ERISA and her requirements

401(k)s are qualified retirement plans subject to all the rules and regulations included in the Employee Retirement Income Security Act (ERISA). Among many other regulations, ERISA imposes fiduciary standards employers must follow including

- » Choosing investments solely considering the best interest of the participants
- » Monitoring these investments
- » Educating participants so they can make informed investment decisions

Dieting won't help top heavy plans

Technically, employers aren't usually required to contribute to their employees' 401(k)s. However, small-business owners are sometimes forced to make employer contributions. This happens when a plan becomes *top heavy* (yes, that's the official term), meaning that more than 60 percent of the money in the plan belongs to the owners of the company and other key employees.

Many organizations that sell 401(k)s to small employers ignore the issue of employer contributions. In my opinion, the first thing to consider when choosing a plan is whether you're likely to end up with a top-heavy plan.

If the plan is top heavy, your company is required to contribute money into each eligible employee's 401(k) account, equal to 3 percent of their pay. You even have to contribute for eligible employees who don't contribute to the plan on their own.

An *eligible employee* is one who has met the eligibility requirements for participating in the plan — for example, one who has worked at the company for the required amount of time. Just because an employee is eligible doesn't necessarily mean that person is actually participating in the plan. I discuss eligibility requirements in more detail in Chapter 5.

The owners of a start-up business usually own more than 60 percent of the plan assets for the first few years of the business because there may be few or no non-key employees. Start-ups often aren't ready to start contributing the minimum 3 percent of each eligible employee's pay that is required when owners and other key employees own more than 60 percent of plan assets.

A small family-held business is often top heavy due to the ratio of family members to non-family employees. The non-key employees in such businesses are likely to be in the lower wage ranges except in the case of a professional or techie business. If that's the case, the family members will probably be limited to lower contribution percentages than desired in order to pass the nondiscrimination tests. The plan will also probably be top heavy requiring a 3 percent minimum employer contribution.

TECHNICAL STUFF

If the combined employee and employer contributions are less than 3 percent for each key employee, the required employer contribution to each eligible non-key employee's account is also less than 3 percent. For example, if the highest contribution for a key employee is 2 percent, your company is required to contribute 2 percent of each eligible non-key employee's pay into the 401(k); if it's 1.5 percent, the required contribution is 1.5 percent, and so on. It is highly unlikely that the combined employee and employer contributions for all key employees will be less than 3 percent; therefore, a 3 percent employer contribution will probably be required if your plan is top heavy.

Key employees include:

>> Officers making over $185,000 for 2020-2021 (adjusted for inflation)

>> Business owners holding more than 5 percent of the stock or capital

>> Owners earning over $150,000 (not adjusted for inflation) and holding more than 1 percent of the stock or capital

TECHNICAL STUFF

In measuring ownership, a participant must include the stock owned by a spouse, children, grandchildren, and parents. This is known as attribution from one family member to another.

ERISA rules require combining commonly controlled businesses. The IRS rules for determining common control are complex and designed to prevent business owners from splitting a business into multiple businesses to provide retirement benefits for some employees but not others.

REMEMBER

As a business owner, you can outsource these responsibilities, but you're still ultimately on the hook for any liability issues. This is why I strongly recommend the non-401(k) alternatives I talk about in the following sections before jumping into a 401(k).

TIP

The probability that you'll end up with a top-heavy plan is high when your company has one or more owners and only a few other employees. If this is the case for you, consider a plan other than a 401(k).

Sticking up for the little guy: Nondiscrimination tests

401(k) plans must pass special nondiscrimination tests at the end of each plan year. (Most plan years run from January 1 to December 31; but you can use a different 12-month period.) The amount contributed by *highly compensated employees* (HCEs) must be compared to the average percentage of pay contributed by those who aren't highly compensated (non-HCEs). (See Chapter 12 to determine whether an employee is highly compensated.)

REMEMBER

In Chapter 12, I explain that the average percentage of pay contributed by HCEs can't be more than 2 percentage points higher than the average percentage of pay contributed by non-HCEs. If eligible non-HCEs as a group contribute 4 percent of salary on average, eligible HCEs may contribute no more than 6 percent. Also, HCE contribution percentages on average can't be more than double non-HCE contribution percentages. So, if eligible non-HCEs contribute 1.5 percent on average, eligible HCEs can contribute only 3 percent (1.5 percent × 2) and not 3.5 percent (1.5 percent + 2 percent).

The nondiscrimination test can result in higher-paid employees not being able to contribute the maximum permitted by federal law ($19,500 for 2021 plus a 6,500 catch-up contribution for those age 50 or older). This catches a lot of people by surprise because they assume that they can always contribute the maximum allowed.

Assume that you're a small-business owner (which makes you an HCE, because you own more than 5 percent of the company), and the eligible non-HCEs in your plan contribute an average of 4 percent of pay. This means that you're permitted to contribute only 6 percent of pay (the non-HCE percentage + 2). If you earn $90,000, you can contribute only $5,400 (6 percent of $90,000) for the year. This amount may be much less than what you wanted to contribute — and it's much less than the maximum amount permitted by federal law.

Nondiscrimination testing of employer matching contributions is also required for employer-matching contributions with a regular 401(k). Failing this test may require a smaller employer matching contribution for HCEs than for the other participants. Not a happy result for HCEs.

TIP

Before you start a 401(k), ask your non-HCEs how much they plan to contribute. This will give you a rough idea of how much you will be permitted to contribute. Typically, the average non-HCE contribution range is 2 to 8 percent of pay. Make sure you have realistic expectations before you decide to go ahead with a plan.

You also need to consider employer contributions. Plans that don't have an employer matching contribution tend to have significantly less employee participation, and employees who do participate contribute less than employees in plans that offer a match. Typically, no more than half of eligible employees contribute when no match is available, while 70 percent or more of eligible employees participate in plans with an employer match of 25 cents on the dollar.

REMEMBER

Participation levels are important, because all eligible employees — even those who don't participate in the plan — must be included when the nondiscrimination tests are performed. Employees who don't contribute pull down the average and reduce the amount that HCEs can contribute.

Another important point is that all eligible employees must be included in the nondiscrimination testing regardless of how many hours they work — unless your plan document has a provision that excludes employees who work less than a specified number of hours. The law requires that you include employees who work at least 1,000 hours during any year, which is an average of just 20 hours per week. This rule usually doesn't help boost contribution rates because part-time employees are less likely to contribute.

The Secure Act requires permitting long-term, part-time employees to participate. Employees who work between 500 and 999 hours per year for three consecutive years must be able to participate beginning in 2024. You can exclude employees younger than 21, and you don't have to vest employer contributions for employees younger than 18. Starting in 2024, you'll be required to give long-term, part-time employees the opportunity to participate, but you don't have to give them employer contributions. You can limit employer contributions to those who work at least 1,000 hours per year; however, you run the risk of disgruntled employees if you decide not to give them employer contributions.

TIP

One way to increase participation in a regular 401(k) is to automatically enroll all eligible employees. The best way to do this is by complying with the eligible automatic contribution arrangements (EACA) that were part of the Pension Protection Act of 2006. An EACA must uniformly apply the plan's default automatic contribution arrangement to all eligible employees after giving them a required notice.

Calculating the bottom line on employer contributions

A matching contribution of 25 cents on the dollar, up to 4 or 6 percent of pay, actually costs you only 1 percent or less of the total payroll. Assume that all your eligible employees combined earn a total of $200,000 per year and contribute an average of 4 percent of pay. Your matching contribution equals one-quarter of the employee contributions, or 1 percent of pay ($2,000). Now say that only 75 percent of your employees participate. You pay less than 1 percent — 0.75 percent, or $750 for every $100,000 of pay. If your eligible employees earn a total of $200,000 a year, the matching contribution will cost you a total of $1,500.

Also, you can make the employer contribution vest over a period of up to three years for cliff vesting or six years for graded vesting. (Check out Chapter 4 for more detailed explanations of cliff and graded vesting.)

REMEMBER

When employees leave your company with unvested contributions, they forfeit those contributions. You can use the forfeited contributions to make matching contributions to your remaining employees' accounts and save some money.

Deciding on other bells and whistles

When starting a 401(k) plan for your business, you need to make decisions about a number of things, such as whether to offer loans and hardship withdrawals, and what vesting schedule to use for your employer matching contributions.

TIP

I generally advise employers who are just starting plans to stay away from offering loans through the 401(k) plan for several reasons:

>> They're hard to administer.

>> No one will have much money to borrow during the first few years.

>> You can add that benefit later. Employers get little (if any) benefit from including loans at the outset, but it can be a nice enhancement to add later.

Virtually all employers permit hardship withdrawals from the start, but they may not let employees withdraw employer contributions. I agree with this approach and usually advise employers to keep their contributions in the plan so that at least that money can provide retirement benefits.

TIP

As for vesting, I generally recommend immediate vesting if the matching contribution is 25 cents on the dollar, or less. Otherwise, I recommend a three-year *cliff-vesting schedule* (0 percent vested for the first three years, and then 100 percent vested after three years).

Comparing 401(k)s

The next sections go through traditional, Safe Harbor, and QACA 401(k) plans. Each has regulations about whether employer contributions are required and if they are, how much they need to be. Plans may have discrimination testing standards. *Nondiscrimination testing* requires tying how much the highly compensated employees may contribute and the employer matching contributions they may receive to the average percentage of pay that the non–highly compensated employees contribute and the matching employer contributions these employees receive. 401(k) plans also have different requirements when it comes to when employer contributions belong to the employee enrolled in the plan. Table 18-1 compares the three different types of 401(k)s.

TABLE 18-1 ## Requirements for Different Types of 401(k) Plans

Type	Employer Contribution	Nondiscrimination Testing	Vesting
Regular	Optional	Yes	3 to 6 years
Safe Harbor	3 or 4%	No	Immediate
QACA	3 or 3.5%	No	2 years

Going it alone: The solo 401(k)

If you're a business owner with no employees who work 1,000 hours or more per year (and no intention to hire any) you can open a one-person 401(k) known as a Solo 401(k). Your business needs to be structured as a sole proprietor or an LLC that's taxed either as a Sub Chapter S or C corporation. The plan can cover both you and your spouse if your spouse earns income from the business, and a business partner can participate as well.

WARNING

Beginning in 2024, the employee rule changes so that any long-term, part-time employees who work 500 or more hours during three consecutive years must be included in the plan.

You can sock away a lot of money for your retirement through a Solo 401(k). The maximum amount you can contribute in 2021 is $58,000.

There are two ways to make contributions to such a plan:

>> Make employee deferral contributions subject to the same limit as a regular 401(k) — $19,500 if you're under age 50 plus a $6,500 catch-up contribution if

you are age 50 or older. *Employee deferrals* are contributions you make by signing a typical 401(k) salary reduction agreement.

There aren't any rules limiting how large a percentage of your pay you can elect to contribute other than 100 percent of your wages for employee deferrals that apply to regular 401(k)s.

>> Have the business make a profit-sharing contribution equal to 25 percent of your W-2 compensation if you are taxed as a Sub S or C corporation. The limit is 20 percent of net income if you're taxed as a sole proprietor.

The combination of employee deferrals and employer contributions may not exceed the $58,000 limit ($64,500 if you're 50 or over) for 2021. All of these limits are adjusted for inflation.

You can elect to have your business operate as a limited liability corporation (LLC) that operates as a Sub S corporation. The W-2 income you take from the LLC governs how much you can contribute.

Assume your W-2 income is $100,000, and you're under age 50. You can contribute $19,500 during 2021 as elective deferrals. This type of contribution must be made during the 2021 calendar year. The LLC may also contribute $25,000 (25 percent of $100,000) as a profit-sharing contribution. This contribution may be made anytime up to the tax-filing deadline for the LLC including any extensions. In this example, you've sheltered $44,500 from taxation as long as your elective deferrals went into the plan as a pre-tax contribution rather than Roth contributions. Your elective deferral contributions may be either pre-tax or Roth contributions. The employer profit-sharing contribution must be a pre-tax contribution.

Choosing a safe harbor in a storm of requirements

A *Safe Harbor 401(k)* or a Qualified Automatic Contribution Arrangement (QACA) 401(k) plan can eliminate the top heavy and nondiscrimination problems associated with a regular 401(k). All you, the employer, have to do is make a mandatory contribution to the plan. The requirements are different for each type of 401(k).

With a Safe Harbor plan, you can choose between two contribution options:

>> A nonmatching contribution of at least 3 percent of pay for every eligible employee

>> A dollar-for-dollar matching contribution of up to 3 percent of pay, plus a 50 percent matching contribution on the next 2 percent of pay that eligible employees contribute.

REMEMBER

The number of eligible employees is generally higher than the number of participating employees. The 3 percent rate will cost 3 percent of each eligible employee's pay. The matching contribution will cost 4 percent of pay — 100 percent of the first 3 percent plus 50 percent of the next 2 percent — if all eligible employees contribute at least 5 percent of pay. The employer contribution is always fully vested with the Safe Harbor 401(k) and after two years with a QACA 401(k).

You have to include provisions in your plan document qualifying your plan as a Safe Harbor plan, and you must notify your employees that it's a Safe Harbor plan. With a Safe Harbor 401(k), the business owner(s) can contribute the federal maximum, regardless of how much the other employees contribute. You don't have to worry about top-heavy and nondiscrimination testing.

The maximum limits for regular and age-50 catch-up contributions to a Safe Harbor 401(k) are the same as for the regular 401(k) plans. Chapter 2 talks more about contribution limits.

The Safe Harbor 401(k) requires a potentially larger matching employer contribution than the QACA 401(k). As an owner, you and all other participants receive this contribution in addition to the amount that you can contribute from your salaries before taxes are taken out. The cost of setting up and running either a Safe Harbor or QACA 401(k) plan is similar to a regular 401(k) except you may get a bit of a break because nondiscrimination testing isn't required.

Spelling out QACA

A QACA (Qualified Automatic Contribution Arrangement) requires automatically enrolling all employees and having them contribute 3 percent of their compensation.

The contribution rate must increase every year, usually by 1 percent per year up to at least 10 percent but not more than 15 percent. The employer contribution must be either of the following:

>> 3 percent of compensation

>> A matching contribution equal to 100 percent of the first 1 percent of compensation plus 50 percent of the next 5 percent of compensation.

The maximum cost to you, the employer, is 3.5 percent with the matching contribution if all eligible employees contribute (1 percent plus 50 percent of the next 5 percent of pay). The employer contribution must be fully vested after two years of service and can't be withdrawn for any financial hardships.

Employees can change their contribution percentages any time, including opting out of the plan rather than sticking with the automatic enrollment percentage. They may also accept or reject the annual contribution increases.

Finding Alternatives to a 401(k) Plan

I have spent the last several years focusing on methods to help small employers work through the maze of employer-sponsored retirement plan alternatives. I have been able to find two ways of setting up a payroll deduction IRA plan with matching employer contributions and ways to package more effectively SEP and Simple IRAs, two other types of IRA-based plans available to small employers.

The top-heavy and nondiscrimination requirements can make 401(k) plans unattractive for small employers, particularly start-ups, family businesses, and other small businesses whose owners earn less than $100,000. (I use $100,000 as a threshold because an owner earning less is unlikely to want to contribute more than what they can contribute to an IRA-based plan.)

FOLLOWING THE RIGHT ADVICE

Small employers tend to follow the advice of a business or family friend when setting up a 401(k). A high level of trust leads them to follow what is recommended without checking out the details. I have seen this happen many times. The following are two recent examples.

The first involves an eight-employee business that was sold a 401(k) that was costing the employer $1,500 plus in annual fees and was costing participants 2.75 percent in annual fees. I helped them change to a Simple-IRA plan eliminating all employer fees and reducing the participant fees to 0.15 percent. The participant fee reduction improved the participants' investment return by 2.6 percent. Such a reduction can result in many years of additional retirement income. The new plan is also much easier for the employer to administer than the 401(k).

The second example involves a web designer netting $65,000 per year. She was able to put $16,000 into a Solo 401(k) and $6,000 into a Roth IRA annually. I initially told her she had received great advice; however, when I dug more deeply, I discovered she was paying $2,450 more in taxes per year than was necessary. And that she was paying her financial advisor 1.75 percent per year for investments she may have acquired for as little as 0.08 percent.

The companies that offer retirement plans to business owners are often interested only in existing plans with lots of money already in them. (That's how they earn their money!) Investment advisors are also trained to sell 401(k)s and the pressure to push 401(k) plans increases as pooled-employer plans gain more attention. (I talk about pooled-employer plans in Chapter 19.)

A growing number of states are requiring employers to establish retirement plans if they don't have one already. Oregon has pioneered this effort, requiring businesses with even one employee to have a plan this year or to start paying a $100-per-employee fine. Oregon established OregonSaves, which is a payroll deduction Roth IRA to help employers establish a plan.

Making it easy with payroll deductions

It's impossible to find an employer-sponsored plan that's easier to set up than a payroll-deduction IRA because there are virtually no rules you have to follow unless you must satisfy a state mandate.

TECHNICAL STUFF

Oregon requires all employers, including even one-employee businesses, to have a retirement plan or to pay a fine; however, Oregon doesn't permit a payroll-deduction IRA other than the OregonSaves plan to qualify as an employer-sponsored plan. Check your state's rules if you're required to offer a plan.

If you're in a state that doesn't have a mandate, a payroll-deduction IRA can cover any employees you want to include — all employers or just certain employees. Keep in mind, however, that the IRS says that if a payroll-deduction IRA is offered to any employees, it should probably be offered to all employees. Employee and any employer contributions are deposited into each participant's IRA.

Employees in a payroll-deduction IRA sign up to contribute a percentage of their pay, just as with a 401(k). This percentage is deducted each pay period by you or the payroll company you use. The contributions are then deposited into the employee's traditional or Roth IRA. The employees can then deduct these contributions from their tax return.

Following are the Department of Labor rules for payroll-deduction IRAs:

>> You may limit contributions to one financial organization you select.

>> If you charge fees for or limit movement to another IRA, you must let employees know about those restrictions before they sign up.

>> As the employer, you must remain neutral about the IRA provider. You can't negotiate for special terms for the employees, try to influence where funds are invested, or receive any compensation except reimbursement for the cost of forwarding the payroll deduction.

The last provision helps you avoid liability exposure by keeping your involvement in the plan to a minimum.

Actions you can take include

>> Providing general information about the payroll-deduction IRA plan and other educational materials that explain why it's important to save, including the advantages of contributing to an IRA

>> Answering employee questions about the payroll deduction plan and referring inquiries to the IRA provider

>> Providing informational materials written by the IRA provider, as long as the materials do not suggest any endorsements by the employer

Make it clear that your role is limited to collecting employee contributions and promptly sending them to the IRA provider.

WARNING

Finding support for setting up and running a payroll-deduction IRA is challenging. The small-business market isn't attractive to the major financial organizations or financial advisors.

That said, currently Charles Schwab doesn't have a minimum for opening an IRA that invests in Schwab-branded mutual funds. The fee for their indexed Target Date Funds is currently only 0.08 percent, making them my first choice for this type of plan despite the fact that they don't currently offer any support for helping set up the plan. But, support in setting up the plan isn't that important because these are all personal IRAs rather than plan-level accounts.

Using an organization like Vanguard is more challenging because they have a $1,000 limit for opening a personal IRA. Using a financial organization with a minimum means you have to deposit the money into a personal non-IRA account until the employee accumulates at least $1,000. At that point, you can open the IRA and deposit all future contributions directly into the IRA.

The state-mandated plans offer limited investment options with fees in the 1 percent per year range. You can set up a payroll-deduction IRA that provides a broad range of investment options with fees as low as 0.8 percent for investments similar to those offered by the state-run plans.

I have written a guide to help small employers set up and operate a payroll-deduction IRA. The guide also contains information about the plan and investing that can be distributed to your employees. The cost is $24.99; email contact@benna401k.com to order a copy.

SIMPLE Simon met a pie man . . .

The SIMPLE IRA is a very good plan for small employers with fewer than 100 employees, particularly during the first couple of years of a new business. SIMPLE stands for Savings Incentive Match Plan for Employees.

You can establish a SIMPLE IRA by completing an IRS Form 5304 – SIMPLE. You shouldn't have to pay any set-up fees, administrative fees, or compliance fees. Avoiding these costs and headaches is a big plus.

WARNING

As an employer, though, you must make a mandatory contribution to each employee's account. You may make either a dollar-for-dollar *matching contribution* to the accounts of only those employees who participate or a *non-matching contribution* for all eligible employees, whether or not they participate in the plan. The matching contribution goes up to 3 percent of pay, although it may be only 1 percent during certain years, which may include the first two years. The non-matching contribution, which covers all eligible employees including those who don't contribute, must be 2 percent of pay. With a SIMPLE IRA, employer contributions are fully vested at all times.

The maximum amount an employee can contribute to a SIMPLE IRA is $13,500 for 2021, plus a $3,000 catch-up contribution if you're 50 or older. Your contribution as an employer is in addition to the employee contribution limits.

Assume you are a 40-year-old small business owner who makes $100,000 from the business. You can contribute $13,500 plus get a $3,000 matching contribution if your plan matches 100 percent of the first 3 percent of your pay for a total of $16,500 per year. An age-50-or-older owner may contribute $16,500 plus get the employer contribution. There probably isn't any reason to consider a 401(k) unless you want to contribute substantially more than these amounts.

You can start a SIMPLE IRA between January 1 and October 1. If you start a new business October 1, you can set up a plan as soon as it's administratively feasible after starting the business.

TIP

The SIMPLE IRA plan is a good starting point for many businesses. You can use it to begin with, and then consider changing to a 401(k) if you have reason to do so, like contributing more than the SIMPLE IRA maximum.

You have to retain a SIMPLE IRA and make all the required contributions for the entire year. If you want to end the plan, you must notify all employees within a reasonable time before November 2 that the plan will be discontinued effective the following January 1.

There isn't any reason to set up a more expensive and much more administratively complex 401(k) plan unless you want to contribute the $19,500 401(k) maximum contribution applicable to a 40-year-old. Whether that's worth doing is questionable in my opinion.

The SIMPLE IRA doesn't require nondiscrimination testing, so you (the owner) and other HCEs can contribute the maximum regardless of how much the lower-paid employees contribute. You don't have to worry about HCE limits or a top-heavy plan. (See the section, "Meeting Regular 401(k) Requirements Is a Pain in the Pocketbook," earlier in this chapter, for more on HCE limits and top-heavy plans.) Another advantage of using the SIMPLE IRA is that you receive the mandatory employer contribution on top of these contribution limits.

Aside from the different contribution limits, other rules for SIMPLE IRAs are the same as for traditional IRAs. One exception is that if you withdraw money within two years of starting the account, you pay a 25 percent early withdrawal penalty rather than the usual 10 percent penalty.

Also, you can make contributions to a traditional or Roth IRA even if you have a SIMPLE. However, your contribution to the traditional IRA won't be deductible if your income is over the limits I discuss in Chapter 2. Sole proprietors and partners deduct their SIMPLE IRA contributions on Form 1040 when they file taxes.

With a SIMPLE IRA, you don't have the responsibility of making decisions about where to invest or what options to offer employees; you just select the financial organization where you want to establish the plan.

In a SIMPLE IRA, the participants pick their own investments. The financial organization you select should offer the same wide range of investments available with personal IRAs including thousands of mutual funds, ETFs (electronically traded funds), stocks, bonds, CDs (certificates of deposit), and more.

Minimum investment requirements are usually waived when participants invest in the financial organization's own funds. Unlike a 401(k), a SIMPLE IRA doesn't require a record keeper, auditor, investment advisor, or a third-party administrator, all of whom have to be paid. This enables participants to invest without any fees other than the standard investment management fees. There aren't any wrap or other extra fees.

Setting up a SIMPLE IRA is much easier than setting up a 401(k); however, it is more complex than the name implies. The name itself leaves something to be desired as well. Ads seeking good employees often include the fact that the employer offers a 401(k) plan. I have never seen one that says the employer offers a SIMPLE IRA plan. The major financial organizations that offer these plans provide basic information, but they don't go beyond that.

I have written a guide that includes more details about designing a plan, setting it up, and marketing it to your employees. The price is $24.99, and the guide may be ordered by emailing contact@benna401k.com.

Contributing the funds with a Simplified Employer Pension (SEP)

Another choice to consider is a Simplified Employee Pension (SEP), also known as a SEP IRA. This may be a good solution if you're your company's only employee, or if your company has several owners and only a few other employees. It, like the SIMPLE IRA, lacks the cost, complexity, and fees of a 401(k) and is a better alternative for many solo entrepreneurs than a Solo 401(k). It's also a better alternative for a small family-owned business than saving for retirement using personal IRAs.

REMEMBER

A SEP is funded entirely by employer contributions. Employees don't make pre-tax contributions of their own.

Because contributions are made entirely by the employer, they're exempt from FICA and other payroll taxes. This is significant because in 2021 Social Security taxes are equal to 15.3 percent of the first $142,800 of your earnings. Consider whether the payroll tax savings will help you fund any contributions to the SEP for other employees. If so, this makes the SEP a good choice for your company, because you can avoid these payroll taxes and the costs of setting up and running a more complex plan.

WARNING

A SEP requires the employer to contribute an equal percentage of pay for each eligible employee. If you're an owner who earns $100,000 and you want to contribute 10 percent to your retirement account, you must also contribute 10 percent of each eligible employee's pay. This may be okay if all or most of the other eligible employees are family members, but it is *not* your best alternative if you have more eligible employees and/or you expect to expand your work force in the future, because it will become very costly for you as the employer.

I recently helped a small family business operated by five family members set up a plan. They had each been contributing $7,000 to personal IRAs. Changing to a SEP-IRA helped them save $5,355 in FICA taxes.

REMEMBER

To set up a SEP, you just need to choose a mutual fund company, bank, brokerage, or other IRA provider that offers SEPs, and fill out a one-page form. You shouldn't have to pay set-up fees or annual fees, or fulfill compliance regulations. You just have to send in the money to be invested in the IRAs. All the advantages of SIMPLE IRAs apply to a SEP IRA. (See "SIMPLE Simon met a pie man . . ." earlier in this chapter.)

The contribution amount is very flexible — up to a maximum of 25 percent of your W-2 income or 20 percent of your net income if you're a sole proprietor (not exceeding $58,000 for 2021) — and there's no required contribution. The employer can make the contribution during the year or wait until the end of the year to determine how much to contribute. You decide how much will be contributed each year, if anything. Each year you can decide how much to contribute for yourself and all other eligible employees.

Employees who are at least 21 years old, worked for you in at least three of the last five years, and received at least $600 in compensation for the year are eligible for the SEP (as of 2021). You can use less restrictive rules, but not more restrictive ones.

I have written a guide to help you set up a SEP IRA including how to make sure you get the biggest tax break. The price is $24.99, and you can order by emailing contact@benna401k.com.

TIP

Rules for withdrawing money from a SEP are the same as those for traditional IRAs. With a SEP you don't have to set up a trust to hold the assets, which frees you from the fiduciary concerns of a 401(k).

A Word about Cost

Many employees have a general perception that a 401(k) doesn't cost their employer anything, because the employer gets a tax deduction for its contribution. It's true that the business can deduct a retirement plan contribution from its taxable income, if it has any, but that covers only a small portion of the cost. And if a business isn't profitable, the employer pays the entire cost of any employer contributions to the 401(k) or an IRA-based plan.

Still, retirement plans aren't too expensive for small employers. Just about every employer can find an affordable alternative. In some instances, you can't afford *not* to have a plan, because you have to hire and keep top-notch employees in a highly competitive market.

Chapter **19**

Offering a 401(k) Plan

I n this chapter, I focus on 401(k) issues that affect small employers from a one-person show to a partnership to a small family-run business to small businesses with fewer than 15 regular, full-time employees.

Meeting the needs of both the company and the employees can be a delicate balancing act. It becomes especially tricky because there are many ways plans can be set up, and lots of financial service companies are vying for retirement-plan business.

This chapter is written to help you clarify the choices. If your company doesn't have a plan, check out Chapter 18 for information about starting a plan. In fact, I strongly recommend doing this before you consider the 401(k) choices here unless you're over 50 and are able to contribute the 2021 $26,000 maximum contribution.

WARNING

Managing retirement funds is a serious matter that can potentially expose the employer to liability. Employees have a very strong interest in the plan. After all, their retirement security is at stake!

First Things First

A 401(k) plan is a big deal to administer. You need an operational structure that begins with deducting contributions from employees' paychecks and goes on to handle everything up to and including benefit distributions for departing employees.

When you set up a 401(k) plan, you'll probably have an eye on the bottom line -- how much your company has to pay to set-up and run the plan. After all, the cost has to fit into your budget. However, getting the best deal for your company shouldn't be the major issue when you set up a plan for you and your employees. The best financial deal for your company may prove to be very expensive if it results in a lot of employee dissatisfaction and possibly a lawsuit.

AN AUDIT IS NEVER GOOD NEWS

Employers must administer hardship withdrawals and loans according to the plan document and the applicable regulations. The primary penalty for violating the law is to disqualify your plan, which creates major tax problems for your company and all participants. The company loses the tax deductions it received (for the matching contributions and employee pre-tax contributions it made), and employees lose the benefits, such as the tax-deferral for investment earnings and the opportunity to roll the money over to an IRA, that come with a qualified plan. Disqualification is rare, but that doesn't mean that a company can feel comfortable in blatantly violating the law. Short of total disqualification, other fines, and penalties may apply.

Both the IRS and the DOL are likely to review both your hardship withdrawal and loan procedures if they audit your plan. Here are steps you should take to protect yourself as an employer:

- Keep the application and other paperwork for each hardship withdrawal or loan on file.

- Be sure to get documentation from the participant to support the reason for the withdrawal. For example, if the participant is buying a home, be sure to get a copy of the contract.

- Make sure that all loan applications include the math showing that the amount of the loan doesn't exceed the applicable limits (for example, 50 percent of the account balance).

Many service providers offer streamlined processing for hardship withdrawals and loans. This processing makes both types of transactions faster and easier for your participants, but you're still required to follow the procedures outlined in your plan document.

A few years ago, the DOL audited one of my clients. The agent spent weeks on site going through all the employer's files. Subsequently, the agent sent a letter to the company's CFO, citing a loan violation. The amount that one participant borrowed supposedly exceeded the 50 percent limit. The CFO was very upset because the letter from the DOL made it sound like his company had committed a horrible crime. We discovered that the agent was wrong and we were right — but getting to that point was a big hassle. The agent wasn't very polite about the whole thing, either — my client didn't receive an apology letter after the agent was informed of his error.

You should operate your plan with the awareness that these audits do occur and are not fun. They're exhaustive and exhausting, and they take you away from important business. Do everything you can to avoid an audit. Some audits are random, but others are triggered by red flags, such as an employer that consistently takes much longer than permitted to put employees' money into the plan.

REMEMBER

The IRS and DOL both have the right to audit any employer's 401(k) plan. Such an audit is like a tax audit. Everything is reviewed to see whether the plan is operating within all the applicable laws and regulations. See the nearby sidebar, "An audit is never good news" for a cautionary tale.

The next sections point out important issues to consider — government regulations and money.

Prioritizing employees: Being a fiduciary

ERISA, the Employment Retirement Income Security Act, includes many requirements for retirement plans and the people who run them. One of those requirements is that a company's decisions about plan investments must be made considering solely what's in the employees' best interest — in other words, the plan administrator has a *fiduciary* obligation. You don't run a 401(k) plan to benefit yourself or even your company; you run it to benefit your employees.

WARNING

Many employers have the misperception that selecting an organization or organizations to run a 401(k) plan gets them off the hook with legal requirements and potential liability. Folks, this just ain't so. You can't get out of this responsibility by hiring someone else. It's like paying someone to prepare your tax return: If that person makes a mistake, you're still the one held responsible by the IRS.

A financial advisor or someone else may share the fiduciary responsibility, but the employer has the ultimate responsibility.

A CEO once asked how he can avoid having fiduciary responsibility. I told him the only way was to not have a 401(k) plan. Regulations have changed since then enabling an employer to reduce but not eliminate its ERISA fiduciary responsibility.

REMEMBER

IRA-based plans are not subject to ERISA regulations, so you don't have fiduciary responsibility if your retirement plan is an IRA.

You must monitor the performance of investments offered by your 401(k) plan and make changes when appropriate. Changing plan providers can be a big deal, so do this only if you have a good reason. (For example, your provider may leave the business or be sold, you may outgrow the relationship, the funds may perform badly, be too expensive, or service may be bad.)

Exploring the world of fees

Who pays the plan fees and how are key considerations of any retirement plan? Participant-paid fees are deducted directly or indirectly from 401(k) accounts and reduce investment return. One sure way to improve the investment return is to reduce the fees paid by the participants.

WARNING

Some organizations' representatives may tell you that you don't pay any fees. Don't fall for this line. (You'd be surprised how many intelligent businesspeople do!) There are substantial services associated with running a 401(k), and companies don't provide these services for free. The question isn't *whether* a specific plan provider gets paid, but *how* and *how much* it gets paid.

Revealing the fees (or not)

Retirement plan providers charge fees in one of two ways:

>> **Directly:** You're presented with an invoice.

>> **Indirectly:** Fees are deducted from assets in the plan.

Direct-billed fees are easy to track because they leave a paper trail in the form of invoices. However, asset-based fees may be hidden because they're paid as automatic deductions from the return investors receive on their mutual funds or other investments. The participant has a lower return because these fees are taken out.

REMEMBER

Indirect fees have no direct connection to the actual value of the services provided because they're based on the value of the investments. The fees increase as plan assets grow even though no additional services are provided. Over time, the total fees can become quite excessive unless you renegotiate them.

These fees are buried, so sales representatives can tell companies that they don't pay any fees. This statement is true in the sense that you don't write a check to the particular financial organization. However, money is deducted from the participants' accounts, reducing the value of the accounts.

Fund management fees must be disclosed in the prospectus for *retail mutual funds* (those available to all investors) but not for other types of investments that may be offered to 401(k) participants. The prospectus includes only the investment management fees. It doesn't include information about other 401(k)-related fees. The provider may deduct additional fees directly from the plan.

The Department of Labor (DOL) requires all employers to disclose all fees before participants join the plan. Not surprisingly, higher-cost providers are usually reluctant to disclose their fees, while lower-cost providers are happy to do so. As a result, the DOL Section 408(b)(2) fee-disclosure forms providing the mandated fee information are often difficult to understand.

WARNING

Larger employers also try to comply with the Department of Labor Section 404(c) regulations, which can provide some relief from fiduciary liability for participant-directed investments. Complying with Section 404(c) isn't required, but Section 408(b)(2) fee disclosure is required. These regulations require employers to provide participants with sufficient information to make informed investment decisions. It's obviously difficult to make informed investment decisions without knowing what fees are paid. As an employer, be aware that if your employees aren't fully aware of the fees charged to them, it can result in failure to comply with Sections 404(c) and 408(b)(2).

TECHNICAL STUFF

Fees are expressed in *basis points*, with one basis point equal to 0.01 percent, and 100 basis points equal to 1 percent. Here's an example of how higher fees can affect participants' accounts. Say your plan has 100 participants and $2 million worth of assets. If it's run with fees of 75 basis points (0.75 percent) or less, including all investment and administrative services, the fees total $15,000 or less. However, if a service provider charges fees of 200 basis points (2 percent), annual costs will total $40,000 (2 percent of $2 million). The $25,000 difference goes to the plan provider rather than to the 401(k) participants' accounts (that's $250 less, on average, for each participant), and this shortfall will get bigger along with account balances each year.

Unfortunately, many employers are only concerned about the fees the company pays. These employers fail to realize that they must also effectively manage the fees that participants pay. A good financial deal for the company doesn't have to result in a bad deal for employees. Those with the largest account balances (usually owners and/or senior executives) are impacted the most by high participant fees.

The level of fees participants pay is determined largely by the way the plan is structured and whether you, the employer, pay the non-investment fees. As the employer and sponsor of the plan, you determine how the plan is structured and who pays the non-investment fees.

The participants may pay as much as 2.75 percent for the same funds that are available via another plan provider for as little as 0.15 percent. The way the plan is structured has the biggest impact on the fees the participants pay. More about that later.

Paying — participant versus employer

Assume employees are participants in different 401(k) plans that include the S&P Fortune 500 fund as one of the investments. One of the plans is structured so that all fees are paid by participants. This plan has a recordkeeper, investment advisor, and a third-party administrator. The total fees paid by the participant are 2.5 percent for the S&P Fortune 500 fund.

The other plan is structured so that all non-investment fees are paid by the employer. The fee these participants pay for this fund is 0.04 percent.

A participant in the first plan with a $10,000 investment in the S&P Fortune 500 Index fund pays $250 in fees during the current year. A participant in the second plan with $10,000 invested in the same fund pays only $40 in the current year. The investment return is reduced by the fees that are paid; therefore, the participant with the 2.5 percent fee will receive a 2.46 percent lower investment return resulting in a much smaller nest egg.

Which plan would you rather participate in?

TIP

The best option for the employer is to pay all non-investment fees. The government will help you do that. This will enable you to offer a plan that will cost participants, including the owners, as little as 0.08 percent instead of 1.5 to 2.75 percent of your account balances annually in fees.

Keeping fees at a reasonable level

Your plan should give participants at least as good a deal as they can get investing on their own outside the plan. The only way to accomplish this for a small employer is for the employer to pay all the non-investment fees, which means you need to carefully consider all the fees charged to the plan.

For example, an investor — call him Joe — can buy essentially any mutual fund through an IRA and pay only the regular management fee charged by the mutual fund company. Joe can do research and find funds that cover different investment categories (large-cap stocks, short-term bonds, ETFs, CDs, and so on) and are among the top performers. It doesn't matter if they're from different fund families, because Joe can invest with different fund companies or go to a fund super-market such as Charles Schwab, Vanguard, or Fidelity. In short, Joe has a lot of investment freedom in his IRA. Joe should be able to get at least as good a financial result through his 401(k) — a broad range of quality funds with total fees equal to what he would pay investing in his own IRA.

He can, in fact, invest in index target date mutual funds (increasingly the most popular 401(k) investment option) for as little as 0.08 percent. The same type of funds offered in a small employer's 401(k) can cost between 1.5 and 2.75 percent, unless the employer pays all the plan's administrative fees. Paying 2.75 percent in annual fees instead of 0.08 percent greatly reduces the value of a 401(k) even when there is a matching contribution. A 50 percent matching employer contribution is a great benefit; however, paying 2.67 (2.75 minus 0.8) more in fees each year for 30 years of participation in a 401(k) plan greatly reduces this wonderful benefit.

Choosing a 401(k) Provider

Getting good advice is challenging for small employers starting a 401(k) plan because the major service providers and qualified financial advisors want plans with $10 million or more of plan assets. Plans with $1 million to $10 million in assets are targeted by insurance companies offering bundled packages that usually involve a financial advisor and third-party administrator. The total fees paid by the participants for this combination of service providers usually are in the 1.75 to 2.75 percent range. The market is much more limited for small employers who are starting a plan that doesn't have any assets.

Employers commonly make bad decisions when they pick their first provider, but they get smart after changing providers a time or two. Employers who are with the top providers tend to change less frequently. Managing the administrative process during a change of providers is challenging for many reasons. Use the information I have provided in this book to select the best plan for your business and to set it up, so it is good for your business and the participants.

Getting up close and personal — why you shouldn't

Small employers are commonly sold a 401(k) plan from someone the business owner knows. In such instances, the business owner typically agrees to whatever their friend or acquaintance recommends, so it's not an informed decision.

A personal friend who is a broker, financial advisor, or 401(k) consultant can add value to the selection process and to your participants, but you need to know what you're buying and have solid reasons for your decision. All costs should be revealed, so you and your participants can evaluate costs versus the services the friend provides.

The most common mistake employers make is to let a personal relationship, rather than economics, influence the selection of a 401(k) plan provider. I have heard stories from participants about bad plans that were run by a friend/nephew/cousin of the boss. Participants are often afraid to complain for fear of losing their jobs.

Unfortunately, higher-cost 401(k) products are usually sold through personal relationships. Blindly buying a 401(k) product from a friend without comparing it to others isn't a good way to handle the ERISA fiduciary requirement of picking investments that are solely in the best interest of your participants. Thoroughly checking the quality of the investments and all direct and indirect costs is in the best interest of all parties involved — including you.

Streamlining the process with outside help

Fees and investment options are not the only things to consider when setting up a 401(k) plan. Streamlined administrative processing is important especially to small businesses that don't have the staff to take on these tasks. Following are ways to streamline the administrative process:

>> Complete online enrollment of participants.

>> Automate payroll deduction of employee contributions, including the data needed to make the payroll deductions.

>> Compute the amount of employer matching and other contributions.

>> Submit employee and employer contributions and investment splits to the record keeper electronically.

>> Monitor maximum employee and employer contribution limits.

>> Provide participants with unlimited online access to account information, including investment information and the ability to change their contribution rate and investments.

>> Automate distribution of all required information to participants, including all the information that must be provided to a participant leaving the plan.

>> Complete Form 5500, an annual reporting form for 401(k) plans to provide specific information to the IRS and DOL. The specific requirements have been and still are in a state of flux; therefore, check the requirements each year.

TECHNICAL STUFF

Currently Form 5500 is required for plans with 100 or more employees, Form 5500-SF is required for 401(k) plans with less than 100 employees, and Form 5500-EZ for a one-participant plan with $250,000 or more of assets. An audit is required if your plan has 100 or more participants. If an audit is required, hire an independent accountant to provide that service.

You can hire a payroll service that integrates these and other 401(k) services with your business's payroll processing. Paychex and APD are the two largest companies providing these and other human resource and benefit outsourcing services for small and medium-sized businesses. One of these businesses can provide all the support you need to start and run a 401(k) plan with or without using a financial advisor. There are also smaller regional firms that can provide 401(k) support; however, you'll probably need an investment advisor and third-party administrator.

Online 401(k) service providers were created to help small businesses start their plans. The employer pays the fees needed to set up and administer the plan. Guideline (www.guideline.com) is one such provider. Their fee for setting up a plan is $500, and the administrative fees are $49 per month plus $8 per active participant per month. Their annual administrative fees for a plan with 10 active participants are $1,548 ($49 plus $8 times 10 times 12).

Guideline also offers

>> A wide range of mutual funds including six managed portfolios that are invested in Vanguard mutual funds that cost only 0.15 percent

>> Direct links to some payroll companies making it easier to streamline the administrative process

Guideline also offers two other levels of service with higher fees and a wider range of plan design options and other additional services. The monthly fee is $79 or $129 for these two tiers, and the active participant fee is still $8 per month.

The $49 base fee option is a good alternative for a new 401(k) plan. Giving participants access to the structured portfolios provides participants sufficient investment flexibility at a cost of only 0.15 percent. That's certainly much better than the plans offered by most of the major service providers that are in the small employer market.

WARNING

When you contact Guideline or any other 401(k) service provider, keep in mind that their primary goal is to sell you their services, which requires getting you to buy a 401(k) plan — even if an IRA-based plan may be a better alternative.

CHOOSING THE WRONG PLAN, THEN GETTING IT RIGHT

I often find examples of small businesses that shouldn't have been sold a 401(k) plan. Here's one example:

Not long ago I helped a small business with eight employees move from a 401(k) plan to an IRA-based plan. The employer was paying $1,500 in fixed annual fees. The participants were paying 2.75 percent annually. The employer had to pay additional fees when the plan had to be amended and when other services were required.

The business's financial manager used one of my $24.99 IRA-based plan guides to change to an IRA-based plan. All employer fees were eliminated, and the participant fees were reduced to 0.15 percent for investments, which was similar to those in the 401(k). Participants also gained access to an unlimited range of investments if they wanted to take advantage of this flexibility.

Some other things that were eliminated include

- Annual filing of Form 5500

- Summary Annual Reports

- Paperwork when employees terminate

- Plan amendments

- Employer investment fiduciary responsibility

An IRA-based plan is often the best choice for a small business's retirement plan.

Going to a third party (the second one was lame)

Another option for a business starting a 401(k) is to retain an independent full-service third-party administrator (TPA). A TPA can provide all the services needed to set up and administer a 401(k) other than choosing and overseeing the investments.

The TPA can suggest the investments, but you must decide which investments to offer. The TPA can also recommend an investor advisor if you want someone to help you pick and manage the investments; however, finding a good advisor is difficult for a plan without any assets unless you're willing to pay a fee for this service.

The fee a TPA charges is a bit higher than an online service provider's, but you gain greater plan design and investment flexibility because a TPA enables you to pick any investments that are legally permitted. The plan can be structured to give each participant access to a brokerage account so that everyone has an opportunity to pick their own investments, choosing from thousands of mutual funds, stocks, bonds, EFTs, CDs, and more.

Trident Retirement Services, LLC, is an independent TPA that purchased a TPA I co-founded and managed for many years. Their fee for setting up a 401(k) plan is $1,000. Their annual administrative fee is $2,500 plus $50 per participant. The annual total is $3,000 for a 10-participant plan. The fees are higher for a plan with a brokerage account structure. Their website is www.trident-retirement.com.

REMEMBER

TPAs specialize in this business, so they're usually good at it, but you still need to be as discerning as you would be with any other supplier of a product or service. For example, a TPA may have strong ties to a major financial organization and may encourage you to use 401(k) funds offered by that company. Make it clear early on that you want investment flexibility. If a particular TPA can't give you the investment flexibility you need, consider another one. As a reminder, a TPA that services 401(k)s is interested in selling you a 401(k) and isn't likely to suggest considering an IRA-based plan alternative.

Choosing Investments and Advisors for Your 401(k) Plan

The quality of the investments offered in your 401(k) is the most important consideration when running a 401(k) plan. Unfortunately, many other issues commonly overshadow the quality of investments when companies decide how to run their 401(k)s. I recommend putting investing at the top of the list.

Most service providers in the small employer 401(k) market offer mutual funds from the same mutual fund families; therefore, a wide range of similar investments should be available regardless of the organization you select to set up and administer your plan.

A *fund family* is a group of mutual funds offered by an investment company. If you invest only at T. Rowe Price, for example, you'll be limited to funds in the T. Rowe Price family. This choice may be fine with you, or you may prefer to own funds from other companies as well.

TIP

Most 401(k) service providers offer mutual funds from a number of fund families; make diversity of investment choice a priority when selecting a service provider.

Your 401(k) plan should make a wide range of funds available to participants so that they can properly diversify among the various classes of investments. The funds your 401(k) offers in all investment categories (asset classes) should have track records placing them in the top half among their peers or even higher.

Fees for these investments shouldn't be more than what the fund company would charge an investor outside a 401(k). Consider using only plan providers that openly and willingly explain the fees that the employer and participants pay.

401(k) products can be packaged in many different ways, making it difficult to evaluate the various alternatives.

Small business seeking a 401(k) advisor

Determining the number and type of investment choices you want your plan to offer is an important first step in setting up a 401(k) plan. Most employers with millions in assets use an investment advisor to help make these decisions. If you're in this situation, an investment advisor can help you select the funds, choose a service provider, and provide the support participants need. It's common for businesses to seek an investment advisor when their plans grow from nothing into millions of dollars.

TIP

I strongly recommend considering an advisor with years of experience who specializes in the 401(k) market and 401(k) plans.

I also strongly recommend retaining a fiduciary advisor who complies with the Securities and Exchange Commission (SEC) standards that became effective in June 2019.

These standards require an advisor to

>> Act in your best interest

>> Act with undivided loyalty and utmost good faith

>> Provide full and fair disclosure of all material facts, defined as those "a reasonable investor would consider to be important"

>> Not mislead clients

>> Avoid conflicts of interest (such as when the advisor profits more if a client uses one investment over another) and discloses any potential conflicts of interest

>> Not use a client's assets for the advisor's own benefit or the benefit of other clients

TIP

Get a written agreement with the advisor that

>> Explains the services that will be provided

>> Explains how the advisor is compensated

>> States that all services provided will be as a fiduciary following the SEC's fiduciary advisor standards

Selecting the investments

The funds you choose should depend largely on the needs of your participants, including factors such as how many participants you have and their level of investment knowledge.

For example, if most of your participants aren't very interested in or knowledgeable about investments, offer fewer than ten funds so that they won't be overwhelmed. However, this limited menu won't satisfy the investment-savvy folks who are used to sorting through thousands of funds when they invest outside the plan. The easiest answer is to give the investment-savvy participants an unlimited fund menu by offering a mutual fund *brokerage window*. Most 401(k) service providers are able to include a mutual fund window or a full brokerage account that gives participants a wider range of investment choices than a typical limited menu.

Figuring out what types of funds to offer

Participants should have the opportunity to invest in large-cap, mid-cap, and small-cap stocks as well as a bond or stable value fund. (I discuss investment classes and funds in Chapter 13.) A money market fund isn't a good long-term option, but it is a good place to park money during uncertain times. An international stock fund is another alternative many participants like. You should also provide a mix of managed and index stock funds and value and growth funds.

It's important to give participants the opportunity to diversify their investments. By this, I don't just mean that you should offer both stocks and bonds (or other fixed investments), although this is certainly true. I mean that you should offer different types of investments within the stock and bond categories.

After you decide what types of funds to offer, you're ready to consider the specific funds to use. Use an independent investment consultant or research to help you through this process because you can't always rely on the descriptions that come from the fund company.

TIP

Another approach if you're starting a plan and want to keep it simple, is to include only *Target Date Funds* (TDFs) for investing and a money market fund for parking money short term. TDFs are mutual funds geared toward and named with a target retirement year, such as 2025, 2040, and so on. Each fund holds a wide array of different stocks and bonds. A participant can easily invest in one of these funds without having lots of investment knowledge.

An easy way out if you're starting a plan is to use a payroll provider such as Paychex or an online 401(k) service provider like Guideline and to include only TDFs or other structured funds.

REMEMBER

Participants need to understand these are funds that will go up and down in value — sometimes substantially.

Establishing your investments in this manner gives you substantial fiduciary liability protection. The Pension Protection Act of 2006 includes a provision for Qualified Default Investment Alternatives (QDIA). Participants who fail to submit their investment options can be placed into QDIA. TDFs qualify as QDIAs. As a result, limiting your plan's investments to TDFs limits your liability exposure because participants are limited to QDIA investments. Doing so also greatly reduces your responsibility to provide sufficient information to participants to help them make informed investment decisions because they won't be building their own portfolios. They don't need to know the difference between large-, mid- and small-cap stocks, and so on because the investment vehicles are determined by the company offering the TDF.

Many financial advisors aren't thrilled about TDFs because they eliminate the need to hire a financial advisor to help pick and oversee a 401(k) investment menu. Picking index TDFs offered by Charles Schwab or Vanguard enables you to provide solid investment alternatives to your participants with fees in the 0.08 to 0.14 percent range rather than the 2 percent and up fee range that is typical with small employer 401(k)s.

Wrapping Up a Package of 401(k) Plans

Some providers offer to run 401(k)s without charging employers any fees. Not surprisingly, these providers win most of the business. You may wonder how they can survive without charging you a fee. The answer is that your plan does pay fees, indirectly. (Check "Revealing the fees (or not)" earlier in this chapter.) In this section, I help you understand the most common ways 401(k) products are packaged.

Major mutual fund companies such as Fidelity, Putnam, T. Rowe Price, and Vanguard control a large segment of the 401(k) business. These fund companies offer full-service *(bundled)* 401(k) products that provide everything you need. If your plan is large enough and has high average account balances, Fidelity, Putnam, and T. Rowe Price will run the plan without charging any fees other than the normal fund management fees. (*Fund management fees* are deducted by the fund company, reducing participants' returns.) Vanguard actually reduces its fund management fees for larger investors. As a result, it may charge participants fees for non-investment 401(k) services such as record keeping and compliance testing. (All fee information was correct at the time of writing, but it may, of course, change.)

For example, the funds you select with Fidelity, Putnam, and T. Rowe Price may charge investment fees averaging around 90 basis points (0.90 percent). If your plan has $30 million of assets, the fees are $270,000 per year. The fund mix you select with Vanguard may average 30 basis points (0.30 percent), or only $90,000. This is why Vanguard may have to charge additional fees for non-investment services.

The fees for non-investment services can be paid from plan assets — in other words, they can be paid from participants' accounts rather than by the employer. Assume that Vanguard charges $15,000 in addition to its $90,000 in investment management fees. That's a total of $105,000. If this money is deducted from plan assets, the total cost to the participant rises to 35 basis points (0.35 percent) — still much lower than what the other fund companies charge.

The point is that you don't have to select higher-priced funds for your participants in order to give yourself (the employer) a break from paying fees. If you select funds with lower investment management fees, any additional administrative fees can be paid by the plan rather than by you, the employer. This can substantially reduce the cost to participants without changing your cost. This is an example of a win-win strategy for both participants and employers.

Of course, fees aren't the only reason for selecting a particular investment. The ultimate goal is to get the best investment return for your participants, which means that you must consider the actual net return after expenses.

The previous example is just that — an example. The situation for your particular company may be different. Be sure to do thorough research before selecting the firm or firms to provide 401(k) services for your company.

Most of you run plans that are a lot smaller than $30 million. Your plan may be so small that none of the fund companies I mention earlier in this section want to handle it. For example, assume that your plan is in the $1 million to $5 million range. The people calling you get paid for selling 401(k) plans. They usually represent a group of providers offering a product that carries additional *asset-based fees* (fees charged as a percentage of the assets in the plan) to cover the compensation paid to the broker and other costs of the provider. These additional charges are usually around 100 to 150 basis points (1 to 1.5 percent). When these fees are added on top of the fund management fees, the total fees are typically in the range of 200 to 250 basis points (2 to 2.5 percent).

If your plan has $5 million of assets, 200 basis points is $100,000 per year — a substantial sum. These fees come directly from plan participants. It's amazing that business-savvy senior executives, who are paying the largest share of these high fees, are willing to accept this result. Your smaller business can avoid large fees with an IRA-based plan, which I talk about in Chapter 18.

TIP

One alternative for avoiding these high fees is to hire a third-party administrator (TPA) to run your plan. (See the section, "Going to a third party (the second one was lame)" earlier in this chapter for more info.) Typically, a TPA charges about $15,000 annually for all non-investment services for a plan with $5 million of assets and 200 participants. Say your current provider is charging 200 basis points (2 percent), or $100,000, in fees for the bundled plan. Further assume that the investment management fees total $50,000 (100 basis points), and the provider charges an additional $50,000 (100 basis points) for non-investment services. You can replace the provider with a TPA that lets you keep the same funds in your plan and lower the total cost of the plan from $100,000 to $65,000 ($50,000 plus $15,000). The additional $35,000 would go directly to your participants.

You may be able to find other ways to lower the plan's costs even further, such as working with the TPA to select lower-cost and better-quality funds.

Joining Up: MEPs, PEPs, and PPPs

How would you like to be part of an MEP (a multiple employer plan), a PEP (a pooled employer plan), or a PPP (a pooled plan provider)? Getting involved in any of these acronym plans gives you and your employees access to a traditional, safe harbor, or QACA 401(k) — the same plans you can choose from if you set up a plan on your own. I talk about the various plans you can offer in Chapter 18.

Benefits of both MEPs and PEPs include the potential for reduced fees, simplified administration, reduced liability, and potential savings.

As a business owner, you're likely to be approached by MEP and PEP marketers at some time. Don't assume that what they're offering is better than what you can do on your own. Check out alternatives rather than making what appears to be an easy decision. MEP and PEP organizations want you to start a 401(k) rather than consider IRA-based alternatives.

TIP

Here is my sales pitch: For a one-time, $200 fee, I will help you decide what type of retirement plan is best for your small business and help you choose one of the 401(k) alternatives or one of the IRA-based alternatives. I have no financial stake in what you decide or in the organization where you decide to set up the plan. I will also help you set up the plan you pick.

Seeking common ground: MEPs

MEPs have been around for many years. A *multiple employer plan* is a retirement plan initiated by two or more unrelated employers. They're available to businesses within a similar industry — auto dealers, construction companies, and so on. The National Auto Dealers Association (NADA) has supported a plan for its members for many years. NADA has assumed the responsibility of selecting the service provider and overseeing their services including pricing. If the structure is already in place, you can move more quickly into the plan set-up stage.

WARNING

A major problem with an MEP is what's known as the "one bad apple" rule. Under this rule, all employers participating in the MEP face consequences if one of the members does something that results in disqualification.

If a plan is disqualified, it loses its tax-favored status. Both the employer and participants suffer tax consequences when this happens. The one bad apple rule can also impact all other employers and participants included in the MEP. The Secure Act provides protection from this rule, hopefully eliminating this problem.

TIP

If you belong to a professional association for your business, check whether one of the membership perks is easy entry into an MEP. Likewise, the ability to join an MEP may be reason enough to become a member of a trade association. I've known auto dealers who joined NADA mainly because it was an easy decision about a retirement plan.

Connecting PEPs and PPPs

A *PEP* is required to follow the same set of regulations and requirements as an MEP except it may include businesses from different industries. A PEP must be administered by a *pooled plan provider* (PPP), which is a financial service company or other entity registered with the Secretary of Labor and the Secretary of the Treasury.

PEPs were included in the Secure Act and became effective on January 1, 2021. The "one bad apple" rule that has been a negative for MEPs doesn't apply to PEPs. PEPs are required to file a single Form 5500 for the PEP, thus eliminating the need for each adopting employer to file a Form 5500. This is a huge plus for employers with 100 or more employees because the Form 5500 requires an independent audit of the 401(k) plan for such employers. Because PEPS are new, they will evolve over time and will grow in popularity if the entities running them deliver the expected benefits.

A 401(k) Is a Terrible Thing to Waste: Educating Employees

If you run your plan on your own, an area where you'll need help is investment education for your employees. One of the many Section 404(c) requirements is to provide adequate information for employees to make informed investment decisions. The TPA that you select may be able to run investment education meetings, but many 401(k) plans don't offer education. If yours doesn't, you'll have to look elsewhere.

TIP

You can check out investment education services via a web search. I don't know any of them; therefore, I can't recommend one. I do recommend, however, finding one that doesn't offer financial services and/or products. That way you don't have to worry that the reason you're being offered a product is because the organization has an interest in offering other services to your participants. Stick to one that provides only educational services.

Chapter **20**

Choosing a Plan for Your Business

R unning a retirement plan is a significant responsibility for any employer. A company isn't required to offer a plan, but if it does, it must comply with the applicable laws and regulations — whether the plan covers only a couple of employees or more than 100,000.

In this chapter, I compare plan options from various types of 401(k)s to various types of IRAs. I also talk about earning credit for setting up a plan.

You're not alone if the first plan you choose isn't the plan you really need. I walk you through the process of switching plans, which isn't pleasant but can be for the best.

Selecting a Plan That's Right for You

Most small businesses want one of the plans that are primarily funded by employee contributions. Each plan has pros and cons. Table 20-1 summarizes the main features of the different plans funded primarily by employee contributions.

TABLE 20-1   **401(k) & IRA Options**

Feature/ Requirement	Regular 401(k)	Safe Harbor 401(k)	QACA 401(k)	SIMPLE IRA	SEP IRA	Payroll Deduction IRA	Solo 401(k)
Maximum under-50 employee contribution	$19,500	$19,500	$19,500	$13,000	25% of W-2	$6,000	$58,000
Maximum 50-and-over employee contribution	$26,000	$26,000	$26,000	$16,000	25% of W-2	$7,000	$64,500
Minimum employer contribution	None*	3%	3%	1 or 2%	0%	0%	0%
Vesting	Up to 6 years	Immediately	2 years	Immediately	Immediately	Immediately	Immediately
Loans	yes	yes	yes	no	no	no	no
Top-heavy rules	yes	no	no	no	no	no	no
Discrimination testing	yes	no	no	no	no	no	no
Set-up fees	yes	yes	yes	no	no	no	yes
Complex document	yes	yes	yes	no	no	no	yes
Form 5500	yes	yes	yes	no	no	no	yes*
Summary plan description	yes	yes	yes	no	no	no	yes
Summary annual report	yes	yes	yes	no	no	no	no
Employee termination paperwork	yes	yes	yes	no	no	no	no
Document amendments	yes	yes	yes	no	no	no	yes
Employer investment responsibility	yes	yes	yes	no	no	no	n/a
Administrative fees	yes	yes	yes	no	no	no	yes

REMEMBER

Form 5500 is required when assets exceed $250,000.

So, how do you choose which type of plan to offer yourself and your employees? Because there are so many options, you have many issues to consider, including the following:

>> **How much do you, the owner, want to save for retirement?** This is important because the maximum amount that can be contributed during 2021 ranges from $6,000 to $58,000.

>> **Do you have employees who work more than 1,000 hours per year?** If you do, you may need to include them.

>> **Do you need a good plan to help you hire and retain the employees required to run a successful business?** Offering a retirement plan can help you attract the quality employees you need, especially if your business is in a competitive or niche field.

>> **How much do you earn from your business?** The amount you may contribute is tied to your earned income.

>> **How long has your business been in existence?** This is important if you have employees because you must be able to meet the same eligibility rules as your employees.

>> **How much do your employees earn?** This is important because higher-paid employees are more likely to contribute. If you have mostly lower-paid employees, they will be less likely to contribute, which will limit how much you can contribute to a regular 401(k).

>> **How much are you willing to contribute for your employees?** If it is less than 2 percent of pay, you need to consider a payroll-deduction IRA or a regular 401(k). If it is 2 percent or more, consider a safe harbor or QACA 401(k) or a SIMPLE IRA (see Chapter 18 for more on those types).

>> **Are you a solo entrepreneur?** If so, a SEP IRA is your best option unless you want to contribute more than 20 percent of your net income, which you can do if you're a sole proprietor or 25 percent of your W-2 if your business is a Sub S or C corporation. A Solo 401(k) is your best option if you want to contribute more.

>> **Are your employees only or mostly family members?** If so, a SEP IRA is a good option because you can structure employees' compensation so that the business will contribute the same percentage of pay for all eligible employees, excluding these contributions from all taxes including FICA.

>> **Do the key employees own 60 percent or more of the plan assets?** If the answer is yes, consider a payroll-deduction IRA, a safe harbor 401(k), a QACA 401(k), or a Simple IRA.

>> **Are you willing to pay the fees necessary to set up and operate a 401(k) and to also deal with the complexity of a 401(k)?** If not, consider one of the IRA-based plan alternatives.

You can change plans at any time; therefore, one type of plan may be best only for a year or two.

Considering Real-Life Examples

Even with all this comparative information, choosing among retirement plan options is often still difficult. The next sections contain examples of small-business owners who found attractive and affordable plans.

Meeting a small business's needs with a SEP

Larry and Helen run a hunting and fishing lodge. They have only one employee, who works less than 500 hours per year, so she isn't eligible for a plan. Larry and Helen each have annual earnings that are less than the Social Security maximum taxable wage base (see Chapter 2 for those limits). As a result, any contributions they make as employee deferrals to either a regular, Safe Harbor, QACA 401(k), or a SIMPLE IRA would be subject to FICA and other employer payroll taxes. Contributions to a SEP aren't subject to these same taxes because the business operates as a chapter S corporation.

They decided to establish a SEP through a mutual fund company. All they had to do was complete one easy form and an IRA application for each of them. Contributions to the plan are deposited into the IRAs set up for this purpose. Larry and Helen can invest in any of the mutual funds, ETFs, stock, bonds, and CDs the company offers for retirement plans. The plan has no set-up fee, no annual fees, and no compliance hassles.

Larry and Helen's business can make contributions during the year, or they wait until the end of the year to determine how much to contribute. The contribution amount is flexible (up to a maximum of 25 percent of their W-2 income), and no contribution is required.

Reaching personal contribution goals with the SIMPLE plan

Manoj and Sarla are medical professionals who have three full-time employees. Manoj and Sarla each have earnings of $170,000. The total gross annual pay for their three employees is $145,000.

The two doctors want to contribute around $17,000 each to a retirement plan. The three employees are willing to contribute a total of $9,800 to the plan. This means Manoj and Sarla will be contributing more than 78 percent of the total employee contributions during the first year. This would create a top-heavy situation with a 401(k) (remember, the cutoff is 60 percent), so their best alternatives are a safe harbor 401(k), QACA, or a Simple IRA.

Each plan would permit them to meet their contribution goals and offer an attractive plan that would help to retain their employees. Manoj and Sarla decide to go with a SIMPLE IRA rather than the safe harbor or QACA 401(k) to avoid the cost of setting up and running a 401(k). Assuming they are each over age 50, the SIMPLE limit for deferrals is $16,500, which gets them close to their desired contribution.

To start the plan, all they did was complete a couple of forms supplied by the financial organization they selected and had each employee, including themselves, complete an IRA application.

Manoj and Sarla decide on a dollar-for-dollar employer matching contribution limited to the first 3 percent of pay.

Table 20-2 shows how Manoj and Sarla's plan works.

TABLE 20-2 **Sample SIMPLE Plan**

Employee	Employee Annual Income	Employee Contribution	Employer Contribution	Total Contribution
Manoj	$170,000	$16,500	$5,100	$21,600
Sarla	$170,000	$16,500	$5,100	$21,600
Lela	$55,000	$4,400	$1,650	$6,050
Alicia	$45,000	$2,700	$1,350	$4,050
Monica	$45,000	$2,700	$1,350	$4,050

Manoj and Sarla's employees, Lela, Alicia, and Monica, can select any of the funds offered by the financial organization that are appropriate for an IRA. The employer simply needs to send the money to be invested each pay period. The participants can go online anytime to access their accounts, change investments, and do much more.

Adopting the standard 401(k) for a growing business

Margaret left her employer six months ago to start her own business producing training programs for the medical community. Her clients are drug companies that want effective educational materials that inform the medical community on how to best use specific drugs. Margaret and an outside investor own the business.

Because her training programs are highly technical, Margaret had to recruit seasoned personnel. During the interview process, she promised candidates that she would set up a 401(k).

Because her business can't handle the additional expense, Margaret isn't willing to make an employer contribution. She's the only participating owner. Three non-owner employees are eligible to participate in the 401(k) plan, and this number is expected to grow. One of the employees earns $95,000 and wants to contribute 10 percent of pay. Another employee earns $55,000 and wants to contribute 8 percent of pay. The third employee isn't interested in participating. The three non-owner employees are contributing an average of 6 percent of pay (10 plus 8 plus 0 equals 18 divided by 3 = 6). The maximum Margaret can contribute is 6 plus 2 or 8 percent because the 401(k) nondiscrimination requirements for a traditional 401(k) limit her to the average percentage of pay the other employees contribute plus 2.

Margaret's contributions are expected to be well below 60 percent of the total employee contributions, so a possible top-heavy status isn't a concern. Table 20-3 summarizes the plan's first-year contributions and shows how employee contributions impact owner contributions.

TABLE 20-3   **How Employee 401(k) Contributions Affect Owner Contributions**

Employee	Employee Annual Income	Dollar Amount Contributed	Percent of Pay Contributed
Margaret	$165,000	13,200	8 percent
Alan	$95,000	$9,000	10 percent
Pen-Li	$55,000	$4,400	8 percent
Cheryl	$40,000	$0	0 percent

Attracting employees with a QACA 401(k)

Rocco and Wes own and run an engineering consulting firm that employs nine other people. The owners are in their fifties and earn $140,000 each. They want to contribute the $19,500 + $6,500 catch-up maximum to their 401(k)s. Rocco and Wes are willing to contribute 3 percent of each eligible employee's pay to help attract and retain good employees in a highly competitive area.

They like a qualified automatic contribution arrangement (QACA) plan because it allows them to contribute the maximum regardless of how much the employees contribute. They like the fact that only employees who contribute get an employer contribution and that it won't be vested until after two years of service. They expect their employees to contribute an average of about 5 percent of pay. As a result of nondiscrimination rules, Rocco and Wes would be able to contribute only about 7 percent of pay — or $10,150 — each to a regular 401(k). The QACA 401(k) allows them to contribute the $19,500 + $6,500 catch-up maximum, regardless of how much the other employees contribute. They and all other participants also receive the employer matching contribution.

Table 20-4 lists the first-year contributions and shows how the combined employee/employer contributions actually work.

TABLE 20-4   Qualified Automatic Contribution Arrangement 401(k) Contributions

Employee	Employee Annual Income	Employee Contribution	Employer Contribution	Total Contribution
Rocco	$145,000	$26,000	$5,075	$31,075
Wes	$145,000	$26,000	$5,075	$31,075
Chitra	$60,000	$3,600	$2,100	$5,700
Willard	$55,000	$3,300	$1,925	$5,225
Denise	$54,000	$2,700	$1,620	$4,320
Laxman	$47,300	$473	$473	$946
Russell	$43,450	$1,304	$869	$2,173
Irene	$36,930	$1,108	$739	$1,847
Darren	$32,110	$321	$321	$642
Sandi	$28,725	$0	$0	$0
Indu	$25,850	$517	$388	$905

Working through all these options isn't easy, and it can take a lot of time. Finding someone who can help a small business that wants to start a plan is also challenging because most financial organizations and financial advisors focus on 401(k) plans as this is the most profitable segment of the market. I am willing to help a small business pick the best plan for a one-time $200 fee. If an IRA-based plan is the best option, you will also receive a guide that will help you set up the plan. Email me at contact@benna401k.com.

Getting Credit to Set Up

The government provides help for employers to set up a 401(k), SEP, SIMPLE IRA, and other types of retirement plans by providing a tax credit of up to $5,000 for three years. The credit may be used for the ordinary and necessary costs of starting and operating a plan. Your business qualifies for the credit if

>> The business had 100 or fewer employees who received at least $5,000 in compensation from the preceding year.

>> The business had at least one plan participant who was a non-highly compensated employee (NHCE) (See Chapter 12 for details about HCEs and NHCEs.)

>> In the three years before the first year you're eligible for the credit, your employees weren't substantially the same employees who received contributions or accrued benefits in another plan sponsored by the business, a member of a controlled group that includes your business, or a predecessor of either.

The rules about controlled businesses are too complex for me to go into here. Just be aware that if you, your spouse, and/or the other owners own more than 50 percent of one business and more than 50 percent of another business, the businesses may be part of a controlled group. Check with your accountant if this may be the case.

The credit is 50 percent of the start-up costs, up to the greater of $500, or the lesser of $250, multiplied by the number of NHCEs who are eligible to participate in the plan or $5,000. First, there must be at least one NHCE participant. If there is at least one, you qualify for at least a $500 credit. If there are more than two NHCEs, then the credit is $250 times the number of NHCEs not to exceed $5,000.

You can claim the credit for ordinary and necessary costs to

>> Set up and administer the plan

>> Educate your employees about the plan

You can claim the credit for each of the first three years, and you may start to claim the credit in the tax year before the plan becomes effective because it takes a while to design and set up a plan. Use Form 8881 to claim the credit.

TECHNICAL STUFF

Tough to understand, right? Just to confuse you further: A business that doesn't have any NHCEs isn't eligible for the credit. A business with one NHCE can claim a $500 credit for each of the first three years. A business with 10 NHCEs can claim a $2,500 ($250 times 10) credit for the first three years.

Changing Service Providers

The need to change service providers is common for a variety of reasons. Costs, investment performance, and poor service are frequent reasons for changing service providers. Selecting a new service provider and smoothly transitioning from one service provider to another isn't easy. It's best to have someone who has lots of experience lead this process — either a fee-for-service consultant or an investment advisor.

Finding a fee-based consultant is challenging because the organizations where they are members permit only members to access their membership directors. These two organizations are the American Society of Pension Professionals and Actuaries and the National Institute of Pension Administrators.

Investment advisors that specialize in the 401(k) business usually have experience in helping employers select new service providers. Obtain a written agreement of what services will be provided and how the advisor will be paid.

Trident Retirement Services, LLC, and Guideline, who I mention in Chapter 19, both have extensive experience handling service provider changes. In both cases, they become the new service provider. Guideline's fees for the first year after the plan is converted are $129 per month plus $8 per active participant per month. You have the option of dropping to the $49 or $79 plus $8 per active participant fee level after the first year. The conversion fee charged by Trident Retirement Services, LLC, is normally $1,000, but it may be more if there are complications.

An independent consultant or investment advisor will help you search for a new provider. Advisors with lots of experience in the business are familiar with numerous service providers. They can determine which ones may be a good fit for your plan. Among the various factors involved are

>> Total asset value

>> Average participant account size

>> Number of participants

>> Total annual contributions

>> Type of employees

>> Services required

>> Desired investment options

TIP

A question I usually ask is, "How high up in the organization can I go if I have a problem?" Encountering problems over several years of administering a 401(k) plan is normal. I knew and had access to the CEO in many instances for the service providers I recommended during my days of providing this type of service.

The process for changing a service provider usually follows these steps:

1. **Notify the old service provider.**

   The change requires transferring the plan assets from the old to the new service provider. You need to inform the old service provider in writing when you have selected the new service provider. The old service provider needs to hand off to the new service provider all plan information including participant account balances, loan information (unpaid loan balances, loan amortization schedules, and so on), and plan documents.

   Both service providers work together to complete the transfer. The old service provider will probably charge an exit fee, and the new one will probably charge a conversion fee.

   The old service provider may or may not regret losing you as a client. In any event they will be cooperative because messing up can expose them legally.

2. **Adopt new plan documents.**

   The new service provider may want you to adopt a new plan document because it's much easier for them to work from their standard plan document than have to struggle through your old one. Plan documents are usually at least 150 pages long, so you can see why working with the old one is more difficult.

TIP

This is a great time for you to consider changes to your plan rather than just keeping all the current plan provisions. I always did this with my clients when they were changing to a new service provider. I provided a summary of the key plan provisions and my recommended changes. I was always able to suggest changes that were incorporated into the new plan document.

3. Select new investment options.

It may or may not be possible to retain all the current investments. It also may or may not be desirable to do so. In fact, I always made the future investment structure the first item to consider before deciding which service providers to pursue. Should the investment menu be restructured? Should the number of options be increased or decreased?

I use one former client as an example: This specific client had a plan with approximately $100 million of plan assets. The investment menu included 12 separate mutual funds plus a group of Target Date Funds (TDFs). A mutual fund window was also available that enabled participants who wanted to pick their own mutual funds to do so. Total participant fees were approximately 0.75 percent annually. I met with the CEO, CFO, and human resource director before doing anything else to discuss the future investment structure. I told them I thought I could greatly simplify the operation of the plan and reduce the cost to the 0.20 to 0.25 percent range. They agreed this would be of interest, which enabled me to hone in on one specific potential service provider.

I was able to successfully move this plan to that service provider and to reduce the cost to 0.20 percent. The new plan investment menu was limited to Target Date Funds plus an open mutual fund window. All participants' accounts were moved into the TDFs. More than 90 percent of the participants left their money invested in the TDFs. The other participants decided to pick their own funds utilizing the mutual fund window.

4. Endure the blackout period.

All activity stops because the old service provider must provide all participant account information to the new service provider. This is impossible to do if there is continuing account activity. This is called a *blackout period* during which participants can't touch their money. Participant accounts must be frozen during the transfer process. This means

- New contributions can't be deposited.
- No investment changes are possible.
- New loans can't be made.
- No benefits can be paid.

The blackout period can last up to two months. Participants must be given written notice of the coming blackout at least 30 days in advance. This gives them an opportunity to consider changes prior to the blackout. Participants must seriously consider the fact that they won't be able to make investment changes during the blackout period. This is a serious issue because the market can drop substantially during the blackout. A participant can cash out and move the entire account into the lowest risk option such as a money market fund; however, doing so will result in a missed opportunity if the market increases a lot during the blackout. As a result, blackouts are troublesome. It is imperative that you make every effort to be sure your participants understand these implications.

5. Manage the transition.

New contributions flow to the new service provider during the blackout period. Determining how they will be invested is another important decision. One option is to have participants submit new investment instructions and to follow them. Another option is to mirror or map the participant's old investment selections and put the money into new funds that are the same or the same type as the current ones.

A decision must also be made regarding how the existing funds will be invested when they are transferred to the new service provider. The new service provider won't be able to end the blackout until it has loaded and reconciled all the transferred participant information. The money will sit in cash unless a different decision is made. This is great if the market drops during this period, but it isn't so good if there is a substantial increase. Sitting in cash simplifies and expedites the transfer process.

6. Reenroll employees.

All eligible employees must be informed of any plan changes plus the new investment options. They need to be told what action to take when the blackout ends, and obviously, they must be told when the blackout has ended giving them access once again to their accounts.

7

The Part of Tens

Find ways to save for retirement.

Get answers to questions about IRAs.

Confirm your choice to join a 401(k) plan.

Chapter **21**

Ten + Two Ways to Save For Retirement

O riginally, the title of this chapter was "Ten Easy Ways to Save for Retirement," but some of these tips require a little time and dedication. But all of them can help you get to your retirement fund goals.

Join an Employer-Based Retirement Plan

Working for an employer that gives you the opportunity to save for retirement is way better than having to do this on your own. Having a retirement savings plan shows that your employer cares about its employees, and this consideration often promotes a good working environment.

Saving becomes the first priority when you join a 401(k) plan. Having a portion of your pay contributed each pay period is the easiest way to save. Otherwise, saving is usually the last thing on your mind. Often, it never happens because there isn't anything left from your paycheck at the end of the month. Getting a matching employer contribution is a big bonus.

Set Up Automatic Withdrawals

You must save for retirement on your own when your employer doesn't offer a plan. An IRA is a great way to do that, so don't miss this opportunity. You can make saving each pay period or month a top priority by setting up automatic transfers from your bank account into your IRA account. This is much easier than waiting to make a year-end contribution.

Start Young

Starting to save for retirement at an early age is important because there are two ways to build a retirement nest egg:

>> The first is contributions you and hopefully your employer make into your 401(k) account or IRA.

>> The second is the investment gains you receive on the invested money.

A dollar invested at age 25 can multiply many times by age 65. A dollar invested at age 55 may not even double by age 65. Start early even if you save only 1 percent of your pay. Then increase the amount by at least 1 percent of your pay each time you get a raise.

Deposit Bonus Money in Your Retirement Account

It may be a huge mental hurdle, but saving a substantial portion of a bonus for retirement is an option worth considering. It requires fighting the urge to do other things with the money, but you won't regret it. I've never met anyone who told me they wish they hadn't saved so much for retirement. I visited a niece yesterday who retired in her early sixties and is helping her parents during the latter stages of their lives. She told me that wouldn't have been possible without her 401(k).

Earmark $20 a Week for Your Retirement Fund

It isn't much, but starting with only $20 per week is $1,000 per year (you can take a couple weeks off your saving plan). This can grow to $490,000 over 40 years assuming a 9 percent average annual return. That won't be enough to retire on 40 years from now, but it's a good start. You can do this regardless of how much you make by eliminating a couple of things a week that you can do without.

Deposit Your Tax Refund into Your Retirement Account

Do you usually get a tax refund because you overpaid your taxes? If so, this is like receiving a bonus because it's also money you can use for purposes other than paying your normal monthly expenses. You have the option of deciding what to do with it. Consider putting some of it in your retirement account.

Cancel Subscriptions You No Longer Use

Magazine subscriptions, online subscriptions, app subscriptions, streaming subscriptions — it's easy to sign up for services that renew automatically. Check your card statement; you may be surprised at what you're still paying for. Cutting out a couple of $5.99 monthly subscriptions and putting that money toward your retirement can provide better entertainment down the road.

Refinance Your Mortgage

Don't do this to increase your mortgage but consider doing it to free up cash each month. For example, if you have owned your home for ten or more years, you can remortgage it taking a longer period to pay off the remaining balance. This reduces your monthly payments enabling you to put more into your retirement savings.

Some financial experts disagree with this suggestion because you'll pay considerably more interest to your lender. They have a point unless you use the reduced monthly payments to invest elsewhere such as your 401(k) or IRA. The investment return on these additional savings should be as much as or possibly more than the additional mortgage interest.

Shop for Better Insurance Rates

I just reduced my auto insurance by approximately 50 percent. If I were younger, this savings could have gone into my retirement account. At my age it is a reduction in expenses, which is a good thing at this stage of life and reduces the amount I need to withdraw from my retirement account.

If you're younger than I am and still looking to boost your retirement savings account, do some comparison shopping. Bundling homeowner and auto insurance can free up some money, as can simply checking the rates you're paying now and seeing whether you can get the same coverage for less money.

Resist Click Bait

Algorithms track your online interests and customize ads specifically for you. Resist the temptation to explore those adorable shoes — you'll only get more ads for adorable shoes.

TIP

Give yourself a click date once a week when you can shop online and explore all the tools, trips, and other tangents that catch your eye. Keep your focus on the main event the rest of the week and cut down on impulse buys.

Think Before You Spend

I learned a long time ago that people are either savers or spenders. Spenders must buy things on a regular basis. As a result, they struggle to save because there just isn't enough money regardless of how much they earn. They keep telling themselves all they need is to earn more; however, earning more doesn't often result in increased savings. This is something to consider when you're looking for a life partner.

Even if you are a spender, you can find many ways to cut down on your spending. Consider whether you really need something and for how long before you pay for it.

If you want a secure financial future, you need to track your expenses, including monitoring those things that you don't really need. I certainly don't like to eat out at places where I pay three times as much for something that I can do rather easily myself.

Reduce Your Transportation Costs

Can you carpool with colleagues? Do you even need to travel to work in a post-pandemic world? If you need to go into the office or into the city periodically, choose public transportation options instead of finding and paying for parking and fuel and wear-and-tear on your vehicle.

If you need to keep a car, check fuel-efficient models or try to downgrade to a less flashy, more economical model. I switched to high-quality used autos years ago after buying many new ones. I now buy models that have great long-term records and that I can get for a fraction of the original cost. This has reduced my car expenses by at least 50 percent, and it has given me cars that I have been able to pass down to various family members.

Chapter 22

Ten Questions about IRAs Answered

A n individual retirement arrangement, commonly called an IRA, is a great way to save money for retirement. This chapter answers some of the common questions about them.

Where can I start an IRA?

Most financial institutions offer IRAs, including banks, insurance companies, mutual fund companies, brokerage firms, credit unions, and brokers. It can be a bit confusing because most institutions offer a wide range of investment products. Some more so than others. For example, a bank is able to offer an IRA that can be invested in mutual funds, and a mutual fund company can offer an IRA that provides a very wide range of investment alternatives including individual stocks and bonds and even certificates of deposit (CDs).

Do I need to hire a broker or financial advisor to start an IRA?

You don't need a broker or financial advisor to open an IRA. A broker or financial advisor can help you decide how to invest your money; however, they don't work for free. They often recommend a managed account that usually is just a mix of mutual funds that have an additional fee other than the mutual fund management fees. You can obtain a similar mix of investments from a mutual fund company without paying any extra fees, and some companies, such as Vanguard and Fidelity, offer a lot more alternatives than just their own mutual funds. They also have staffs that can help you select your investments with or without an extra fee.

How much can I contribute to my IRA?

You can contribute $6,000 per year plus an additional $1,000 if you're 50 or older and if you have at least this amount of taxable income during 2021. The contribution limits are the same for traditional and Roth IRAs.

The amount you can contribute is reduced or eliminated if you or your spouse is covered by an employer-provided retirement plan.

What tax breaks do I get for having an IRA?

You get a tax deduction for contributions you deposit into a traditional IRA, plus your contributions grow without being taxed. All withdrawals are taxable, including a 10 percent penalty tax if they're withdrawn prior to age 59½ unless the withdrawal is for a reason that is exempt from the penalty tax.

Contributions to a Roth IRA aren't tax deductible but they grow without being taxed. Withdrawals aren't taxable if you follow all the rules.

How do I take money out of my IRA?

You can take money out of a traditional IRA or a Roth IRA anytime you want to by notifying the institution that holds your account.

REMEMBER

Taking money out often means tax consequences. Chapter 16 has more information on withdrawal issues.

How much tax do I have to pay when I withdraw money from my IRA?

Withdrawals from a traditional IRA are taxable as part of your adjusted gross income when you file taxes each year. You may also have to pay a 10 percent tax penalty if you withdraw funds prior to age 59½.

Withdrawals from a Roth IRA are not taxable if you are over age 59½, and your account is at least five years old. Withdrawals prior to age 59½ are also not taxed if they are made for certain special reasons. See Chapter 16 for the details.

What can I invest in through my IRA?

You may legally invest in just about anything except life insurance and collectibles. You can invest in real estate; however, you may not receive any direct benefits such as receiving rental income that is paid to you rather than your IRA account, and you may not live in the property. You will need a special custodian rather than a bank or other financial institution when you invest in non-traditional investments.

Having so many options is a huge plus for those of you who like a lot of investment flexibility; however, it can be intimidating if you're not investment savvy. Target Date Maturity mutual funds are an easy solution for those in the latter category because the fund manager puts your money into a broad mix of stocks and bonds that are considered by investment professionals to give you the right mix for your age.

What's the safest way to invest my IRA money?

I have found the biggest fear people have when investing is that they will lose everything. When I speak to an audience of retirement plan investors, I tell them that there isn't any place they can invest their money and be sure they won't be wiped out during a major worldwide financial meltdown like the Great Depression. I then say I know some of you will tell me your money will be safe if you put it into CDs. I then explain that CDs that have federal backing through the Federal Deposit Insurance Company (FDIC) work successfully when the number of bank failures each year are within a predictable range. FDIC protection won't be sufficient during a total economic meltdown.

REMEMBER

The best protection you can have over the long haul is to be widely divested — that is, to be invested in many different things. You can do well even when one or more of your investments are terrible. I can confirm this because I have made some really bad investments; however, I have made enough good ones that I am okay.

Is my IRA insured?

Your IRA receives FDIC protection if you invest in CDs that are FDIC protected. Many CD buyers get them from banks, but FDIC-backed CDs are also available through brokerage firms. However, as I mentioned in the preceding section, the FDIC has limited resources.

Your other IRA investments aren't insured even when you use a bank to buy them.

Can I start an IRA for my spouse and/or children?

There isn't any minimum age for opening a traditional or Roth IRA; however, a child must have earned income to have an account. The account must also have a custodian if the child is a minor. People 18 and older are considered adults in most states, but the age of maturity is 19 or 21 in other states.

You can also open an IRA for a non-employed spouse. The contribution limit is $6,000 under age 50 plus an additional $1,000 when the spouse is age 50 or older during 2021. The employed spouse must have sufficient earned income to cover all the IRA contributions. The employed spouse's participation in a 401(k) can reduce or eliminate the spouse's traditional IRA contribution.

When do I have to start taking money out of my IRA?

Required minimum distributions (RMDs) must begin once you reach age 72 for a traditional IRA. The initial distribution must be taken no later than April 1 of the year following the calendar year during which you reach age 72. There are several different ways of computing the amount that must be withdrawn. No RMDs are required for a Roth IRA until the account holder's death. There is a severe tax penalty for failing to comply with the RMD requirements. Chapter 17 explains RMDs.

Chapter **23**

Ten Reasons to Participate in a 401(k)

Y ou have absolutely no reason not to save for retirement — especially if your employer makes it easy by offering a 401(k) or similar plan.

This chapter offers the obvious and not-so-obvious benefits of 401(k) plans.

You Can't Afford Not To

Most people can find $20 a week if they really try — that's about $1,000 a year. Invest $1,000 a year for 40 years, at a 9 percent annual return, and you end up with $338,000. That's certainly better than nothing — and you'll probably be able to afford to save a larger amount sooner than you think.

Don't make the common mistake of expecting it to get easier to save after you start making more money. It never gets easier, so start now. Most people can find ways to reduce expenses without feeling any pain. See Chapter 11 for some suggestions. Also, a tax credit is available to retirement plan participants with low and moderate incomes. Details are in Chapter 2.

The Stock Market Can Be Your Friend

Although a reluctance to invest in stocks is understandable, it's not a good reason to ignore saving for retirement. Even if your investments don't produce spectacular results, you'll still be a lot better off in your retirement years if you save for retirement than if you spend all the money now.

TIP

401(k)s often offer some investments that aren't stocks. Some may offer a stable value fund and other lower-risk investments. If you're really stock-shy, you can consider lower-risk alternatives available to you. However, remember that historically (on average), stocks have provided the highest return over long time periods than other types of investments and have done the best job of beating inflation, so you should consider including them in your investment portfolio.

The first step to conquering fear is finding out more about what you're afraid of. Part 4 of this book is a good place to start educating yourself about investment basics.

You May Get Contributions from Your Employer

Many employers make what's known as *matching contributions*. These are additional contributions that you get only if you contribute to the plan. The matching contributions usually range from 10 to 100 percent or even more of the amount you contribute. It's usually limited to the first six percent of pay or less of the amount you contribute.

Some employees I meet suspect this matching-funds stuff is too good to be true and believe there must be a catch. There isn't. The only way you lose out is if you don't play — and by play, I mean participate in your employer's 401(k) plan.

Your 401(k) Money Is Placed Safely in a Trust

The money you contribute to a 401(k) is placed in a trust. The assets of the trust don't belong to the company, so they aren't at risk in a bankruptcy. If your employer goes bankrupt, you should eventually get your 401(k) money — although it may take a while. Of course, if you hold company stock in your 401(k), it will be worthless if the company goes out of business.

You can lose contributions that have been deducted from your paycheck but not yet deposited into the 401(k) by your employer. Employers are supposed to deposit contributions into the plan fairly quickly, but some employers violate this requirement. One month's worth of contributions is the most you'd be likely to lose if your employer is making deposits on time.

Any Plan Is Better than No Plan

If you don't like your 401(k) plan because you think that the fees are too high or the investment selection is inadequate, don't simply throw in the towel and not participate.

One strategy you can try is to contribute only enough to get the full company match. (If your employer contributes 50 cents for every dollar you contribute, that's a 50 percent return on your money right there.) Then, contribute the maximum to an IRA as well if you're eligible, to boost your retirement savings. You may not get a tax deduction for the IRA contribution, depending on your salary, but you may be able to contribute to a Roth IRA, which allows tax-free withdrawals. See Part 3 for more details about IRAs. Also, try to convince your employer to improve the plan, as I explain in Chapter 14.

Your Account Is Portable

You may be hesitant to join your 401(k) because you're thinking of changing jobs. Well, unless you have a firm job offer to start next week, I have news for you — things don't always go the way you plan. You may be at your job longer than you think. And when you do change jobs, you can roll over your 401(k) money into your new 401(k) if permitted or an IRA. Take advantage of the opportunity to save for retirement at your current employer, even if it's only for a few more months.

You May Be Able to Take Out a Loan

Most plans permit "hardship withdrawals" and/or loans from your 401(k) for approved purposes, such as higher education expenses, buying a home, or financial hardship. I explain the rules in detail in Chapter 16.

TIP

Consider saving for other purposes in different types of accounts. For example, keep an emergency fund in something easy to access, such as a money market fund. Save for your children's college in a tax-advantaged college savings fund. Then put retirement money into your 401(k) or IRA.

Social Security Isn't Enough

Social Security benefits received during retirement generally replace about 20 to 40 percent of pre-retirement income for someone who retires at Social Security's "normal retirement age." (The higher your pre-retirement income, the lower the percentage replaced by Social Security.) But financial planners estimate that you'll need 70 to 80 percent of your pre-retirement income to have a comfortable retirement.

TIP

If you don't get a pension, you're left with a gap of 30 to 60 percent. A pension benefit, if you have one, may provide an additional 15 to 25 percent, reducing the gap. How do you fill this gap? Unless you have certain wealth from another source, you need to save on your own. The more you save in a 401(k) or other retirement account, the better off you'll be.

The Younger You Start, the More You Can Save

Why start planning now (and deprive yourself of cash every month) for a retirement that's 30 or 40 years away?

To that I answer, *compounding.* Small amounts of money saved regularly over time can grow to large sums, especially in an account like a 401(k) or IRA-based plan that lets you save without paying taxes on your investment gain each year. Invest $1,000 a year from age 20 until age 65, with a 9 percent average return, and you'll end up with $525,000. Start saving five years later, at age 25, and you'll only have about $338,000. See how much better off you are if you start early?

You don't have to start big, either. Just $20 a week adds up to about $1,000 a year. As you move up in your career and your salary increases, you can increase your contributions, as well — especially if you're already in the habit of saving. Participating in the plan makes it even easier because your employer does all the work of deducting and contributing to the plan.

Chapter 11 gives tips for developing a savings plan and examples of the benefits of starting young.

You Can Contribute More as You Get Older

Some people in their 50s and 60s worry that they're starting the retirement savings game too late. If you're just beginning to save at that age, indeed, you have some catching up to do. But guess what? The age-50 catch-up contribution and increasing federal contribution limits that I discuss in Chapter 15 help baby boomers who haven't saved enough for retirement save more.

Don't berate yourself if you're in this situation. The retirement landscape has changed dramatically in the last 10 to 20 years, and many people were caught unaware by the increased need to save for retirement rather than depend on Social Security and a company pension.

TIP

It's never too late to save in a 401(k) or an IRA-based plan. For as long as you work, even if you're older than 70½, you're allowed to contribute to your employer's 401(k) or IRA-based plan provided you don't own 5 percent or more of the business. The important thing is to have a plan. Life goes on whether you're ready or not, so be prepared.

Index

E

P

partial rollovers, IRAs, 120

part-time work, as source of income in retirement, 133

passively managed funds, 161

payroll deduction
  401(k), 10, 17, 56
  IRAs, 17, 254–256

payroll service, as 401(k) provider, 268

Pension Protection Act of 2006, 248, 274

PEP (pooled employer plan), 11, 278

percentage-of-pay limit, contributions, 198, 199

personal IRA, 200

Plan Disclosure Form, 401(k), 82–83

plan document, 401(k), 54

pooled employer plan (PEP), 11, 278

pooled plan provider (PPP), 11, 278

potential annuity income report, 401(k), 83

pre-tax contributions, 198

probate, 35

prospectus, mutual funds, 78

Publication 590, IRS, 98

Q

QACA (Qualified Automatic Contribution Arrangement) plan, 11, 56, 251–253, 285–286

QCDs (qualified charitable distributions), 39–42
  donor-advised funds, 40
  overview, 39
  RMDs and, 40–41
  taxes, 41–42

QCE (qualified charitable entity), 40

QDIA (Qualified Default Investment Alternatives), 274

QMAC (qualified matching contribution), 147

QNEC (qualified nonelective contribution), 147

Qualified Default Investments, 66

R

Reagan, Ronald, 32

refinancing mortgage, 295–296

rental properties, 133

repayment rules, 401(k) loans, 212–213

required minimum distributions (RMDs), 224–227
  IRAs, 303
  QCDs and, 40–41
  Roth conversions and, 121

retail mutual funds, 76–77

retirement, managing
  401(k) withdrawals
    72(t) withdrawals, 221–224
    early withdrawal penalty, 89, 92–93, 221–222
    leaving with previous employer, 222–223
    overview, 218–220
    SEPP, 221–222
  consolidating accounts, 235–236
  home as income-producing asset
    expenses, 239–240
    home equity loan, 240
    reverse mortgage, 240
  improving quality of, 143–144
  investments
    annuities, 232–235
    inflation and, 230
    overview, 229
    realistic expectations, 230–231
    risk management, 231–232
  IRA withdrawals, 223–224
  making workable retirement plan, 150–154
  overview, 218
  planned withdrawal strategy, 237–239
  protecting nest egg, 236–237
  retirement calculator, 154
  RMDs, 224–227
  tax strategies, 227–229

reverse mortgage, 240

risk, investment
  debt instruments, 180
  determining risk tolerance, 192–194
  diversifying, 183–185
  dollar cost averaging, 186–187
  downturns, 185–187
  equity instruments, 181

About the Author

Ted Benna is commonly referred to as the "Father of the 401(k)" because he created and gained IRS approval of the first 401(k) savings plan. He has received many citations for his accomplishments including the 2001 National Jefferson Award recipient for Greatest Public Service by a Private Citizen, the 2001 Player of the Year selected by Defined Contribution News, and one of eight individuals selected by *Money Magazine* for its special 20th Anniversary Issue Hall of Fame. He was selected by Business Insurance as one of the four People of the Century, was one of ten selected by Mutual Fund Market News for its special 10th Anniversary Issue "Legends in Our Own Time," received the Lifetime Achievement Award by Defined Contribution News 2005, and was the recipient of the Icons and Innovators Award — Investment News 2017.

Ted has authored five books including *401(k) For Dummies* and *401(k) — Forty Years Later.* Ted has been featured in many interviews and broadcasts including CNBC, *Wall Street Journal's* "Future of Everything," Politico, the *New York Times*, the *Washington Post*, and many more.

Acknowledgments

401(k)s & IRAs For Dummies wouldn't have happened without Tracy Boggier's ability to convince Wiley that this was worth doing. I thank Tracy for the effort it took to get this project launched. The writing stage was challenging and frustrating at times because Wiley has such high standards, especially for its *For Dummies* books. Kathleen Dobie was of tremendous assistance during this stage. Her guiding and prodding resulted in many changes and additions that have resulted in a much better and more useful book than would have otherwise been possible. I thank Kristie Pyles, Christy Pinglelton, and Linda Brandon for their help during the final editing and pre-production stage. Sherry Gensemer of Trident Retirement Services, LLC's role as a technical reviewer was greatly appreciated. Finally, I am very thankful for Google, which enabled me to easily access many sources that were necessary to confirm the accuracy of many portions of the book.

Publisher's Acknowledgments

Senior Acquisitions Editor: Tracy Boggier

Managing Editor: Kristie Pyles

Development Editor: Linda Brandon

Copy Editor: Christine Pingleton

Technical Editor: Sherry Gensemer, ERPA, RPA

Dummifier: Kathleen Dobie

Production Editor: Mohammed Zafar Ali

Cover Image: © jygallery/Getty Images

Take dummies with you everywhere you go!

Whether you are excited about e-books, want more from the web, must have your mobile apps, or are swept up in social media, dummies makes everything easier.

Find us online!

dummies.com

dummies
A Wiley Brand

Leverage the power

Dummies is the global leader in the reference category and one of the most trusted and highly regarded brands in the world. No longer just focused on books, customers now have access to the dummies content they need in the format they want. Together we'll craft a solution that engages your customers, stands out from the competition, and helps you meet your goals.

Advertising & Sponsorships

Connect with an engaged audience on a powerful multimedia site, and position your message alongside expert how-to content. Dummies.com is a one-stop shop for free, online information and know-how curated by a team of experts.

- Targeted ads
- Video
- Email Marketing
- Microsites
- Sweepstakes sponsorship

20 MILLION PAGE VIEWS EVERY SINGLE MONTH

15 MILLION UNIQUE VISITORS PER MONTH

43% OF ALL VISITORS ACCESS THE SITE VIA THEIR MOBILE DEVICES

700,000 NEWSLETTER SUBSCRIPTIONS TO THE INBOXES OF

300,000 UNIQUE INDIVIDUALS EVERY WEEK

# of dummies

Custom Publishing

Reach a global audience in any language by creating a solution that will differentiate you from competitors, amplify your message, and encourage customers to make a buying decision.

- Apps
- Books
- eBooks
- Video
- Audio
- Webinars

Brand Licensing & Content

Leverage the strength of the world's most popular reference brand to reach new audiences and channels of distribution.

For more information, visit dummies.com/biz

PERSONAL ENRICHMENT

Staying Sharp
9781119187790
USA $26.00
CAN $31.99
UK £19.99

Facebook
9781119179030
USA $21.99
CAN $25.99
UK £16.99

Guitar
9781119293354
USA $24.99
CAN $29.99
UK £17.99

Investing
9781119293347
USA $22.99
CAN $27.99
UK £16.99

Beekeeping
9781119310068
USA $22.99
CAN $27.99
UK £16.99

Digital Photography
9781119235606
USA $24.99
CAN $29.99
UK £17.99

Meditation
9781119251163
USA $24.99
CAN $29.99
UK £17.99

Pregnancy
9781119235491
USA $26.99
CAN $31.99
UK £19.99

Samsung Galaxy S7
9781119279952
USA $24.99
CAN $29.99
UK £17.99

iPhone
9781119283133
USA $24.99
CAN $29.99
UK £17.99

Crocheting
9781119287117
USA $24.99
CAN $29.99
UK £16.99

Nutrition
9781119130246
USA $22.99
CAN $27.99
UK £16.99

PROFESSIONAL DEVELOPMENT

Windows 10
9781119311041
USA $24.99
CAN $29.99
UK £17.99

AutoCAD
9781119255796
USA $39.99
CAN $47.99
UK £27.99

Excel 2016
9781119293439
USA $26.99
CAN $31.99
UK £19.99

QuickBooks 2017
9781119281467
USA $26.99
CAN $31.99
UK £19.99

macOS Sierra
9781119280651
USA $29.99
CAN $35.99
UK £21.99

LinkedIn
9781119251132
USA $24.99
CAN $29.99
UK £17.99

Windows 10
9781119310563
USA $34.00
CAN $41.99
UK £24.99

SharePoint 2016
9781119181705
USA $29.99
CAN $35.99
UK £21.99

Fundamental Analysis
9781119263593
USA $26.99
CAN $31.99
UK £19.99

Networking
9781119257769
USA $29.99
CAN $35.99
UK £21.99

Office 2016
9781119293477
USA $26.99
CAN $31.99
UK £19.99

Office 365
9781119265313
USA $24.99
CAN $29.99
UK £17.99

Salesforce.com
9781119239314
USA $29.99
CAN $35.99
UK £21.99

Coding
9781119293323
USA $29.99
CAN $35.99
UK £21.99

dummies.com

dummies
A Wiley Brand

Learning Made Easy

ACADEMIC

Algebra I dummies

Mary Jane Sterling

9781119293576
USA $19.99
CAN $23.99
UK £15.99

Basic Math & Pre-Algebra dummies

Mark Zegarelli

9781119293637
USA $19.99
CAN $23.99
UK £15.99

Calculus dummies

Mark Ryan

9781119293491
USA $19.99
CAN $23.99
UK £15.99

Chemistry dummies

John T. Moore, EdD

9781119293460
USA $19.99
CAN $23.99
UK £15.99

Physics I dummies

Steven Holzner, PhD

9781119293590
USA $19.99
CAN $23.99
UK £15.99

1,001 Practice Questions SAT dummies

Ron Woldoff

9781119215844
USA $26.99
CAN $31.99
UK £19.99

Organic Chemistry I dummies

Arthur Winter

9781119293378
USA $22.99
CAN $27.99
UK £16.99

Statistics dummies

Deborah J. Rumsey, PhD

9781119293521
USA $19.99
CAN $23.99
UK £15.99

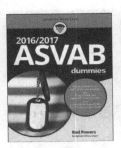

2016/2017 ASVAB dummies

Rod Powers

9781119239178
USA $18.99
CAN $22.99
UK £14.99

Includes Online Practice Tests
1,001 Practice Questions Praxis Core dummies

Carla Kirkland
Chan Cleveland

9781119263883
USA $26.99
CAN $31.99
UK £19.99

Available Everywhere Books Are Sold

dummies.com

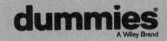

dummies
A Wiley Brand

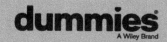